BAD-ASS SOLUTIONS
For Today's BIG-ASS Problems

"People who are crazy enough to think they can change the world are the ones who do."
—STEVE JOBS

"One of us is bat-shit crazy. God, I hope it's not me."
—MITCH

BAD-ASS SOLUTIONS
For Today's BIG-ASS Problems

MITCH FRANCIS

Copyright © 2024 by Mitch Francis

All rights reserved. No part of this book may be reproduced, distributed, or transmitted in any form or by any means, including photocopying, recording, or other electronic or mechanical methods, without the prior written permission of the author, except in the case of brief quotations embodied in critical reviews and certain other noncommercial uses permitted by copyright law.

Published by Silver Bullet Press LLC
bad-asssolutions.com

ISBN (paperback): 979-8-9908131-0-6
ISBN (ebook): 979-8-9908131-1-3

Book design and production by www.AuthorSuccess.com

Printed in the United States of America

For Sandy

I found her lost while skiing in a Colorado white-out snowstorm. She said I saved her life so she had to marry me. The truth is, she saved MY life. It's been 42 incredible years so far…My life is filled with love and joy beyond my wildest dreams because of her.

Sandy is an incredibly talented actress and writer. She taught high school English and public speaking. Sandy is the editor of *Bad-Ass Solutions*. The price was right. She kept me on track and helped make the book coherent and pleasurable to read. Her fabulous sense of humor added tremendously—as it does to my life every day.

CONTENTS

FOREWORD   IX

INTRODUCTION   1

CHAPTER 1: DIPLOMA FOR MINIMUM WAGE   11
Education
Make public schools better than private.

CHAPTER 2: THE AMERICAN FALL OF ROME   19
The US Economy
Pay-off the entire deficit/US debt forever.

CHAPTER 3: ROCKY MOUNTAIN BEACH FRONT   33
Global Warming / Rising Oceans
Stop the oceans from rising due to melting ice caps.

CHAPTER 4: BAZOOKA FOR A HIGH SCHOOL GRADUATION PRESENT   49
Guns and Assault Weapons
Destroy every assault rifle in 30 days and enforce reasonable guns laws

CHAPTER 5: I'M FILING FOR DIVORCE   57
China and Russia
Divorce due to irreconcilable differences.

CHAPTER 6: I'M SO SCREWED   74
Identity Theft, Robo Calls, Fraud Scams
Declare war to rid the US of this scourge immediately.

CHAPTER 7: ONE TRICK PONY   80
The Federal Reserve
Stop this unelected, ill-equipped group from ruining the US economy.

CHAPTER 8: LIKE HERPES—IT'S NEVER RESOLVED   103
Abortion
Immediate resolution for all sides that applies
to more than 94% of all current abortions.

CHAPTER 9: BEND OVER   112
Healthcare
Provide great healthcare to all.

CHAPTER 10: CALL IN THE TROOPS   122
Crime
Stop crime and protect citizens immediately.

CHAPTER 11: THE RICH PAY YOUR SHARE TOO   136
US Taxes
Enact a fair tax system that will actually yield excess funds for the US.

CHAPTER 12: WATCH YOUR ASS   150
Lawsuits
Stop the pain and waste in the current legal system.

CHAPTER 13: DRUGS COST A LOT MORE IN PRISON   155
Drugs
Immediately dismantle the entire criminal drug world.

CHAPTER 14: PAY TO PLAY   166
Elections
Take special interests out of election funding immediately.

CHAPTER 15: NOT TO DIE FOR   176
Military and Wars
Never lose another US soldier on the battlefield.

CHAPTER 16: PLACE YOUR BETS   185
Securities—The Stock Market
Close the casino.

CHAPTER 17: WTF? 22,000 GOVERNMENTS IN THE US?   210
State & Local Government Restructure
Bring government out of the horse and buggy era.

CHAPTER 18: THROWAWAY PEOPLE   216
Homeless / Mental Illness
House and treat everyone who needs it—at very low cost.

CHAPTER 19: MOM'S BASEMENT HILTON   225
Housing Shortage
Use the basics of US capitalism to oversupply/cheapen housing.

CHAPTER 20: FREE-FOR-ALL   231
Immigration
Fair laws for immigrants and US citizens.

CHAPTER 21: NOT MY PROBLEM   238
So Now What?
Do something!

SOURCES   249

ACKNOWLEDGEMENTS   257

FOREWORD

by Jack Canfield, Coauthor of the Chicken Soup for the Soul® series

Bad-Ass Solutions surprised me in that Mitch Francis has taken on how to solve twenty of the most dire problems currently facing Americans and even the world. The problems range from: 20 million assault rifles currently in the US; to our disastrous public schools; to the crippling US deficit and debt. Even more surprisingly, he has actually devised amazing, real solutions that are fascinating and actually doable. For example, one of my major interests and concerns is global warming and environmental sustainability. Mitch's solution for stopping the rising ocean levels due to the melting polar ice caps is really new and extremely interesting to me—a truly fabulous Bad-Ass Solution!

We are facing massive problems that politicians and news pundits constantly argue about but rarely do anything to resolve. As a society, we need to change the current discourse from complaining and blaming to successfully resolving these problems without the restraints of rigid political party ideologies. Mitch's refreshingly non-political work sets the table for this new direction of actually solving our problems together.

While I don't totally agree with every one of Mitch's solutions, I found the book to be an enjoyable, interesting, and highly educational read. If any of the solutions offered in the book catch on, which you can help create, it could spark real change that would benefit millions. If you agree with me, once you read this book, I encourage you to buy another copy and send it to someone who can join with you in pushing one or more of these ideas forward. Let's start a movement to implement some of these solutions and actually get things done.

INTRODUCTION

Problems. Big-ass problems. We're not talking about what to order for dinner. We're talking about solving the biggest threats to ourselves and even our civilization, such as global warming, homelessness, and mass killings.

I began writing this book shortly after my brother-in-law's brother was shot and killed during a Fourth of July parade near his home in Highland Park, Illinois, by a crazed young man with assault rifles. Steve Straus was an incredibly kind and brilliant man who was deeply loved and respected by his family and all who knew him. His surviving brother is someone with whom I'm extremely close. He will suffer from this terrible loss forever. This family tragedy hurt and frustrated me. It ultimately made me expand my view to all of these problems and kicked my ass into doing something—including writing this book.

I'm sure you have your own story about how the problems addressed in this book have negatively impacted you or someone you care about.

This nonpartisan book explores and provides solutions for problems that are coincidentally identified as many of the most important issues to *all* Americans by Gallup Polls, one of the most trusted analytics and advisory companies known for its public opinion polls conducted worldwide.

For example:

> ✓ Guns and crime are totally out of control. Americans are not safe. We are being robbed, beaten, addicted, and killed. We are fearful for our lives.

- ✓ The homeless, addicted and mentally ill, are suffering terribly and are living in horrible conditions throughout the US.
- ✓ The US economy is fragile, with Americans' jobs, income, and retirement savings always vulnerable.
- ✓ The economic differences between the wealthy and the poor in the US is tragic and frightening. Revolution is not unthinkable.
- ✓ Carbon emission pollution is not even close to getting resolved, so global warming will continue to cause the ice sheets to melt so much that the ocean levels will likely rise enough this century to flood and destroy all coastal cities and islands.
- ✓ Russia and China have always been threats. However, they are currently more joined together and are escalating tensions against the US and its interests.
- ✓ The problems of abortion, immigration, taxes, healthcare, drugs, wars, elections, and housing costs are daily frustrations to most Americans.

Can these nightmare problems really be solved? Yes!

Many of the discussions in this book include some truly fascinating facts, such as that the ice sheets on Antarctica and Greenland are melting at a rate that would fill approximately twenty Olympic-sized swimming pools—every second! We're all screwed, right? Guess what? We're not. You'll discover incredible solutions in this book!

Most of us believe these immense problems are too enormous to do anything meaningful about them, much less have any idea where to start. This book addresses these seemingly impossible challenges.

Do you want to help make things better? Are you concerned, frightened, frustrated, or angry:

- ✓ That our lives are so vulnerable to the many different big-ass problems?
- ✓ That our government dances around the problems and does little or nothing other than blame the other party?

- ✓ That our country is so polarized by political ideologies and party lines that our fellow citizens feel like enemies rather than partners?
- ✓ That you've lost loved ones or have been hurt yourself because of drugs, gangs, gun violence, or mental illness?
- ✓ That our polluted planet is literally gasping to survive the damage from humans?
- ✓ That treatment for an illness for you or your loved ones will be unaffordable, inaccessible, or even bankrupt you?

Me too! That's why I wrote this book. It's for all of us who care about these issues and want them solved. There really are good solutions to help us solve these seemingly impossible problems.

More good news: I'm not a professor or academic, so the problems and the solutions in this book are addressed in a way that we "normal" people can relate to and even enjoy.

I'm also not "political." That's important, because there's little room for partisanship when trying to tackle important issues that affect all of us. It makes sense to problem-solve together. Having no horse in the race is just what's needed for unbiased perspective and creativity.

That said, you will likely read some solutions or statements that you will hate me for, assuming I'm a liberal asshole, or alternately, a conservative asshole. At some point, you will probably think you have me pegged. You'll be sure I'm a Democrat, then sure I'm a Republican. I never declare.

I (perhaps like you) have become extremely critical of both parties and their intractable "party positions" that just serve to feed on our differences and only exacerbate hate and distrust of each other. I am also sick of the red-state / blue-state categories that try to succinctly define a US state and its entire population of millions of diverse Americans as if there is only one issue involved, as there was for the Civil War. Is that what they're trying to duplicate? Feels like it. This political polarization is dangerous stuff. We need to be brought together, not separated for the benefit of political parties and the convenience of the press.

In the real world, apart from the party-line politicians, aren't we all actually liberal on some issues and conservative on others? It seems everyone I talk to is this way. This thoughtfulness and flexibility I find in real Americans gives me hope. We need to bypass the intractable loyalty to rigid party positions to actually accomplish something.

So, who the hell am I to be proclaiming I have answers to the most challenging problems our nation is facing? I'm not the smartest guy in the room, but one thing I've always been good at is solving problems. My strict, conditional—love father caused me to become skilled in being a pleaser, which evolved during my teen years into the development of really good problem-solving abilities. I prefer problem-solver in this context to "kiss-ass." Perhaps I should have titled this book: *Kiss-Ass to Bad-Ass*.

You'll note that I drop some F-, S- and A- bombs in this book. I'm not trying to offend anyone with that. It's just the way we all talk now. We need to be authentic, and it's hard not to get frustrated and agitated when talking about the problems in this book.

You'll also see many lists in this book. This may be due to my loving mother, who clearly forced potty-training (main cause of obsessive/compulsive behavior), which resulted in the development of my obsession to list and number everything.

I also often begin sentences with "And" and end sentences with a preposition.

You may have heard this before, but it's a story worth retelling: A freshman just arrived and was walking the grounds of Harvard. He stopped a senior and asked, "Can you please tell me where the library's at?" The senior replied, "You're at Harvard now, so never end a sentence with a preposition." "Okay," replied the freshmen, "can you please tell me where the library's at, asshole?"

I've founded, directed, and managed private and publicly-traded companies as CEO across many fields, such as commercial real estate development and international entertainment. One company I founded became the largest ticket broker in Las Vegas, selling more than $1 billion of show tickets, attractions, and dining. I own and manage commercial properties throughout the US. I have a California Real

Estate Broker license that I don't use (like everyone else in California). My inventions have yielded four United States patents, with another three inventions currently patent-pending.

My lifetime in business has revealed an axiom: roadblocks are continually thrown in the way of every single step a businessperson must take toward his/her goals. To succeed, you need to develop really good problem-solving skills and be relentlessly tenacious. Solving cultural and national problems is no different.

As an aside, I have been a founding director of two charitable organizations and remain on those boards. Though important, neither organization deals with the twenty topics addressed here.

I despise the term "thinking outside the box." It's so overused that people who come up with an idea, no matter how mundane, such as putting the jelly on the bread before the peanut butter, believe they're thinking outside the box. Thinking outside the box is not very different from coloring outside the lines.

Here are two examples of the type of problem-solving I'm talking about: the kind that exemplifies creative thinking to yield solutions to problems which, in fact, were right in front of everyone's eyes. You may be familiar with these. If so, please indulge me because they're worth repeating and great for those who haven't heard about them. I just want to believe they are true.

Stuck Truck

Somewhere on a mountain two-lane highway, a large truck got stuck in a tunnel. Really stuck. No amount of rocking helped. In fact, it only wedged the truck into the solid rock ceiling even more. Traffic was backed up for miles in both directions. Road and tunnel contractors along with engineers were helicoptered in. No one could devise a plan other than to jackhammer the solid rock ceiling that was imprisoning the truck. Construction crews with heavy equipment were on their way.

With nothing to do while their car was parked on the road with all the others, a father and daughter took the half-mile walk up to see the spectacle for themselves. Upon reaching the stuck truck and all the hot tempers that were on display, the little girl walked up to the enormous truck. She carefully walked around all four sides as if she wanted to buy it. Finally, she tugged on her dad's coat and motioned for him to bend down. When his ear reached her mouth, she whispered, "Why don't they just let some air out of the tires?"

In minutes, the air was released, the truck lowered just enough to back out of the tunnel and the little girl was cheered. Her picture was on the front page of every newspaper in the state.

The problem had a simple solution that only a small child with an unbiased perspective could resolve.

Stuck Toothpaste

One of the major manufacturers of consumer goods had a critical meeting of their board of directors. Their stock was stagnant and there were rumors of activist shareholders plotting to replace the entire board. They called in the president of their toothpaste division, the largest division, and had him sit at the end of the long conference table. They acknowledged that his division and in particular their brand of toothpaste remained the number one selling toothpaste in the US. Just as the president began to thank the board, they interrupted him, talking one after another, actually getting somewhat upset at the president. They explained that the company, and in particular, his toothpaste division was stuck in the same place, year after year, just treading water. True, it was the best-selling toothpaste, but shareholders expect growth, and if he can't deliver 10 percent growth in sales from his toothpaste division within one year, the board would not renew his employment agreement and they would find another president who could deliver growth.

The president left the board room upset, dejected, and frightened. He quickly assembled his management team to attack the problem of how to grow their toothpaste sales by at least 10 percent within a year. Over the next two weeks, the team responded with all kinds of ideas:

"Make the toothpaste taste better."

"Have promotions to give a free toothbrush with every tube."
"Put a numbered ticket in every tube with the winner getting a trip to Disneyland."

None of the ideas were worth betting their futures on.

The team decided that they needed outside help. They called in a seasoned (euphemism for old) marketing consultant who had innumerable marketing successes over his long career. He came into their office and sat quietly as they described the problem and all of the solutions they had devised. Finally, the president leaned in toward the consultant and said, "If you can come up with a plan to help us achieve a 10 percent increase in sales of our toothpaste, we'll pay you $1 million upon success."

The consultant sat for a moment and said, "I would like to think about this a bit and will come back here in one week and either give you a plan or tell you I can't assist."

In the meantime, he asked that the company provide a contract with the million-dollar terms. They agreed, saying he would have the agreement the next day. They all confirmed to meet again in exactly one week.

At the appointed day and time, the consultant sat down at the conference table with the president and his management team. Of course, they were all anxious to hear about their future. The consultant took the agreement from his briefcase and placed two copies on the table. He said, "I have signed the agreement, please sign for your side." The president signed both copies immediately and returned one to the consultant.

The consultant smiled broadly, put both hands on the table and stood up. "I have the answer to your problem. You will absolutely increase your toothpaste sales by 10 percent within one year, without games, without advertising, and without new flavors."

The group gasped in unison. Then they all assumed he was a quack. "Okay, how? How can we do this?"

The consultant held up his hand with the a-okay sign (index fingertip touches the thumb tip, making a circle, the other three fingers straight up). He then spread the two fingertips apart, just a bit, making the circle just a bit bigger, then said, "Make the toothpaste tube hole 10 percent larger!" He paused just a moment, then continued, "Your customers will still squeeze toothpaste along the entire length of their toothbrush, only they'll be using an imperceivable bit more toothpaste. Of course, over time, your customers will need to buy 10 percent more toothpaste and your sales will have increased by 10 percent."

The plan worked. The president and his team kept their jobs (with bonuses); the company's stock rose due to the increased profits, thereby retaining the directors; and the consultant got his $1 million check for solving a problem with remarkable perspective and creativity.

Here are some truths about problem-solving:

1. Identifying a problem is easy.
2. Creating a viable solution is difficult.
3. Executing the solution is damn near impossible.

Each chapter in this book provides a discussion about the major problem(s) having to do with that topic. The information is presented as a 10,000-foot-high perspective because each topic could easily require an entire book to investigate its problems thoroughly.

Following each description of the problem are one or more solutions that are so logical and reasonable that you may be shocked they're not already being implemented. They are effective solutions because their development was not restrained by bias or cost restraints, and they are therefore outside conventional thought, politics, and bureaucracy.

At the beginning of every chapter are relevant and often humorous quotes from people you likely know of. I hope you enjoy their wit and wisdom as much as I have, collecting their quips for decades.

With all my bitching about our problems in this book, you might think I hate America. You would be 100 percent wrong. I'm more grateful to live here and for what this country has provided than you could ever imagine. Our country is doing badly right now on delivering the promise of America to so many of its citizens who are struggling and have little hope. America itself is facing decline in myriad ways. I want to help the US survive and to see it and my fellow citizens thrive. This is my way: to offer solutions that just might ameliorate our worst problems.

Many of the issues are timeless, so the solutions will apply for decades. These include topics such elections, education, healthcare, taxes, China and Russia relations, legal reforms, military war strategies, and the housing shortage. However, some topics reflect enormous and immediate threats such as rising ocean levels, gang and gun violence, the Federal Reserve's economic screw-ups, and immigration. These topics require solutions that must be implemented as soon as possible.

Feel free to jump directly to chapters that have particular interest to you. That said, I'm confident you'll find each chapter provides great information and even a fun experience. And, most importantly, be sure to read the final chapter in this book, which provides solutions to one final problem, perhaps the most critical of all: How to help get the bad-ass solutions in this book enacted!

> "When the people lead, the leaders will follow."
> —MAHATMA GANDHI

CHAPTER 1
DIPLOMA FOR MINIMUM WAGE

EDUCATION

Make public schools better than private

"One-half of all people are below average."
—UNKNOWN

"You know there is a problem with the education system when you realize that out of the 3 Rs, only one begins with an R."
—DENNIS MILLER

"I became so frustrated with visiting inner-city schools (in America) that I just stopped going. The sense that you need to learn just isn't there. If you ask the kids what they want or need, they will say an iPod or some sneakers. In South Africa, they don't ask for money or toys. They ask for uniforms so they can go to school."
—OPRAH WINFREY

> "I just cannot understand why we can't have better schools. That private schools are the only option for the kind of high net-worth crowd, I think, is ridiculous. It should be a major initiative. It should be something we're all working on. We have to get our head out of the clouds.
>
> — MARC BENIOFF

THE PROBLEM

The single most horrifying report ever on the health and sustainability of the entire US economic system came from *The Ascent*, a Motley Fool Service, stating that approximately HALF of American households don't have $400 cash to cover an emergency. No other statistic could better evidence that the United States is on the brink of failure. This illustrates a massive chasm between those who can spend $400 for a nice dinner and those who can't pay $400 cash to repair their car so they can get to work.

The United States has millions upon millions of citizens who are unqualified for virtually any real work that could lead to their financial success. Further, those same people often don't want menial jobs. So, what do they do? I know what I'd do—ANYTHING to get money for my family and me to live. Why is crime so prevalent? Why are drugs and sales of drugs everywhere? Why are thousands living on sidewalks in every American city? Duh. These people have been left behind and have no way out of their hell, except for those who turn to illegal activities.

Per the National Taxpayers Union Association, just 25 percent of the population pays nearly 90 percent of the country's taxes. The top 1 percent pays 46 percent—NEARLY HALF of the taxes. More than 50 percent pay virtually nothing. There is a Grand Canyon between the haves and the have nots—and the divide is getting bigger all the time. It can be said that America is for the rich. Guess what, that's who's paying the bills. Is their enormous success fair? Do the poor deserve their struggle? Both answers are of course not.

When the economy is failing most people, don't they lose their sense of nationalism? Why should they support a system that's not working for them? How do those people feel when they're subjected to a constant bombardment of the insanely rich Kardashians, Musk, Bezos, etc.? Natural human response is awe, then jealousy, then upon realization that they will never be like them, anger.

Historically, when the majority of people are desperate, hungry, and angry, there is revolution. How far from revolt is America? Didn't we get a taste of it during the summer of 2020? Thousands of extreme liberals chanted "defund the police" while they looted, torched, and attacked. They didn't give a damn about order or that innocent property owners were being terribly hurt. The January 6, 2021 attack on the Capitol was an opposite force of extreme conservatives taking a stand for preserving their version of America at all costs. They too didn't care who they hurt or even killed while they desecrated our nation's sacred Capitol. Sides may have been chosen. Perhaps the revolution has already begun.

People with nothing to lose want revolution. You can look it up.

The most valuable component for success is EDUCATION. The greatest possible equalizer of Americans is to receive an equal education. If America is to continue and succeed, it must look to education as the answer. Educate workers with skills for new jobs that become careers. Educate workers whose jobs have become obsolete to be valuable elsewhere. Most importantly, educate children to give them tools to succeed in America. They need skills in reading, writing, mathematics, sciences, American history, and new technologies such as computer coding, artificial intelligence, and the next new important technological skill set.

Americans need to understand why their country (with all its faults) works better than all others. They need to know the difference between capitalism and socialism/communism and why capitalism won the enormous economics experiment of the last century. Socialism and communism lost. Capitalism won. Americans need to know why, so they continue to support the system that works.

The education system in the US is guilty of being the main divider between the haves and have nots in America. Education should be the gift of living in America, where all children get an equal education.

In America, people who value education are involved in seeing that their children are well-educated and are ensuring their children's success, while people who do not understand the critical need for education are dooming their children to generational poverty.

The founding fathers of America referred often to the idea of equal education for all being the cornerstone of democracy. They understood that equal education made a level playing field for all, subject only to one's drive and abilities. Of course, for those guys, equal education for all meant all white males. Thankfully, most Americans have evolved to include all people as all people.

According to the National Center for Education Statistics, there are 130,930 K-12 public schools in the US. There are 32,461 private schools, or approximately 20 percent of the total 163,391 schools. Privateschool-review.com reports that the national average private school tuition is $12,269 per year (2022-23). The private elementary school average tuition cost is $11,295 per year and the private high school average is $15,792 per year. The state with the highest average private school tuition is Connecticut with a $28,053 average tuition cost. The state with the lowest tuition cost is South Dakota with an average cost of $3,825.

The Studio City section of Los Angeles houses a private college prep school (grades seven through twelve), whose annual tuition is an incredible $46,900! For perspective, just over the hill from that school is the famous University of California Los Angeles (UCLA), whose annual tuition is $14,479. It's not hard to grasp the unfair advantage of the fortunate rich kids at that prep school who are programmed for massive success compared to kids in public schools.

BAD-ASS SOLUTION

- **PRIVATE SCHOOLS MUST BE IMMEDIATELY ELIMINATED**

Only great public schools can deliver the equal opportunity promised in the United States. Currently, parents who value education and can pay put their children into private schools. Private schools ensure the continuation of rich people being rich because their kids receive a great education. Private schools often take the best teachers for higher pay and a better work environment. Private schools take the wealthy parents who care deeply about education completely out of the public-school world. They don't care what happens in public schools—their children are safe and getting well prepared for their futures in private schools.

This is insane. America is saying, "All those who are successful and appreciate a good education, go over there to have your children highly educated, and all those who don't understand the value or can't afford private schools, have your children go over there where your kids will start the race far behind the rich kids."

Clearly, the kids with a private school education should beat the pants off a kid who attended a public school when it comes to careers and likelihood of success.

Okay, okay. Yes, some public schools are pretty good. There are millions of parents who fight hard to make their children's public schools as good as possible. Many kids work extremely hard and excel in public schools. But below is a new plan that may be even better for those parents and students.

No private schools means everyone is in public school. **The parents who now pay enormous sums to keep their entitled progeny in private schools to ensure they get the best education will have to work within the public school system, which will benefit all children.**

This is clearly a critical direction that the US must pursue. It's not going to yield instant magic. This takes time. Bussing in the early 1970s was a nightmare. Undereducated kids can't immediately compete with well-educated kids. It's not fair and is too frustrating for any possibility of success. Undereducated kids must be slowly brought up to speed in a non-threatening, encouraging environment.

Public schools must be places of learning—not babysitting for gangster kids. A positive environment for students and teachers is all-important. It may be unfashionable, but schools must once again have order and discipline. Unruly kids need to be removed, first to special classes or schools, then expelled completely. Students cannot graduate automatically. They will have to earn it. They actually have to be educated to proceed.

Students who don't graduate must go into the US Military or to be trained elsewhere to contribute to society, not be parasites on it. The military and trade schools should be valued, not be deemed a punishment. We need to get very serious about this.

Instead of spending time arguing about teaching critical race theory and woke-ism in schools, we need to be sure that kids get a solid education in American history that is brutally honest with accurate racial information. This is not a political party or liberal/conservative issue. The focus must be on quality education because of how poorly educated most young people are today. They barely have passable reading and writing skills, let alone a working knowledge of mathematics, sciences, and US history.

To ensure the continuation of our economic system in the US, curriculum must include a working knowledge of capitalism versus socialism. Although not perfect by any stretch, the last century's experiments of socialism, communism, and capitalism resulted in very clear evidence that capitalism brought a much higher standard of living to populations than socialism and communism. In fact, it was only after communist and socialist governments such as China and Russia allowed capitalism into their economic structures that they began to flourish with a higher quality of life for most of their populations.

We need to refocus on force-feeding kids the information and skills they'll need to survive out there as adults. Education is serious business. Make it fun and interesting but make it valuable.

Finally, to the elite people who are incensed at the idea of sending their royal offspring to public schools: you should realize that the US you and probably your ancestors thrived in, is changing quickly. The spread between poverty and wealth is growing fast. The poor people with few options to improve their and their children's financial opportunities will become disheartened and angry as they watch the top 10 percent of Americans reaping the majority of rewards in this country.

Can you imagine what it would be like to park cars for a living and deal with the BMW, Tesla, and Mercedes owners all day long while you need to take three buses and walk the final two miles to work every day and still can't get by? Can you imagine what poor Americans feel when they watch the Kardashians arguing over whose private jet to take on vacation this week? I'll tell you again. Awe, then jealousy, then anger that neither they nor their children could ever attain even a piece of that golden pie.

This is serious. You don't want a revolution in the US. And it could easily happen in your lifetime. You want your royal heirs to actually have the things and opportunities you wish for them. You had better reconcile that poor people must have improved opportunities and wealth, or you are Nero playing the fiddle while Rome burns. Your heirs may actually be refugees at some point in their lives.

Just make sure everyone has equal opportunities in the US. If you want a great education for your kids, make sure poor kids get the same thing. Public schools in wealthy communities cannot be better than public schools in poor communities. The thousands of localized school districts must be eliminated so that each state, or even the federal government, can establish uniform, excellent education for all. Think about it.

As citizens of the US, we can prioritize EXCELLENT education for all. We can demand and pay for outstanding teachers, cutting edge curriculum and materials, quality school buildings, safe environments, and high educational standards.

According to Time.com, John Adams achieved one of the most significant accomplishments in educational history: he wrote the Massachusetts Constitution of 1780 and placed education at the center of the state's understanding of government. The Constitution declared that "wisdom and knowledge . . . diffused generally among the body of the people [are] necessary for the preservation of their rights and liberties... . [Thus,] it shall be the duty of legislatures and magistrates, in all future periods of this commonwealth, to cherish the ... public schools."**

This is one of the bad-ass solutions that has a clear path toward implementation. Assume that the majority of American voters agree that dramatic improvement of public schools can happen if we eliminate all private schools as discussed in this chapter. Their gargantuan voting strength would likely be a power for change that has rarely been seen in US history. Any opposition who wants to continue private schools would clearly constitute just a small fraction of the anti-private schools voting bloc. This is because there are approximately five times more children in public schools than in private schools. The enormous constituency will have the power to force the US federal and state governments into action. Representatives who work for the change can earn the title of "Bad-Ass Politician." It could become a badge of honor.

This is a long, difficult journey. Begin with the first steps. If you agree with this bad-ass solution, tell other people. Let's create the groundswell. Make this happen for the happy and successful future for all Americans.

> "I am very fortunate I can send my kids to private school, but everybody does not have the money. If you cannot get your kid in a good school today, your kids are going to be behind the eight ball.
>
> —SPIKE LEE

CHAPTER 2
THE AMERICAN FALL OF ROME

THE US ECONOMY

Pay off the entire deficit/US debt forever

"The only reason economic predictions exist
is to make astrology look respectable."

—J. K. GALBRAITH

"The inherent vice of capitalism is the unequal sharing
of blessings; the inherent virtue of socialism is
the equal sharing of miseries."

—WINSTON CHURCHILL

"An economist is an expert who will know tomorrow why the
things he predicted yesterday didn't happen today."

—LAURENCE J PETER

"Two-thirds of Americans live paycheck to paycheck.
This system ain't workin'."

—MITCH

THE PROBLEM

The problem with the science of economics is that it's not a science at all. It just thinks it is. Everyone who had the privilege of attending a decent university had to take, or really endure, Econ 101 and usually Econ 102. My own privilege included Econ 101 taught to a cozy group of 500 freshmen by Dr. Ruben Zubrow, the oldest and highest paid professor at the University of Colorado. He advised lots of presidents; we assumed going back to Grant. The time frame was the early seventies. Hippies were just phasing out; drugs weren't; Vietnam was raging; Nixon was being Nixon, and the US was mired in inflation and a rash of economic problems. Economists argued opposing positions against each other constantly.

Dr. Zubrow was a dynamic and wonderful speaker. He had the worst stutter I had ever heard, but he was so brilliant and still somehow connected with 500 kids in such a way that we just didn't seem to notice the machine-gun stammer. The poor man's head actually lurched violently with every syllable. Certainly, no one dared mention it, even in private. The guy was just too revered for anything so trivial as a speech impediment to matter.

His entire first lecture was about how moronic we freshmen were to even consider taking economics. He avoided the fact that it was required. He said there was clear evidence every single day that no economist knows what the hell they are talking about. At best, they just had opinions. And those opinions could be dangerous. Yes, we were imbeciles for studying economics.

Zubrow continued to point out that our enormous textbook, simply called "Samuelson," after the author, was of little to no value other than as a doorstop. Yet, we would be expected to digest every word in that goddamn fifty-pound tome for testing by the man who was telling us what garbage the stuff was.

His proof was that literally every passage containing an axiom or economics rule of some kind began with the admonition, "all things being equal." Those words were used so much that they haunt me to this day like a song verse stuck in my head.

Economists say that their rules are true if nothing else changes at all. Of course, all of the other variables change continually, so what good is the rule? Was it just to work our little minds into a froth? Was it for people to leave university and sound erudite at parties? Was it so economists could have employment of some kind—regardless of whether or not the crap works? Guess what? It doesn't work.

Economics is not a science, and its theories, rules, and conclusions should be taken as guesses when applied to the real world. Bitter? Nah, just pissed when people present themselves as experts whose statements must be revered, when at best, they are just guessing.

Moving On

There is an old adage as advice to politicians running for office: "It's the economy, stupid," attributed to James Carville. This is also known as, "people vote their pocketbooks." No other subject is more impactful to all of us than The Economy. You'll note that the economy is involved in many other topics in this book: The Federal Reserve, Securities, Taxes, Accounting, Crime, and Housing Costs. Come to think of it, every topic in this book ultimately has some link to the economy.

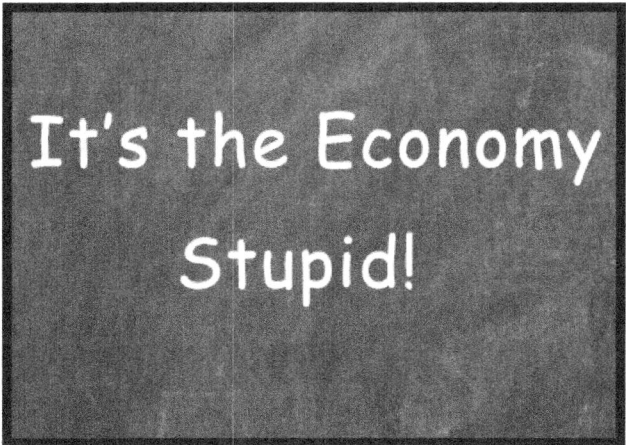

Attributed to James Carville, a strategist for Bill Clinton's successful 1992 presidential campaign.

All of us make up the economy. Everything we buy, every expense we incur, our jobs, our investments, our healthcare, and on, and on, and on, and on. Couldn't there just be a central committee to deal with all this stuff so we don't have to? Oh, right. That's communism. That one really doesn't work.

There are so many moving parts to the US economy that it's awfully difficult for us to really get our arms around it, so no one really does. Instead of boring you with in-depth discussions about each part, I'll just name a few that affect all of us—almost daily. Interest rates, inflation, housing costs, healthcare costs, Democratic and Republican fiscal ideologies, the deficit, welfare needs, the military, infrastructure (roads, bridges, utilities), and international factors such as the value of the US dollar versus foreign currencies and US financial and military support of other countries.

Again, too much crap to wrap our little myopic brains around. Actually, our government doesn't seem to comprehend the interrelational workings of the whole economy, so it's understandable how they mess it up—daily. Still, we're all players in a massive corporation called the United States.

The US now spends trillions of dollars per year more than it takes in. Every idiot knows that you can't keep spending more than you earn unless your goal is bankruptcy. So how does the US accomplish this magic trick? Simple: The US has a printing press for paper money in the basement.

Not really so simple. In order for the US to spend money it doesn't bring in from taxes, it has to first borrow the money. The US constantly sells treasury bonds and notes, which are actually loans from individuals and even other countries to the US treasury. Of course, the interest paid on the bonds and notes comes right from the same general funds of the US. Try borrowing money from someone using the same logic. Even your mom would be laughing at you while she refuses.

The resultant illness of the US government spending more money than it takes in is called the deficit. The deficit grew from almost nothing just forty years ago to now more than $34 trillion. *Fox Business Live* states that this equates to about $101,000 for every single person in the US. Worse, it amounts to more than $264,000 per taxpayer. Pay up. *The*

Washington Times reported in March 2024 that the "US national debt is spiraling out of control, rising $1 trillion every 100 days."

The US is drowning in its own debt.

It would be helpful to have a good understanding of how much a trillion really is. For that matter, few of us have a grasp of how much a billion is. Here's a really good commonly used relative analogy:

A million seconds pass in **11.6 days**. Six zeros.

1,000,000

A billion seconds pass in **32 years.** Nine zeros.

1,000,000,000

A trillion seconds pass in **32,000 years.** Twelve zeros.

1,000,000,000,000

Another common analogy:

A billion seconds ago it was 1992.

A billion minutes ago Jesus was alive.

A billion hours ago our ancestors were living in the Stone Age.

A billion days ago no one walked on the Earth on two feet.

A billion dollars ago was just over TWO HOURS AGO at the rate our government is spending it.

Ingest this concept so you can puke every time some bozo politician throws around multi-billion-dollar or even trillion-dollar programs to buy votes.

The low interest rates of the last nearly twenty years (prior to 2022) has made paying the debt service on the US government's deficit in the forms of bonds and notes relatively cheap. During 2022, interest on the ten-year Treasury Note went from approximately 1.25% to well over 4%. In other words, the cost for the US to pay interest on its debt TRIPLED that year. Interest on the $34T (twelve zeros) deficit at 1.25% is $425 billion. The same $34T at 4% is $1.36 trillion ($3.7 BILLION PER DAY). The difference is $935 billion—per year. Just this additional interest exceeds the entire current US military annual budget, and the total interest payment equates to approximately $4,100 for every single American, every year—and growing. Your invoice is in the mail.

Interest on the national debt is now one of the three largest single expenses of the US government and will soon be the largest. Paying more interest means increasing the deficit even more—and more and more and more. A deficit death spiral.

Who's running this shit show? What does bankruptcy of the US look like? How do our grandchildren pay for what we're spending today? That's just not fair, and a terrible plan because those kids can hardly do more than play video games anyway.

Americans want stuff. We want security, so big military. We want good roads, schools, parks, infrastructure, police, fire departments, subsidized housing, Medicare, Social Security, jails, social welfare programs, and much, much, much more. What politician would say, "No, we have to cut those things because we don't have the money?"

So, what do we do? We're spoiled to the point of believing that all of these things are our RIGHT to have. When politicians tell Americans that they'll receive free this and free that, the response is joy and votes. When did we start wanting and even expecting something for nothing? All of us should have learned that lesson when we were children—oh right, Americans behave like children.

The US is doomed. History repeats itself. We're actually re-living the fall of Rome.

CONUNDRUM: THE US IS BANKRUPT YET REMAINS AS THE STRONGEST ECONOMY IN THE WORLD. HUH???

According to *Investopedia*, the US has the largest economy in the world. China is in second place, even though it has four times the population. The businesses based in the US are the strongest in the world. The US provides goods and services to its people far better than any other country. If only the US didn't have the economic mess from its too-generous government programs and deficit spending.

The Peter G. Peterson Foundation reports that, "interest costs will eventually become the largest 'program' in the federal budget." Further, "interest costs on the national debt are projected to total around $66 trillion over the next thirty years."

FACE IT: THERE IS SIMPLY NO WAY THAT THE DEFICIT WILL EVER BE PAID OFF. IT WILL CONTINUE TO SPIRAL COMPLETELY OUT OF CONTROL. SOMETHING MUST BE DONE, YET NO SOLUTIONS ARE EVEN BEING DISCUSSED.

BAD-ASS SOLUTION

Can you picture how successful the US would be if it had no deficit, no interest payments, and was required to spend no more than the taxes it brings in? **It can happen**.

For decades, perhaps even millennia, countries had currencies based on what became known as The Gold Standard. In the US, it meant that every paper dollar bill had real gold behind it. Really! There was actual gold in Fort Knox equal to the total amount of paper money. Americans were supposedly even able to exchange paper money for the gold itself. Somehow, the government learned it could print and spend more money than we had in actual gold. In 1971, the US moved away from the concept of gold-backed money, so under President Nixon, the Gold Standard was abandoned. This psychological shift may have been the beginning of deficit spending. The politicians could go wild—and did.

Hundred-million-dollar jets? Sure. Three-billion-dollar aircraft carriers? Of course. Gold toilets? Why not? Fund other countries' wars? Have to. Fund every possible social program imaginable? Hell yes!

> "An elephant is a mouse built to government specifications."
>
> —LONG'S AXIOM

Here is an idea for a new magic wand that will completely wipe out the deficit. Take caution that this magic wand can only be used once. This genie must be immediately put back into the bottle after granting just this one wish. This solution can save the US. It could ruin the US. The safeguard is that using this magic wand once will have to be coupled with an ironclad law against any future deficit spending so that it will never have to be used again.

Let's take a look at a business balance sheet that details its assets and liabilities (debts). For this purpose, we'll look mostly at the assets. Companies list assets such as cash, real estate, equipment, investments, and goodwill. A healthy company will have a "clean" balance sheet, meaning that its assets far outweigh their debt liabilities. Typically, a company can borrow money against its assets for things like investing in new plants or purchasing new inventory.

What if a new set of laws was enacted to say that a business could only borrow money against its cash? Most businesses simply could not borrow enough to operate and grow. This restriction would likely spell the end for a large majority of businesses.

This illustration is analogous to the Gold Standard. In the case of the US, the government effectively could only print dollars equal to the amount of gold it had stored at Fort Knox. Rather than printing money against all of its assets, the US printed dollars ONLY against its gold.

What does the balance sheet of the US look like?

US assets include gold, massive lands, parks, infrastructure, schools, buildings, hospitals, un-mined natural resources, planes, ships, weaponry, military installations, brand value, etc. An accounting would likely arrive at a value of the US assets in quadrillions or even quintillions.

THE US CAN SIMPLY PAY OFF ITS DEFICIT BY PRINTING MONEY AGAINST ITS REAL ASSETS. YUP, BAD-ASS. LET'S "COIN" A NEW PHRASE, THE "ASSET STANDARD."

Based on accepted accounting practice, this makes sense. The US has assets that are many times the value of its gold. Why not use those assets to back the currency of the United States?

Rattle this around your brain for a while. Suppose the US government sent a check to every person, entity, and country that currently holds its bonds and notes (all the creditors of US debt) with a thank you note saying that the debt is hereby paid back. That's right, we send China a check for $1 trillion (China's ownership of treasuries is roughly 13 percent of the US national debt per Investopedia.com). What would they do? Would they return it and say it's no good, like a bank for insufficient funds?

The Chinese, Japanese, and your aunt Betty will rush to deposit the check into their bank account and wait for it to clear. Will it clear? Hell yes. Who, other than the Federal Reserve, would be in a position to say it won't clear—and the check was drawn against its own (US Central Bank) account!

This truism is proof of the whole concept. As long as everyone takes US government checks, the currency is valid and valuable. This phenomenon is already in place. **According to current economic and accounting thought, the US is already bankrupt because its debts exceed its assets. Yet, its credit rating is AAA, and the entire world continues to lend the US money by purchasing its treasury notes and bonds. Clearly, those same people already believe that the US is not bankrupt and that they will be paid back—with interest! NOBODY SEEMS TO REALIZE THAT THE US IS ALREADY ON THE ASSET STANDARD!**

This Asset Standard provides a one-time opportunity for the United States to pay off all its debts and even ensure its obligations for the funding of its underfunded social programs like Medicare, Social Security, and perhaps even one or two more long-term gifts to the US citizens such as universal healthcare and funding for real quality education. Effective endowments can be created for a truly wonderful future for American citizens and their offspring. A multi-trillion-dollar emergency account (think Covid funding) could be funded to ensure that deficit spending is over. Any use of the emergency fund would require repayment over a brief period of time.

- **UTILIZE THE ASSET STANDARD TO PAY OFF ALL US DEBTS AND TO FULLY FUND UNDERFUNDED PROGRAMS.**
- **ENACT A CONSTITUTIONAL AMENDMENT REQUIRING A BALANCED BUDGET WITH DEFICIT SPENDING MADE ILLEGAL.**

Here's the same thinking by Thomas Edison roughly a century ago: **"It is absurd to say our country can issue $30 million in bonds and not $30 million in currency. Both are promises to pay, but one promise fattens the usurers and the other helps the people."**

Wow, this is big stuff to get your head around. Issuance of debt and issuance of currency by the government feature the same promises. So why should the US take on debt instead of issue more currency?

SIDE TRIP

Our mail includes at least one solicitation every day from a US Veteran charitable organization, begging for donations to improve the housing, medical care, and opportunities for Vets. Although my wife sends something to each of them, we should all resent this entire situation. The US government should be funding all of the needs of our veterans so generously, so completely, that there is no need for this constant begging to citizens who are already paying their taxes that should be going toward this priority.

US Veterans and active-duty military AND THEIR FAMILIES deserve appreciation and support in every way. This Bad-Ass Asset Standard Solution for changes to the US economy can fund veterans' needs now and into the future as job one.

Okay, so what are the problems?

1. Economists

The arrogant economist don't-know-it-alls, who know nothing for sure, will bitch and denounce this solution. They'll come up with a zillion reasons why this can't or should not be done. Of course, they can't prove any of their concerns.

They'll say the currency will be devalued by the rest of the world. Why will it be devalued? We've already shown that the US has more than enough assets to back its dollars.

They'll say that this concept will encourage the US government to simply write checks for anything and everything it ever wants. True. That's why this Asset Standard must be enacted concurrent with a constitutional amendment to require that the US government have a balanced budget—forever. That is, the government can no longer spend more than its revenue from taxes. Massive emergency reserves will need to be maintained for wars, famine, pandemics, and disasters.

2. Effects on Our International Trade

A strong US, with no debt, fully funded social programs, and a new, fair tax structure (see Chapter 11 on US Taxes) will yield a strong dollar and probably the best environment for economic growth of any country in history. A strong dollar always sounds good, but we trade with people, companies, and nearly all countries on the planet. A strong dollar compared to other currencies means that what we buy from other countries can be relatively cheaper for us and what they buy from the US such as food is more expensive for them.

So, what's the answer against the US economy becoming even stronger than virtually all other countries who can't wipe out their debts by going onto their own Asset Standard? International currency exchanges will naturally come into play to balance international economic values.

3. Other Countries Will Want to Do This

Using this logic, it would appear that countries that have land, natural resources, public buildings, precious metals, and equipment, such as military, can do this to a degree. Once again, the international currency exchanges kick in. Just the way that everyone will cash the checks from the US, most will cash the checks from other countries—if they're viewed as financially secure.

4. Financial Professionals and Inflation

Financial professionals will tear this bad-ass solution apart. They'll say it's the most dangerous program they have ever heard of. If the US government pays off its debts completely by simply sending out checks with the explanation that the assets of the US more than back up the payments, there will be chaos in the streets all over the world. They'll also warn that government spending always sparks inflation and the dollar will be impacted severely.

Government programs usually create spending that goes into the economy for jobs, construction, and services. It's true that putting money into the general economy for those things has a multiplier effect that is inherently inflationary. Companies and workers who are paid from these programs buy other goods and services, whose businesses and employees buy other goods and services, and so on and so on.

Important: This bad-ass solution is not purchasing anything in the economy. It's REPAYING companies, individuals, and countries back who LENT THEIR OWN MONEY to the US. Don't forget that the money was theirs in the first place, just loaned to the US. The money from this bad-ass program goes to return investment dollars, likely for reinvestment, or will go completely out of the US economy, such as the $1 trillion owed to China. Sure, trillions of dollars being invested into other investments such as real estate and securities has some trickle-down and multiplier effect through the economy, but not anywhere near the multiple that other, more normal government programs do.

5. Imagine the Benefits

The US would be incredibly economically healthy after this. Imagine that the US never has debt or interest payments; has all its important social programs fully funded; has a fair, yet vibrant tax structure; and requires a balanced budget in the future? Simple. The US would come out of intensive care with a totally clean bill of health and be prepared in every way to provide opportunities for growth and happiness of its citizens for generations.

The US has already borrowed the unbearably massive $34 trillion, effectively bankrupting the US, and yet the dollar is the strongest currency in the world and the US has the strongest economy in the world. Think about that conundrum. By all CURRENT definitions, the US is literally bankrupt, meaning that it has more debt than assets—and US trade partners don't care!

The dollar constantly fluctuates against other international currencies. **Within the US, the international strength or weakness of the dollar makes no difference at all**. It only comes into play in the following circumstances:

1. A strong dollar relative to other currencies makes goods and services from other countries cheaper, so Americans benefit. Nikes that are made in other countries would cost us less.
2. Conversely, a strong dollar makes US goods and services more expensive for other countries to buy from us. Our export products such as food would cost more for other countries to buy from us.
3. A weak dollar makes goods and services from other countries more expensive for Americans. Nikes made in other countries would cost us more.
4. A weak dollar means that US goods and services are cheaper for other countries to buy from us. Our export products, such as food, would cost less for other countries to buy from us.
5. Multinational companies are affected by currency differences as illustrated above. A strong dollar makes it more difficult

to sell their products internationally. A weak dollar makes it easier to sell their products internationally.

Additionally, multi-national companies are affected because the money they earn in other currencies has to be converted into US dollars for their financial reports and if they actually bring the funds into the US. Most just keep the money offshore and avoid US taxes as and if they can. That loophole needs plugging. How much should we really give a damn about this? Don't lose sleep worrying about the currency exchange for multinational companies. They're not losing sleep about you . . .

Yes, the critics, politicians, smart-ass financial experts, and non-scientific economists will have a field day tearing this bad-ass solution down. Wouldn't we all rather they spend their time and effort to make this work? It could be one of the greatest things to happen for the US in its history. Remind them that **continuing to do nothing about this immense, ever-growing deficit is much, much, much worse than their fears of implementing this bad-ass solution.**

If the experts aren't happy with this solution, they should at least try to tweak it until it can work. Americans are sick and tired of all of these assholes complaining about everything and doing nothing, who act like, "If there's no solution, there's no problem." We need actions. We need people who can and will make this happen. **Demand that our leaders be Bad-Ass.**

CHAPTER 3
ROCKY MOUNTAIN BEACH FRONT

GLOBAL WARMING / RISING OCEANS

Stop the oceans from rising due to melting ice caps

"It isn't pollution that's harming the environment. It's the impurities in our air and water that are doing it."
—DAN QUAYLE

"The radical right is so homophobic that they're blaming global warming on the AIDS quilt."
—DENNIS MILLER

"The last time the earth was four degrees warmer, as Peter Brannen has written, there was no ice at either pole and sea level was 260 feet higher."
—DAVID WALLACE-WELLS
THE UNINHABITABLE EARTH: LIFE AFTER WARMING

THE PROBLEM

Extreme weather somewhere on the planet is nearly a weekly event. There are massive rains and floods. Little or no rain for prolonged periods is causing unprecedented droughts with vast crop losses and drastic water conservation restrictions. Massive wildfires are regular occurrences. There are devastating storms, hurricanes, typhoons (Asian hurricanes), and severe tornados. We're just starting to see significant acceleration in the melting of the polar ice caps and glaciers that are projected to result in a catastrophic rise in ocean levels. As was predicted in *Jaws*, "We're gonna need a bigger boat."

Our forty-ninth state is now called "Baked Alaska."

Some countries and governments are aggressively doing what they can to reduce the causes of global warming, mostly by reduction of carbon dioxide emissions. Many of the largest countries that are the worst contributors of carbon dioxide emissions do little more than bullshit about their intentions.

Many carbon pollution mitigation ideas seem like great solutions that will take care of the problems. Not so fast. Solar power, wind power, thermal power . . . these alternative energy sources will take a very long time to reach critical mass and it's unreasonable to believe they will address the entire problem in time.

Consider electric cars. Americans are being told that electric vehicles (EVs) that replace internal combustion engines (ICEs) will save the planet. Hey, California already mandated that only EVs can be sold in the state after 2035—just eleven years from now. Cool, right? Not really.

To recharge your EV, you will probably plug it in to a 220-volt outlet in your garage overnight. Wait. Have you ever asked yourself, or anyone else, how does the electric company get its electricity? Guess what, Dorothy? Your electric company burns fossil fuels to spin turbines to make electricity that gets sent over wires and into your house. What? Then what's the damn point if we're burning oil and coal to power EVs anyway? Their answer is, an EV requires less fossil fuel burning than your current gas car. Big whoop. As great as electric vehicles will be, we're being sold an illusion right now.

Oh, great—we still must pump, frack, and beg for oil and gas in the future? Damn it! I'm selling my Tesla shares and buying Chevron and Exxon stocks again. What about nuclear power plants? Well, sure. Try getting that accomplished quickly . . . Then, there's the nuclear waste and Chernobyl-style meltdowns.

Here's the one real path toward a truly green EV. If you have a really big roof, gobs of money, and several big battery packs hanging on your garage wall, you can generate enough solar electricity to power your home AND charge your electric car batteries. I've checked on this for myself. I have a large house and my roof still isn't big enough to power my home and one EV, let alone enough power for two EVs.

By the way, with just a small fraction of the cars in the Los Angeles area being electric, the local utility company ordered owners of EVs not to charge their vehicles because the grid was at capacity last summer. Seriously? It's true. It is thought that the electric grid size would have to double to have enough power to charge a critical mass of EVs. It does not appear that there are any current plans to do this.

WHEN ADDRESSING A PROBLEM, YOU CAN FIX THE CAUSE OF THE PROBLEM, OR FIX THE RESULT OF THE PROBLEM.

The latter is generally pursued when the former can't be fixed. If you can't change the cause of a problem, you will have the best likelihood of success by trying to repair the damage. Unfortunately, this is the situation we have with the planet's greenhouse gas problem and the resultant catastrophes that will cause more human and animal suffering than anything on this planet since the asteroid wiped out the dinosaurs.

Climate change will affect the planet and all of its inhabitants in innumerable ways. Warming oceans will change fish migration and even wipe out entire species that cannot adapt to even slightly higher temperatures quickly enough. Surface weather patterns will change, possibly constantly as we've seen recently with increases in storm strength, tornados, hurricanes, flooding, severe draughts, and massive fires. Global crop failures will be devastating.

It became clear to me that one of the very worst effects of climate change can actually be remedied by a bad-ass solution. It is the rise in ocean levels due to melting ice sheets and glaciers. In fact, we have two bad-ass solutions.

Three-quarters of this planet is covered with our most precious commodity. No one can live without it; man, beast, or plant. Water. The planet's savior—and nemesis.

According to earthdate.org, the melting polar ice caps and glaciers store 66 percent (two-thirds) of all fresh water on earth. The melting of ice is the most devastating result of global warming. There does not appear to be anything close to a real near-term solution that will resolve this enormous problem before our planet is impacted beyond repair.

Imagine the global impact of a significant rise in ocean levels. Projections from the Intergovernmental Panel on Climate Change (IPCC) report that we can expect as much as a thirty-five-inch increase in the level of the oceans by the year 2100. Some think that accelerating models show a possible rise of the ocean level by as much as eleven feet. Even at the thirty-five-inch projection, virtually all beaches will be absorbed into the oceans. Innumerable islands will cease to exist. Manhattan streets will be underwater. Low-lying cities such as Venice and New Orleans will be just memories—maybe good ones, but just memories.

There is big-ass bad news and big-ass good news.

The bad news is that no group has a good working model of the melting ice sheets, either in terms of how much will melt or how fast it will melt. *Discover Magazine* reports that the ice sheets from Antarctica and Greenland are currently adding about 1.1 BILLION TONS of water per day to the oceans, causing about ten inches of ocean rise by 2100.

This number doesn't include glacial melting or the Arctic ice, because that ice is already in the oceans, not on top of land as with the Antarctic and Greenland ice sheets. But then, most other scientific efforts to understand this problem vary in estimates, typically agreeing that we can expect about one meter (thirty-nine inches) higher ocean levels by the end of the century. It really gets depressing when they continue that it could double or even nearly triple that amount based on exponentially accelerating warming models.

Motherjones.com reports that three feet of sea-level rise would cause massive and frequent flooding of all cities along the coastlines and many islands would lose most of their land mass. At a six-feet rise, approximately 12 million people in the US alone would be displaced, with other major vulnerable cities being submerged. At eleven-feet, land inhabited by hundreds of millions of people will be underwater. The higher water will yield flooding tides and frequent storms on the order of Hurricane Sandy.

The good news is that the press paints a totally false picture of the ice sheets melting eminently. I must be a dumb-ass because I actually thought the ice would melt in a few years, leaving no more ice in the near future. According to *National Geographic* and Motherjones.com, the size of the ice sheets in Greenland and Antarctica are millions of square miles in area and between one and two MILES thick! Some scientists project that total melting would take 3,000 to 5,000 years! Peaks in Colorado won't be beachfront property for thousands of years. Still, as we've seen, the amount of melting we can actually expect can and will be devastating to the planet and its inhabitants.

BAD-ASS SOLUTION

Now try to imagine our planet without the threat of rising ocean levels and all that water from melting ice being channeled to irrigate parched, arid areas of the planet.

Yes, the world will continue to try to reduce greenhouse gases that cause global warming, but it won't happen soon enough to avoid catastrophe.

- **FOCUS ON FIXING THE PROBLEM OF RISING OCEANS SEPARATELY FROM FIXING THE CAUSE OF GLOBAL WARMING.**

Simple logic:
If you have a swimming pool that is being overfilled by a mythical fire hydrant at one end that cannot be turned off and is flooding your yard with water about to reach your house, you have to figure out how to pump water back out of the pool and move it somewhere else.

This is our planet's quandary. Too much fresh water is overfilling the oceans. How do we take fresh water out of the oceans? **Bad-Ass Solution: On the other hand, can we stop other fresh water from going into the oceans to compensate?**

If melting ice cannot be stopped from adding enormous amounts of fresh water into the ocean that will flood a large percentage of the Earth's land, what other source of water can be reduced from supplying fresh water to the oceans? Will it be enough? Then, what can we do with all that water that's not going into the oceans?

The river systems on every continent serve to efficiently distribute rainwater and snow melt along their paths, then dump the excess water into oceans. Think of the Mississippi River that delivers billions of gallons of fresh water per day into the Gulf of Mexico. This happens all over the planet. This massive infusion of fresh (unsalted) water effectively contributes along with the melting ice to raise the oceans.

Shut off the rivers? No, just partly reduce discharge flows into the oceans. The continued flows will still serve the critical ecological necessities at the places where fresh water feeds into the oceans.

About now you're probably thinking this guy is just too crazy-ass and you want to put this damn book down. Don't—it gets really interesting.

Can we offset the volume of water from melting ice by stopping that much water from rivers going into the oceans? **YES!**

The really great news is that the water from melting ice that goes into the ocean is just a small fraction of the total water flowing into the oceans from rivers!

- **STOP A FRACTION OF THE WATER GOING INTO THE OCEANS FROM THE MAJOR RIVERS AND MOVE IT TO ARID LANDS.**

The byproduct of having all this fresh water to distribute will be an incredible abundance of food production to make starvation and thirst on Earth a thing of the past. The lives of people in arid regions will be immeasurably enhanced. Wouldn't the bounty from all of this water be a justifiable cost? You bet your ass. Too cool—save much of the planet and at the same time, greatly enhance the lives of billions.

The United Nations World Water Development Report 2023 states that 26 percent (a quarter) of the world's population doesn't have access to safe drinking water and 46 percent (nearly half) lacks access to basic sanitation. This is truly stunning, particularly as we argue over which billionaire's spaceship will be the first to land on Mars.

Water must be moved from rivers either by gravity or pumps. Pumps require significant amounts of power. Massive amounts of power must be generated to pump huge amounts of water uphill, or even level. It doesn't make much sense to use fossil fuels to power this solution to global warming. So, what green power is available? Water running downhill or from reservoirs can generate electricity. Great. Solar and wind farms can supply power adjacent to pumping stations. Small nuclear power plants could be utilized.

Businesses and countries have utilized vast pipelines to distribute oil and gas from production in distant sites to metropolitan areas for decades. Two thousand years ago, the Romans created a network of aqueducts to bring water from far away to Rome for its baths and fountains—without electric pumps! Incredible advanced engineering.

Finally, the people of Arizona, along with the state and federal governments, created a model system to bring critical water from far away. The Phoenix and Tucson region would be tiny, parched communities without this surprisingly forward-thinking effort by the people, government, and utilities. We'll look at this more closely in a few minutes.

How do we move all this water?

After identifying rivers that have reliable excess water, holding lakes and reservoirs (for hydroelectric power generation) will be created at strategic locations along the rivers. All kinds of methods for moving water will be utilized, such as canals and pipes. Water can be moved above ground that is already owned by state and federal governments, including lands adjacent to highways and railways.

Rising ocean levels will represent financial devastation on a level never before seen. Human and animal suffering and property and business losses along the coasts will be incalculable. Billions? Trillions? How about hundreds of trillions of dollars? This will be a global effort beyond anything ever undertaken, including world wars.

River systems already serve as efficient water distributors. Think if some water from the Mississippi River is diverted through pipes that go underneath the Gulf of Mexico, then back onto land in West Texas and up to the Colorado River in Colorado or Utah to supply and refill Lakes Powell and Mead, delivering fresh water along the way. From Powell and Mead, the water is used for hydroelectrical power generation as it is released back into the Colorado River for distribution throughout the Southwest. Hundreds of miles of efficient water distribution already exist.

Here are some really amazing statistics. Don't get scared, they're fairly easy to ingest.

Many of these statistics are extremely difficult to obtain. Many were gleaned from several sources with Discovermagazine.com particularly helpful in understanding the increase in ocean levels relative to the amount of square meters of water per second from melting ice. My tenth grade Algebra teacher would certainly be happy with the hours of calculations that ensued. Much of the math that follows is from a non-expert citizen dilettante.

To raise the ocean levels forty inches by 2100:

> Tons of melted water added to the oceans per day:
>
> (4.4 billion tons)
>
> 4,400,000,000 tons
>
> Number of cubic meters of melted water per day:
>
> (Units used for water volume)
>
> 3,992,000,000 cubic meters per day
>
> (A square meter of water is equal to 264.17 gallons)
>
> Number of cubic meters per second of melted water:
>
> (Measured in flow of water in rivers)
>
> 46,200 cubic meters per second
>
> Round up that number:
>
> 50,000 cubic meters per second of melted water to be replaced by river relocation.

This means that approximately 50,000 cubic meters of water from melting ice are being added to the ocean levels every second. For context, Justintools.com reports that an Olympic sized swimming pool holds 2,500 square meters of water, so **ice is melting and adding to ocean levels at the rate of approximately the water in twenty Olympic pools PER SECOND.** Don't wet your pants. Remember, this massive amount of melted water can be stopped elsewhere from going into the oceans to balance out.

Now, let's look at the twenty largest rivers in the world based on their average water flow (discharge) into the oceans, using square meters of water per second:

	RIVER	CONTINENT	AVERAGE DISCHARGE (METERS/SECOND)
1	AMAZON	SOUTH AMERICA	224,000
2	GANGES	ASIA	43,900
3	CONGO	AFRICA	41,200
4	ORINOCO	SOUTH AMERICA	37,740
5	GUAINIA/NEGRO	SOUTH AMERICA	35,943
6	YANGTZE	ASIA	35,000
7	MADEIRA	SOUTH AMERICA	31,200
8	RIO DE LA PLATA	SOUTH AMERICA	27,225
9	BRAHMAPUTRA	ASIA	19,825
10	YENISEI	ASIA	19,800
11	PARANA	SOUTH AMERICA	19,706
12	GANGES AT FARAKKA	ASIA	18,691
13	MISSISSIPPI	NORTH AMERICA	18,434
14	JAPURA	SOUTH AMERICA	18,122
15	LENA	ASIA	17,067
16	SAINT LAWRENCE	NORTH AMERICA	16,800
17	MARANON	SOUTH AMERICA	16,708
18	MEKONG	ASIA	16,000
19	IRRAWADDY	ASIA	15,112
20	TAPAJOS	SOUTH AMERICA	13,540
	TOTAL AVERAGE DISCHARGE (METERS/SECOND)		686,013

Chart from: en.wikipedia.org
The Amazon is massive! Does Bezos own that Amazon too?

Remember, melting ice is adding 50,000 square meters of water per second to the oceans. The total average flow discharge of water from just these twenty largest rivers into the ocean is 686,000 square meters, or approximately fourteen times more than the amount of water from melting ice!

In other words, the additional ice-melted water is only about 7.3 percent of the water going into the oceans from Earth's twenty largest rivers. Whew. I thought we had a real unsolvable problem here.

Although a massive undertaking, doesn't it seem easily within our reach to remove just 7.3 percent of the water flow from the twenty major rivers and distribute that water where it can be used so positively?

An even smaller amount of water could be diverted if more rivers are utilized. Great bad-ass solution!

You're thinking this is just ridiculous and nothing like this could ever be accomplished. Well, as mentioned earlier, a fantastic project similar to this (on a smaller scale) already exists, right in our own US backyard.

WE HAVE A MODEL!!!!

The parched region of Arizona that encompasses Phoenix and Tucson could never have grown into the vibrant, attractive places to live and work they now are without importing water. The place is a real desert after all. According to CAP-AZ.com and Americanwatercollege.org, a twenty-year massive project call the **Central Arizona Project** diverts water from the Colorado River over 336 miles via canals that includes lifting the water nearly 3,000 feet in elevation via a series of fourteen pumping plants, one hydroelectric pump/generating plant, thirty-nine gate structures, fifty turnouts, and storage reservoirs to serve the water needs of 5 million people in Arizona, or 80 percent of the state's population.

The project is an engineering masterpiece. It delivers 456 billion gallons of water per year. The project was accomplished between the state of Arizona and the US federal government. Can you believe that Congress actually passed something so magnificent and valuable? The Colorado River Basin Project Act of 1968 was signed by President Johnson and heralded at the time as one of the most celebrated bipartisan achievements of the twentieth century. Cooperation from the federal government was critical for the land and funding.

This amazing project was completed in 1993 (thirty years ago) at what can be considered an incredibly low price of only $4 billion. Fantastic. The long-term human and economic benefits make this cost immaterial.

Again, moving vast amounts of water over, under, and through terrain to deliver it where you need it has been done already. The planet can save itself with this bad-ass solution on every continent. Let's go!

How much will it cost to transport water from these rivers to arid areas? Perhaps the question should be how much will it cost if we don't move the water?

Unlike oil pipelines where the commodity being moved is costly, the water is free. Only the cost of the infrastructure is involved. If the pure water that will be used for humans and irrigation is sold for a fraction of a penny per gallon, trillions of dollars will be generated annually to pay for the system's continued utilization.

A cost/benefit analysis is skewed enormously toward actually doing this program—immediately. The scale and cost to build these systems on many continents may be the largest effort ever undertaken on planet Earth. Labor, materials, and construction will take years and trillions of dollars. This will support local economies with jobs and materials. Offset this cost by the literal saving of coastal areas and the benefit to the arid lands transformed into verdant oases.

How can we (the whole planet) not do this? We have to do this—and right now.

SECOND BAD-ASS SOLUTION

Again, we need to either stop other fresh water from pouring into the oceans or remove water from the oceans to stop the rise from melting ice. Here's another idea to balance out water levels from flooding much of the populated planet and can be utilized in concert with the previously-described bad-ass solution.

The problem with all of this ocean water is that neither man, beast, nor plant can use the salty crap. What the hell kind of God joke is that? Okay, he/she likes fish. Joe Rogan stated the obvious, "We don't have a water problem on this planet, we have a salt problem."

Fortunately, the world has experienced a technological explosion. The planet evolved from agrarian to starships in just a couple hundred years—about the same time humans have been destroying the planet and its future.

- **REMOVE WATER FROM THE OCEANS AND REMOVE THE SALT SO IT CAN BE USED FOR PEOPLE AND IRRIGATION.**

Imagine that we could take water from the oceans, remove the salt, and use that pure, clean water to quench and irrigate the parched soil and its inhabitants. Can you picture desalination plants located along virtually all coastlines that back up to parched land and people? CA.gov reports that there are twelve desalination plants already in California and Greencitytimes.com reports approximately 20,000 operational desalination plants in 120 countries. We need many thousands more. Again, this would easily be the largest public works program in world history. But, with the biggest payback. This program, if done in a new way, will also (with the first bad-ass solution mentioned above) remove massive amounts of water from the oceans that are being overfilled by the melting ice caps and glaciers.

As an aside, remember your history books that described when ships going from the Atlantic to the Pacific, or vice versa, had to sail all the way around South America? It more than doubled the length of the voyage and obviously more than doubled the cost and time for the transportation of people and goods. That was solved by funding from the US to create the fifty-one-mile-long waterway, the Panama Canal. According to History.com, The project took ten years (between 1904 and 1913), and its cost was monumental at $375 million (only $8 billion in today's dollars). But the result was truly magnificent and a great achievement whose massive benefits are continuing 111 years later. A truly incredible feat. We can do this kind of massive project again, even bigger, with more universal benefits.

Many massive projects like the Venice flood gates that hold back the rising tide from flooding the city have just the one purpose. Only a truly great project can have two enormous benefits like both bad-ass solutions we have here. Stop the rising oceans that would otherwise destroy the world's coasts, and at the same time bring fresh water to parts of the planet that will flourish to unimaginable heights because of the water.

Besides saving the planet, the increased food production and quality of life for the poorest, most desperate people—and everyone else on Earth—will yield miraculous results. It's difficult to imagine a more global benefit, except maybe forcing a huge asteroid away from a direct Earth hit.

Current desalination technologies have three very significant limitations:

1. They are incredibly expensive.
2. They service a relatively small number of people.
3. They return even saltier water to the ocean, which could negatively impact marine life, which we've polluted enough already.

Here's the Bad-Ass Solution for fixing the desalination problems:

1. Place the desalination plants on government-owned lands and do not allow local governments and neighbors to slow down approvals. This must happen very quickly, without red tape.
2. Deal with the excess salt in a number of ways:
    a. Remove the salt and transport it inland for burial like a landfill.
    b. As is starting to occur with new desalination plants, add the extra salt to the community's wastewater system which was flowing as unsalted fresh water into the ocean, thus averaging out the excess salt impact.
    c. Remove the salt and ship it to the poles to combine with the new fresh water from the massive melting.
    d. Remove the salt and ship it to be mixed in small amounts with the freshwater discharge from major rivers into the oceans.

PLEASE: Start somewhere. Do something. Don't spend your time criticizing. That's easy and worthless. Spend your time solving problems by creating solutions and working toward achieving them.

Make these or other bad-ass solutions work for this destructing planet. Just do it now!

Think big. Stop the rising tide—literally.

The entire planet wins.

CHAPTER 4
BAZOOKA FOR A HIGH SCHOOL GRADUATION PRESENT

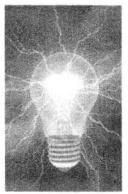

GUNS AND ASSAULT WEAPONS

Destroy every assault rifle in thirty days and enforce reasonable guns laws

"Hunt or be hunted."

—UNKNOWN

"They say if you outlaw guns, only outlaws will have guns. Well, those are precisely the people who need them!"

—GEORGE CARLIN

"I have grown up with guns all my life, but people who like assault weapons—they should join the United States Army, we have them."

—GENERAL WESLEY CLARK

"I went to buy an assault rifle today. Astonished by the price, I asked the clerk: Do I get a student discount?"

—UNKNOWN

> "I don't think we need more gun control laws."
> —PRESIDENT JOHN F. KENNEDY

THE PROBLEM

There are **433.9 million** civilian firearms in the US, which is approximately **100 million** more guns than people. Source: National Shooting Sports Foundation

The US has two cataclysmic situations:

1. Criminals have guns—and use them.
2. Mentally ill people, particularly young white men, can get their hands on assault weapons—and use them to carry out mass shootings. Strike that. Mass killings.

There are now approximately two mass shootings in the US—every single day. (Mass shootings are four or more people.)

The entire subject of guns polarizes the US. Some want all guns banned. Some want all guns legal. Some want some guns banned and some guns legal. Some want to carry guns on themselves at all times. Some want no one but police to carry guns. Of course, the criminals have their guns. What a dangerous mess.

The anti-gun folks are inflexible, worried that guns in the hands of normal citizens create all sorts of needless deths and injury. The pro-gun folks are inflexible, worried a ban on guns will leave them defenseless when an intruder breaks into their home. The lobbyists for both sides are well-paid and have their feet firmly planted in cement. No compromises. As with most polarizing topics, the extremes of both sides take ridiculous positions. No guns for any citizen versus teens toting assault rifles under their trench coats.

The wild, wild west conundrum:

The bad guys have guns. How do the good guys protect themselves, their families, and their property without guns? So everybody is armed? "You better not give me that parking ticket, or else . . ."

Citizens have a real constitutional right to have guns. Okay, but the US has an enormous problem. ***Forbes* reported in May 2021 that there are at least 20 million assault rifles in America.** Really? WTF? Are we assembling a citizen militia to invade Canada?

There is no reason other than a military operation for anyone to possess assault weapons. These are mass-killing machines, period. They are not for hunting. They are totally unnecessary for home defense. The wackos who believe these military weapons are a right, apparently haven't been watching the news every single night to understand the constant death these things are inflicting on all Americans—and their children. Demanding the right to keep assault rifles is just plain nuts.

My brother-in-law's brother was shot and killed while watching a Fourth of July parade near his home in Highland Park, Illinois, along with six other people. If you haven't lost someone to this horrible assault weapon nightmare, you will. Then you may also think these effing things are too dangerous. Let me just add that Steve Straus was a warm, kind, and brilliant man who was and remains deeply loved.

BAD-ASS SOLUTION

How do we resolve this scourge on the US?

- **BAN AND SIEZE ALL ASSAULT WEAPONS—FOR REAL.**
    1. Immediately ban the sale and possession of all assault weapons.
    2. Require all assault weapons to be turned in for an immediate return of their full cost, paid by the US government.

Oh sure, no one would believe that everyone, especially the bad guys, will turn in their assault weapons, unless:

    3. We allow thirty days to turn in assault weapons for refunds, no questions asked.
    4. **After the thirty days, anyone found in possession of an assault weapon (utilizing gun sale and registration information) will have an immediate trial and mandatory one-year jail sentence, which will be immediately implemented.**

Remember all the old westerns, where the judge rode into town, held a short trial, and the convicted killer was hanged right then and there? That's exactly the kind of legal system that must be applied where the US needs it so desperately.

This kind of immediate criminal justice must happen throughout the US NOW. The US must actually use its power to create the laws that are needed and enforce those laws with total cooperation from the courts. **STOP PUSSY-FOOTING AROUND WITH CRIMINALS. WHY THE HELL IS OUR SOCIETY PROTECTING CRIMINALS MORE THAN VICTIMS?**

Keeping guns at your home or business is not the only issue. One issue is that if a bad guy breaks into your home, you can't just shoot him. Unless the bad guy has a weapon, AND THREATENS YOU WITH THAT WEAPON, you can't shoot. You'll be in jail, perhaps even for murder, if you do shoot him.

We are literally supposed to wait to shoot until the bad guy tries to kill us. This is insane. Recently, a bad guy held up a convenience store in New

York. He physically abused the elderly shop owner and threatened him with a knife. The old man actually wrestled the knife away from the bad guy—and killed him! A store video showed the entire incident. Incredibly, the old man was arrested and remained in jail until the public outcry forced authorities to release him. Can't make this shit up.

Here's another incident that may be just a great urban legend: A couple was followed home from a restaurant. Upon arriving at their house, a bad guy approached them as they exited their car, held them at gunpoint, and made them take him into their home. The couple yelled to their children, ordering them to stay in their rooms. The criminal barked at the terrified couple while holding the gun and demanded they take him to get everything of value in the house that he could carry. As the husband turned to climb the stairs, he tripped and pulled on a coat rack to stop his fall. The coat rack slammed down on the criminal's arm. The gun fired, thankfully not hitting anyone, and was flung into the air as the criminal fell back.

The husband somehow caught the gun and turned it on the criminal who was now on the ground. "Don't move, asshole."

He then told his wife to call 911. The criminal yelled, "WAIT. If the police come and arrest me, I'll be out within a day or two. I know where you live. I know you have children. Let me go and you'll never see me again. If you call the police, I'll come back and kill you and your children."

The husband thought for a second, then shot the criminal in the head, dead. The husband wasn't charged because he told a somewhat different story that the criminal continued to come at him as the gun was flying, then the husband was able to grab and shoot. It was termed self-defense.

Some states have "stand your ground" laws. Ncsl.org explains this as, "people have the right to use reasonable force, including deadly force, against an intruder in their home." Under such a law, people have no duty to retreat before using deadly force in self-defense, meaning you can defend yourself and your property by shooting a **threatening** invader.

Until the government can adequately protect us and our property, which is their number one obligation, the public needs to be armed in their homes and businesses and have the right to use necessary force against intruders who are attempting to rob or attack them or others, with the perceived danger of bodily harm. It is important that citizens understand the laws and even their state's court rulings to know what they can and cannot do.

What about carrying a gun when you're out among the general public? This is normally called concealed carry. That is, wearing a hidden gun. What about open carry, that is, wearing a gun that is not concealed? Is that okay? Yes, to at least some degree in most states. Weird.

The bad guys have been emboldened. Right out in the open and in broad daylight, groups are doing smash-and-grab thefts daily; robbing and beating citizens right on our streets and following citizens home to burgle their homes and, in many cases, beat and even kill the victims.

The idea of the general public being armed conjures up visions of the old West, with shootings in the street at high noon. Didn't we end that about 150 years ago? How about the movie cowboys with their pearl-handled six-guns that would twirl in circles before they went back into the holster? If someone tried to twirl a real gun, wouldn't they end up shooting their own armpit? (Couldn't resist that.)

To address this reasonably, try to imagine walking with your spouse to your car after a nice dinner. Suddenly, two guys approach, show a gun or knife, and order you to give them your wallets, purse, and jewelry. You comply (as you should) because "things" are replaceable but lives are not.

But this isn't over. Now, they demand that you take them to your home to give them everything of value there. Remember, they're yelling at you, being extremely aggressive, and you're scared to death. You're sure that when you give them everything in your home, they're going to kill you, your spouse, and heaven forbid, your children who may be at home. What do you do? Shit yourself. Too late . . .

These types of crimes are everywhere. Why? Because the bad guys have learned that people will eagerly hand over their possessions because they know what was said before, that things can be replaced, but not people. "Here, take everything, just please take it and go!"

Wouldn't we all do this? Of course. But this is what the bad guys have learned about us. Why would they not commit this crime? There is nothing to stop them. They may even shoot their victims anyway—just for fun.

But what if you're armed and shoot or even kill them? What if this becomes more the rule than the exception? Will these crimes stop? Yup.

Take a deep breath, because you'll hate this like I do. Unless or until the government (police) can protect you, you must be prepared to protect yourself. Learn how to use a gun. Learn what an officer learns. For example, know that when you shoot, you will also hit anything behind your target. If there is an innocent person behind them, or even through a wall, you can't shoot.

If you can survive an ordeal by giving them what they want, for Christ's sake, GIVE IT TO THEM. If you don't think you and your family will survive, start shooting (if no bystander can be hit). Them or you. Choose you. Just know very well what you're doing. Of course you don't want to do this. No one does!

Additionally insane, mostly young men are committing mass killings by going into schools, concerts, businesses, etc. with assault weapons to just shoot everyone possible as if they're inside a video game. I don't know about you, but I would pray that someone in that room has a weapon and can shoot the lunatic in the head before dozens more are killed. This is damn serious and may be worth the government and the public agreeing that they need to help to keep Americans safe.

What about deputizing lots of people to carry weapons? It now makes sense to highly train a citizen force of people who are capable and willing to protect people during a mass shooting before the real police arrive. Don't you like the idea of an undercover air marshal on your passenger plane to protect against terrorists? I do and hope they're on every flight.

- **TRAIN A CITIZEN DEPUTY FORCE TO CARRY CONCEALED WEAPONS TO PROTECT AMERICANS (AND THEMSELVES) IN MASS SHOOTING SITUATIONS.**

The Supreme Court recently ruled that the Second Amendment includes citizens' right to carry a concealed weapon, even while they are away from their homes. States are rushing to figure out how they can comply with the ruling, while still keeping as many people as possible from carrying concealed weapons. You should get permitted to carry if possible. If not, consider carrying anyway and risk committing the crime of illegally carrying a concealed weapon without a permit. In California, you'll go to jail, but will likely be out quickly because you've committed a misdemeanor.

Your call. And it's a very tough one. Doesn't it just suck that we're having this discussion because we are not safe?

- **GET TRAINED TO CARRY A CONCEALED WEAPON TO PROTECT YOURSELF AND OTHERS.**

Hopefully, this is a temporary solution. The permanent solution is to have less crime because:

1. Criminals become fearful of being shot by their victims.
2. Criminals have better options for making a living.
3. Law enforcement and the justice system regain control to keep citizens safe.

It's a dangerous jungle. Stay safe out there.

CHAPTER 5
I'M FILING FOR DIVORCE

CHINA AND RUSSIA

Divorce due to irreconcilable differences

"The capitalists will sell us the rope with which we will hang them."
—VLADIMIR LENIN (PROBABLY)

"You know, without China there is no Wal-Mart and without Wal-Mart there is no middle class and lower-class prosperity in the United States."
—ARTHUR LAFFER

"The problem with socialism is that you eventually run out of other people's money."
—MARGARET THATCHER

"We had a very successful trip to Russia. We made it back."
—BOB HOPE

THE PROBLEM

What is it with Russia and China? No matter what side of an issue the US is on, Russia and China are on the opposite, dark side.

We support Israel, South Korea, Ukraine. They back Pro-Palestinian terrorist groups like Hamas and Hezbollah, North Korea, Iran, Venezuela. We think our choices are for good regimes and intentions and that their choices are for evil regimes and bad intentions. It's axiomatic that each side in a conflict believes they are right and their cause is just. Westerners just can't understand what the hell Russia and China are thinking. They probably feel the same—classic roots of conflict. Doesn't it suck that the US, Russia, and China can't have a similar, or at least compatible, notion of good and evil?

RUSSIA (A basic background)

Let's not go back too far, leave the Czars out of this. The Soviet Union was actually allied with the West during both World Wars. Let's shorten the time frame even further, going back only to World War II. The alliance was actually kind of surprising, because Joseph Stalin was the Russian leader during that time. He and the Soviet Union were certainly not friendly toward the West. They could not have been more ideologically polar opposites

Per History.com, Stalin was the leader of the Communist Party (along with other titles) of the Soviet Union after Lenin, from 1922 through 1952. He was the effective dictator after the 1930s and adhered to Leninist Marxism, with some of his own interpretations.

Under Stalin's tyrannical control, the Soviet Union had purges, forced labor camps, ethnic cleansing, repression, famine that killed millions, and executions of 700,000. What a guy.

At the beginning of World War II, there was a non-aggression pact between the Soviets and Nazi Germany. It ended quickly because Germany (Hitler) actually invaded the Soviet Union in 1941. Thus, the Soviets became allied with the West. It was a clear case of "the enemy of my enemy is my friend."

By the end of the war, the Soviets annexed much of Eastern Europe and parts of Asia. The West was busy rebuilding Europe via the Marshal Plan. The end of the war left two clear superpowers: the Soviet Union and the United States.

It has been rumored for more than seventy years that General George Patton wanted the US (Eisenhower) to allow him to use his Third Army after the war in Europe concluded to invade and conquer the Soviet Union, which Patton thought would be a cakewalk after they were so decimated and exhausted from the war with Germany. Of course, this didn't happen and probably led to the "retirement" of Patton. However, what if . . . ?

After the war, there was serious distrust between the Soviets and the US/Great Britain. The West was rebuilding Western Europe, which included democratic/capitalist influence. The Soviets controlled Eastern Europe and spread socialism/communism.

The years that followed continued the trend with arms races, space races, and political ideology differences. The distrust on both sides was dangerous. There were continuous aggressive incidents like in Hungary, Czechoslovakia, the Cuban Missile Crisis, and the division of Berlin via the infamous wall. Both sides routinely showed their might by endless missile and nuclear weapons testing, aka warning shots.

The reality of a nuclear war between two powers having similar planet-destruction capabilities yields no winner. The certainty that everyone loses has kept the sides in check for the better part of a century, while the leaders maintained their fingers just inches away from being able to push "the buttons."

The major turning point in the Cold War was during the 1980s under Ronald Reagan's presidency. Reagan detested the Soviets' communism, military escalation, and support of "evil" countries and terrorists. That said, he was correct in his determination that the USSR's economy was doing very badly and that they would not be able to continue the arms and minds race against the US.

According to Heritage.org, through a series of strategies and directives that included backing the Solidarity movement in Poland, Reagan continued to hurt the Soviet economy by reducing their access to Western technology and by driving down the price of oil and limiting natural gas exports to the West. Sound familiar forty years later? Big boy Monopoly.

Reagan continued to make the Soviets try to keep up with US military spending while he actually caused them to spend eight times more just to catch up. Finally, the Strategic Defense Initiative (SDI), more affectionately referred to as "Star Wars," was the trump card in the arms race that the Soviets simply couldn't duplicate and which frightened the bejesus out of them.

Also, per Heritage.org, by the end of Reagan's presidency in 1989, the Reagan Doctrine had achieved its goal. Mikhail Gorbachev, the last leader of the Soviet system, publicly acknowledged the failures of Marxism-Leninism and the futility of Russian imperialism. Could somebody please tell Putin?

Reagan succeeded with his demand, "Mr. Gorbachev, tear down this wall." The Berlin Wall came down shortly thereafter. Margaret Thatcher (British Prime Minister) said, "Ronald Reagan has ended the Cold War without firing a shot."

The new Russia retained the Kremlin but permitted many changes to their economy in the form of capitalism. The changes transformed the country from constant images of bare grocery store shelves and long lines for staples like bread, into a much more prosperous population and standard of living. Still, the old guard boys of communism have held on to their beloved days of socialist poverty for all. Of course, they feel this way while, as oligarchs, they sit on their mega-yachts in the South of France.

It is widely believed that the Russian President, Vladimir Putin, is dedicated to returning Russia back to the glory days of the USSR, including the return of all the former Soviet Eastern European satellite countries that have been on their own for decades now. It is also believed that Putin stashed away so much of Russia's wealth that he is the richest person in the world. Sorry, Elon.

Putin has ruled Russia as prime minister or president via sham elections since 1999. He's one of the main guys always causing or supporting trouble in the world. His latest, greatest criminal act has been the unprovoked attack and invasion of Ukraine. His and his soldiers' brutality has been laid bare for the world to see. Calling them wild animals would be a compliment for these rapists, torturers, and murderers.

Vladimir Putin
Владимир Путин

Putin in 2021

President of Russia

Incumbent

Assumed office
7 May 2012

Prime Minister Dmitry Medvedev
Mikhail Mishustin

Preceded by Dmitry Medvedev

In office
7 May 2000 – 7 May 2008
Acting: 31 December 1999 – 7 May 2000

Wikipedia

Putin has weaponized his country's only real assets, oil and gas, using them to raise money to fund his war efforts while at the same time extorting the countries and people who need the energy. He jails, poisons, and murders political adversaries. The most recent was his most ardent and popular rival, Alexei Navalny. Putin had him poisoned, then after he recovered miraculously, had him jailed and finally killed in February 2024. Putin arrests Western citizens on trumped-up charges to be used as hostages.

Guess what? Incredibly, the asshole may lose the war against Ukraine! Perhaps there is justice and karma.

Some interesting facts about Russia:

1. According to Worldmeters.info, Russia's population was 144 million in 2023, 43 percent of the US population of 332 million. Russia is the largest country by land mass.
2. Per Investopedia's rankings:
    a. Russia has the eleventh largest economy in the world, with just $1.48 trillion GDP, representing only 1.31 percent of the world's economy.
        i. US GDP is $23 trillion—fifteen and a half times the size of Russia's economy.
    b. California, Texas, and New York each have larger GDPs than Russia. But Russia has its own nukes!
    c. **RUSSIA'S ECONOMY IS 25 PERCENT SMALLER THAN ITALY'S!** This is amazing. What happened to being a superpower?
    d. This isn't an "apples-to-apples" comparison, but worth considering: Russia's annual GDP is less than half of Apple's stock market value.
        i. Russia's main assets are its vast supplies of natural resources, most importantly oil and gas.
        ii. Jason Furman, who chaired the Council of Economic Advisers in the Obama Administration told the New York Times, "Russia is incredibly unimportant in the global economy except for oil and gas. It's basically a big gas station."

- **MAKE NO MISTAKE. PUTIN AND THEREFORE RUSSIA ARE NOT TO BE CONSIDERED FRIENDS OR EVEN POTENTIAL FRIENDS OF THE US.**

CHINA (A BASIC BACKGROUND)

News flash. That is, you probably didn't know this, or never actually thought about it, but China was also an ally of the West during World War II. According to CNN.com, In the few years prior to the war, China and Japan were embroiled in an all-out war, with Japan likely headed toward a victory.

China's leader, Chiang Kai-shek, a nationalist (not a communist), refused to surrender to Japan, which effectively merged China with the Allies after Pearl Harbor in 1941. As with the Soviets, China joining the Allies was another case of "the enemy of my enemy is my friend." China contributed to the war effort by keeping Japan busy fighting while the Allies spent most of the early war effort fighting Hitler in Europe.

Per the BBC.co.uk, Mao Zedong came to power after being on the opposite side of Chiang Kai-shek in a Chinese civil war. In 1949, Mao founded the People's Republic of China (PRC). He tried to have a Chinese form of communism, which led to famine and the deaths of millions. Mao attempted to reestablish his authority with the "Cultural Revolution" in 1966, and the result was that 1.5 million people died and much of the country's heritage was destroyed. He continued to lead with the backing of the army, but his health began to fail.

Toward the end, Mao tried to build bridges with the US, Japan, and Europe, culminating with a famous visit to China by President Nixon in 1972, where they watched ping-pong. Relations between the US and China began a period of building since that event. Dating, but not lovers.

To their credit, China transformed in a shockingly short time from a pathetically poor agrarian country prior to World War II into a thriving, dynamic, industrial, and technological powerhouse society. Of course, they still have more poor peasants than they can count, but their standard of living has increased tremendously. They now have the number two economy in the world behind the US.

How did they do it? The communist country learned that capitalism works. Sure, they're still tyrannical and murderous, but now they're also communist-capitalist boorish pricks, to coin a phrase.

How is it that our own college students don't know what China and Russia know about the benefits of capitalism over socialism/communism?

As expected with a 4,000-year-old society, the Chinese are wise. They have seen that Western businesspeople and their governments will sell their very souls for a few bucks. They take advantage with their 1.4 BILLION people in two ways. First, they have cheap labor to make all the goods for the West. Second, their people buy goods and services from the West that are manufactured and sold in China, so they are critically important trade partners. They've made it virtually impossible for the US to wean off the Chinese teat.

For many years, the Chinese have dictated the terms of doing business there. Catch this: if a Westerner wants to manufacture in China, they must give China the specifications of the product—and patents don't matter! Every US company manufacturing in China succumbs to this—yes, apparently including Apple. Are we insane? Yes, because we bow to their demands like children.

Regardless of your feelings about Donald Trump as president, he was tough on China. He imposed tariffs and demanded fair dealing. Along with Trump, that policy didn't last very long, and China moved back to taking advantage in every way possible. They must just laugh their asses off at us dumb-shit Americans.

Their President Xi Jinping took office in 2013 and now (like Putin) declares himself to be president for life. Can you say emperor of China? Also, like Putin, Xi supports all the bad guys such as North Korean President Kim Jong-un. Xi too is always on what we consider to be the evil side of issues. Xi has allied with Putin, but at times seems to be backing away as the Ukraine war crimes and failures keep multiplying.

Oh, and Xi's and China's gift to the world? COVID.

Xi Jinping

Xi in 2019

General Secretary of the Chinese Communist Party

Incumbent

Assumed office
15 November 2012

From Wikipedia

Some interesting facts about China:

1. According to UN statistics, China's population is 1.434 Billion, 19 percent of the global total and 4.32 times the US population of 332 million.

2. Per Investopedia's rankings:

    a. China has the second largest economy in the world, with $17.7 trillion GDP.

    b. US GDP is $23 Trillion—1.3 times the size of China's economy. It's worth noting that the US has the larger economy with less than one-quarter of the population.

    c. Per Prosperousamerica.org: China is the world's largest manufacturing economy and exporter of goods. It is also the world's fastest-growing consumer market and second-largest importer of goods. China is also the world's largest consumer of numerous commodities.

3. According to the Office of the United States Trade Representative:
   a. Total US goods and services trade with China in 2022 totaled $758.4 billion.
   b. China exported $562.9 billion to the US.
   c. China imported $195.5 billion from the US.
   d. Therefore, the US sold $367.4 billion less to China than it bought from China (a trade deficit).
   e. The US sold $14.9 billion more services to China than it imported from China (a trade surplus).

4. Per heritage.org, China may have one of the world's largest economies and be the world's biggest exporter, but its income per capita is below the global average.

5. Per worldbank.org, China accounts for 27 percent of annual global carbon dioxide and a third of the world's greenhouse gas emissions.

6. Fentanyl is made in China and is currently killing approximately 300 Americans every day. **SO FAR, WE'VE LOST APPROXIMATELY FIVE VIETNAMS OF AMERICANS TO FENTANYL.** This alone should mean war. Really. War. Send drones in to attack and bomb the fentanyl manufacturing facilities. Fuck China if they don't like it.

- **MAKE NO MISTAKE. XI AND THEREFORE CHINA DO NOT GIVE A DAMN ABOUT THE US AND ARE NOT TO BE CONSIDERED FRIENDS OR EVEN POTENTIAL FRIENDS.**

Note: Some governments perform badly on the world stage, but most people living in those countries rarely have any real input about the activities of their governments. Therefore, Evil Countries means the governmental regimes and not necessarily the people.

BAD-ASS SOLUTION

- **CHINA AND RUSSIA ARE EVIL EMPIRES.**
- **THE US AND ITS ALLIES MUST IMMEDIATELY GET DIVORCED FROM CHINA AND RUSSIA, CITING IRRECONCILABLE DIFFERENCES.**
- **BOTH SIDES RETAIN CUSTODY OF THEIR OWN LOYAL CHILDREN COUNTRIES.**
- **THIS NEW ERA WILL MARK THE END OF BUSINESS GLOBALISM, CALLED DEGLOBALIZATION OR ON-SHORING.**
- **THE US AND ITS ALLIES MUST BE FINISHED DEALING WITH EVIL COUNTRIES.**

The past several decades championed the idea of a global economy where goods and services would be produced wherever costs are most efficient. Simply put, the consuming world chased cheap labor to produce its goods. China and India thrived by having billions of people working for pennies. This included Japan for a while, until they got too rich from all the business. Manufacturing spread to many other countries with masses of poor people whose labor cost very little.

At its best, globalism signaled world peace through economic interdependence. How sweet.

Think about this: forty years of cheaper goods produced offshore gave US consumers continually lower prices. This is precisely what kept US inflation almost non-existent during that period. It had NOTHING to do with the Federal Reserve. Read the chapter on the Federal Reserve for the real reasons for the massive return of inflation in 2022.

The US has an unprecedented opportunity right now for its long-term economic security. Following is the roadmap:

1. The US has enough oil and gas resources (if liberated by the US government) to keep itself and probably its allies energy independent. This will support the divorce from the energy bad guys: Russia, Saudis, OPEC, and Venezuela.

    a. The US has taken the lead in renewable energy sources and technologies that will continue to supplement and replace fossil fuels into the future.

    b. A recent announcement of successful nuclear fusion power generation portends a remarkable future for the entire planet. This is literally the same power source as the sun and stars. It's completely clean, safe, and uses hydrogen as its fuel, the most abundant element in the universe. The US and its allies should retain complete control and throw Russia out of the original, decades-old fusion partnership. Call it punishment for Ukraine. Unfortunately, this amazing technology will take many years to become commercially accessible. This will change the world. Can you imagine what can happen with cheap, non-polluting, never-ending energy?

2. US companies own and continue to develop superior advanced technology in the fields of automation, artificial intelligence and robotics. These are incredible advantages that support bringing all manufacturing back to the US because fewer workers are needed to actually produce more goods. Robots equate to the cheapest labor possible.

    a. For decades, US developers of advanced technologies have freely sold them to rival countries such as China, who reverse engineer and duplicate the technologies for their own uses.

Remember Lenin's quote from the beginning of this chapter? "The capitalists will sell us the rope with which we will hang them."

b. The time is right now for US businesses to grow up and think more defensively for the country rather than just short-term profits for their shareholders. Congress MUST immediately demand and legislate that US businesses restrict trade of these vitally important technological advantages.

c. President Biden recently restricted US computer chip companies such as NVIDIA and AMD from providing their most advanced chips (particularly the best artificial intelligence chips) to foreign countries like China. About time!

d. President Biden also signed the Chips Act in August 2022, which included $52 billion to build semiconductor foundries in the US. Very impressive that the US government saw this danger and actually did something! Hey, we need to give kudos when they're deserved.

e. There's a reasonable argument for computer chips being as important to the security of the US as fighter jets.

3. The end of globalization should protect the US against the kind of supply chain problems experienced during Covid that proved disastrous. US consumers couldn't get goods that were desperately needed. As always, low supply causes higher prices, and thus was one of the main components of the inflation that roared back from the dead during Covid.

4. US companies who created computer chips and manufactured them in the US and Europe thirty years ago moved the manufacturing to lower-cost countries, particularly China, Taiwan, and throughout Asia. The US now only produces approximately 20 percent of the world's chips. Chips are in everything and will continue to be critically important for the foreseeable future. They can be viewed as the new most important commodity, even more critical than oil.

a. The US and its technology companies are racing to get chip production back onto US soil because of the possible or even likely event of China invading Taiwan and taking its chip manufacturing. The US and the West would be paralyzed. Even Taiwan Semiconductor Manufacturing Company (TSMC) (the largest in the world, manufacturing up to 90 percent of the world's most advanced chips, according to voanews.com) is spending tens of billions of dollars to recreate itself away from China's Taiwan threat—in Arizona!

5. This vulnerability resulting from the US not currently having control over chip manufacturing represents the biggest potential danger from the China divorce. The US had better triple its efforts to return semiconductor manufacturing back home immediately.

6. The US is rapidly creating a huge workforce that has cheaper labor than even China, India, and Vietnam. How can this be? ROBOTICS. A robot can work twenty-four hours, 365 days, with no vacations, sick time, or even bathroom breaks—and no union negotiations. The capital investment in a robot, even just a robotic arm can be repaid in labor cost savings very quickly. The need for US companies to chase cheap labor offshore has passed. This is one of the main engines for the successful divorce. For the first time, perhaps ever, the US can compete against global labor costs and also have significantly reduced shipping costs and time savings. Amazing, and perfect timing.

Robotics' wide use should be able to further lower the cost of manufactured goods for Americans. This is enormous future inflation protection. Best of all, every side of the business stays within the US to further ensure the success of the economy well into the future.

- **ROBOTICS WILL MAKE THE US SELF-SUFFICIENT AND COMPETITIVE AGAINST GLOBAL LABOR COSTS.**

- **BRING MANUFACTURING OF GOODS TO THE US AND ITS FRIENDS' SHORES: ON-SHORING.**
- **DO NOT PURCHASE ENERGY FROM ENEMIES.**
- **ARTIFICIAL INTELLIGENCE IS ABOUT TO CREATE THE NEXT GREAT INDUSTRIAL, MEDICAL, AGRICULTURAL, AND SOCIAL REVOLUTION THAT WILL PROPEL THE US INTO A BRIGHT FUTURE. THIS EXTREME TECHNOLOGICAL ADVANTAGE MUST BE MAINTAINED AS PROPRIETARY TO THE US.**

The US and its people are mostly benevolent and kind (except the gangbangers). Americans generally want peace and prosperity for everyone around the world but are often too trustworthy. Conversely, the governments of Russia and China are not altruistic and certainly do not deserve trust. Perhaps their people are like Americans but lack the political power to influence direction of their governments. Sadly, it doesn't alter the need for the divorce. Divorce is because of the parents, not the children.

Unfortunately, it is time to treat our enemies as enemies. The US must assemble all the kids on the block and choose sides. Us or them. Good or bad. The time has come for a real cold war.

- **DIVORCE AND CHOOSE SIDES.**

All countries on the US side will be accepted based on their recent histories of loyalty and support for basic Good Side tenets. Those who aren't on the Good Side are on the Bad Side (BS). Sides are not based on geography, race, religion, political structure, or economic structure.

Following are the new Good Side platforms:

1. The Good Side supports all member countries with fair trade and defense. (Similar to NATO.)
2. The Good Side does not trade with the Bad Side and takes active, strategic measures to stop trade considered dangerous between Bad Side countries, such as the Iranians selling weapons to Russia to support their war against Ukraine.

3. The Good Side manufactures goods and services only within Good Side countries for use exclusively by Good Side countries.

4. Good Side countries close all of their business operations within Bad Side countries. It will be illegal for domestic US companies to do business in or with the Bad Side countries.

5. Individual Bad Side countries can leave the Bad Side and welcomed to join the Good Side under a strict period of probation.

6. It is the goal of the Good Side to have all Bad Side countries eventually join the Good Side as one, good planet.

Sound too simple? Of course it does. But not impossible. We really don't need to make this too complicated. Everyone already knows where each other stands. In many ways, much of the world is already divided up between Good and Bad countries.

Get used to having divorced parents—without having to split holiday dinners.

One more thing: nothing about this divorce changes the face-off situation regarding nuclear weapons. All parties will continue to have their fingers above the buttons that could destroy the world, which keeps us all safe as long as the evil guys don't get too batshit crazy on us.

The Good Side better continue to do everything possible to keep evil countries like Iran and North Korea from getting nukes. They already have the batshit crazies who would push the button, regardless of the consequences.

- **CONTINUE TO DEVELOP MISSILE DEFENSE SYSTEMS (LIKE ISRAEL'S IRON DOME) TO SHIELD THE US AND OTHER GOOD SIDE COUNTRIES AGAINST MISSILES AND NUCLEAR WEAPON THREATS.**

CHAPTER 6
I'M SO SCREWED

IDENTITY THEFT, ROBO CALLS, FRAUD SCAMS, CYBER SECURITY, RANSOMWARE

Declare war to rid the US of this scourge immediately

"I don't need to worry about identity theft because no one wants to be me."

—JAY LONDON

"If you spend more on coffee than on IT security, you will be hacked."

—RICHARD CLARKE

"Someone cracked my password. Now I need to rename my puppy."

—UNKNOWN

THE PROBLEM

The US has another epidemic beside Covid. It may not be as lethal, but it certainly is debilitating and has us fearful because so many of our fellow citizens have been infected by this scourge: cybercrimes. There are a few protections available, such as LifeLock and enterprise-level computer security systems for big businesses and governments, but our collective pants are around our ankles. The bad guys are having a field day because the government and its myriad bureaucratic agencies are doing next to nothing.

Once our personal stuff like a social security number, driver's license, and credit card is breached, the bad guys have everything they need. They get your identity, then borrow money in your name; get mortgages against your property and even try to deed your home away. Really scary-ass shit.

Why are social security numbers and driver's licenses so vulnerable to cybercrimes? Because these are called "static identification;" they can never change. If the bad guys get these, they have you. Really? Is that really necessary? Do we need to keep the same social security number even after hackers all over the world have it and are destroying our financial lives? Yup. Stupid system? Yup. Anything being done about it? Nope. Fucked up? Yup.

Here is probably only a partial list of the cybercrimes plaguing the US:

1. Identity Theft as described above.
2. Fraud schemes, particularly against the elderly, are usually over the phone. These scams try to convince people that they owe money and they are in trouble; or that the IRS is after them for a payment; or their grandchild is in trouble somewhere overseas and needs cash wired immediately. Sounds like only a fool would fall for these, but we're dealing with professionals who have devised scams that seem extremely real. They gain control over your computer that can alter even your bank information to appear real. It's actually difficult to challenge their authenticity.

You have to doubt EVERYONE. When you get this type of call, you must hang up or log off, then call the entity that supposedly contacted you with a number you have or that you obtain independently online. Ask if they contacted you with a problem. NEVER reply to texts or emails that advise you that something is wrong. Don't even respond to a text supposedly from your credit card company asking if you made a charge that they are questioning. YOU CALL THEM at a number on the back of your credit card or that you obtain online. Do not call the number provided in the email or text.

1. Robocalls include companies or organizations you do business with. These occur constantly and are huge, unwanted intrusions into our daily lives.

2. Computer hacking, viruses, and infiltrations. What a pain these are. Once infected, you have to fix this by wiping your computer and reinstalling software and your data. New advice is to keep no data on your computer, and instead keep everything in the cloud so it's away from the vulnerability of being hacked.

3. Malicious software is being injected into personal, business, and government computer systems to kidnap the entire system until a ransom is paid. This extortion is euphemistically called ransomware. In addition to individuals, hundreds of the largest companies like MGM Resorts in Las Vegas and even major US government agencies are routinely targeted. Systems that run entire business operations are literally shut down and the release of customers' personal information is threatened until money is paid as ransom. This problem is much bigger than you likely know. There are ransomware gangs comprising thousands of English-speaking hackers (young-ish men from the US, UK, etc.) who partner with nefarious professional Russian hackers. These are serious crimes and must be stopped. The criminals must be severely prosecuted and even stopped militarily as described in the next paragraph.

4. Political hacking has been alleged in recent campaigns, including for the presidency of the US. Russia and other nefarious

countries and others use considerable computer power and expertise to try to influence election outcomes. So much is at stake here. How can this not be considered an act of war? It's equivalent to bombing. Fire up the drones. Attack these computer hacking installations and their operatives. The US government knows where they are. Foreign participants have to be routed out and attacked by our military and intelligence agencies. Really? Yes! Take no prisoners. Not kidding. War is war, and this is simply a new kind of war.

The government is trying to assist with the global ransomware matter for big business and government agencies. However, the threat of cybercrimes on individuals is horrific and frightening to all of us. Any of us could easily be next. Where is the government to help us with this? They keep passing the buck from the FBI to the states to the local police. It seems clear that no one wants to take on this fight that is growing exponentially. This is unacceptable. Why aren't Americans demanding help on this? It may be like whistling past the graveyard. Let the people who have been damaged by this fight the fight to get something done. Meanwhile, the rest of us will just keep whistling and hope it doesn't happen to us.

Once a cybercrime has begun, there's little one can do to stop it. It's like a dam breaking just up the road, and we know the trickle we're seeing will soon become a tsunami over us. Money and even homes are lost, credit is destroyed, elderly citizens lose their money, and businesses and governments are paralyzed until they pay ransomware (usually in Bitcoin—the only real use for that crap is to pay and hide criminals). Everyone is annoyed by robocalls and

computer invasions that require massive cost and time spent fixing them and rebuilding data. Probably no real deaths, just massive damage. SOS to the government—get off your bureaucratic asses and help us!

Who's doing these cybercrimes? The answer partly explains why it's so difficult to stop. Cybercrimes are being committed by governments, international spies, domestic and international gangs, domestic and international computer hackers, individual smart-ass teens, and adult computer wizards who get off on messing with people and businesses.

All of these piss us off, but two of them are simply incomprehensible. The hackers messing with people just for fun are pathetic and need to be stripped and lashed (spanked) in public.

I just hope that no one actually does business from a robocall. Please, please, please, either do not answer or immediately hang up. Stop being nice. Don't feel badly if it's a real person—hang up on them! Maybe they'll quit and get a real job that is productive and contributes to society.

BAD-ASS SOLUTION

If Americans live in fear because of a real threat of being hurt either physically or financially, the US government is obligated to step in to help.

Who the hell do you call when your identity has been stolen? No one knows because there really is no one to call. The police, sheriffs, local and state agencies, and the CIA/FBI don't want the responsibility. Some local governments are creating laws.

The US needs a one-stop shop for everything in the cybercrime realm. A new department needs to be set up under the direction of both the FBI and Department of Homeland Security and will be called the Cyber Crime Squad (CCS). The CCS will have access to the best technologies and individuals to assist with the efforts to stop infiltrations, correct damage, prevent cybercrimes, and catch the perpetrators.

- **CREATE THE CYBER CRIME SQUAD (CCS) TO ATTACK AND RESOLVE CYBER CRIMES.**

- **THE CCS CAN ISSUE NEW SOCIAL SECURITY AND DRIVERS LICENSE NUMBERS WHEN NECESSARY.**

The CCS will have very broad powers. They must respond immediately to notification of a problem and carry the ball completely for the victim, be they individuals, businesses, or government.

The CCS will have the following abilities:

1. Freeze entire computer systems as necessary.
2. Freeze credit that has been hacked.
3. Reverse damage to victims.
4. Issue new social security numbers.
5. Issue new driver's license numbers.
6. Assist victims to reestablish their new numbers and credit.
7. Infiltrate suspected networks and computers for evidence.
8. Investigate all evidence to determine actual perpetrators.
9. Utilize the US Military to attack foreign hacker pods.
10. Have broad powers to charge domestic and international suspects, including extradition from foreign countries back to the US for trial.
11. Pursue and freeze assets of perpetrators to compensate victims and deter perpetrators.
12. Prosecute the criminals.
13. Enact extremely severe penalties and get courts to fully participate with fast trials and limited appeals.

The Cyber Crime Squad have to be so competent, so fast, so tough, and so effective that cybercrime effectively ends. Come on, this can and should be fixed right away.

To dream the impossible dream . . .

CHAPTER 7
ONE TRICK PONY

THE FEDERAL RESERVE

Stop this unelected, ill-equipped group from ruining the US economy

"A recession is when your neighbor loses his job. A depression is when you lose yours and recovery is when Jimmy Carter loses his."

—RONALD REAGAN, WHO DEFEATED JIMMY CARTER

"There are two things that can disrupt business in this country. One is war, and the other is a meeting of the Federal Reserve Bank."

—WILL ROGERS

"Fed data has too much latency. Mild recession is already here. It's not like just the canary in the coal mine (Silicon Valley Bank) died, one of the staunchest miners (Credit Suisse Bank) died too and the cemetery is filling up fast! Further rate hikes will trigger severe recession. Mark my words."

—ELON MUSK

LET'S BEGIN WITH A FEW SHORT DEFINITIONS

THE FEDERAL RESERVE (The FED):

The Federal Reserve (FED) is the Central Bank of the US and establishes monetary policy to achieve its objectives; particularly to keep inflation under control (PRICE STABILITY) and positively enhance employment. The FED has two main tools to use: raise/lower interest rates and buy/sell securities.

Per Federalreserve.gov, the FED has a chairman and a board of governors of which there are seven, including the chairman. The chairman and governors are appointed by the president and confirmed by the US Senate. The chairman and vice chair have four-year terms, and each governor's term is fourteen years. (Fourteen years—really? Few people can choose a spouse they'll even speak to for half that time.) There are twelve Federal Reserve Banks, each with its own president. All of the governors and the bank presidents make up the Open Market Committee that meets regularly and sets monetary policy (basically interest rates). The chairman leads those meetings.

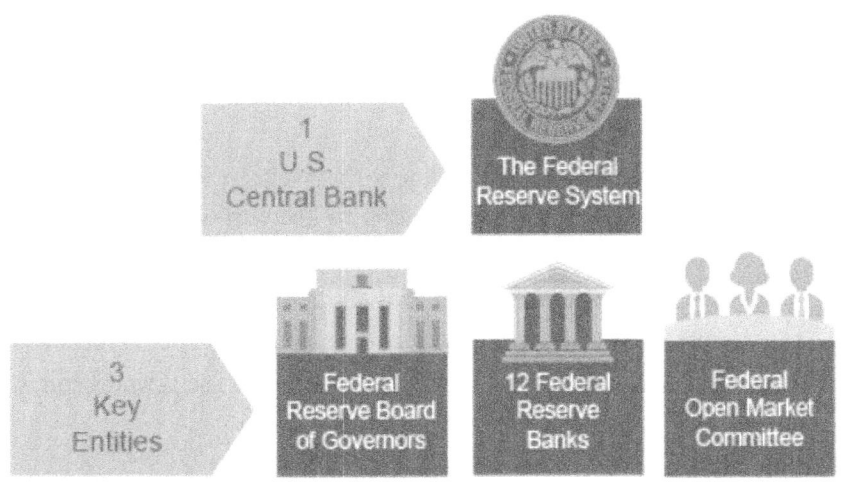

From federalreserve.gov

According to Investopedia.com, the Federal Reserve/Central Bank did not exist until 1913. It has always been highly criticized for not stopping the Crash of 1929 or the resulting Great Depression. In fact, the FED really had very little impact on the US economy until the 1970s, when persistent inflation became a reality.

INFLATION

Inflation is the percentage increase in which goods and services increase on an annual basis. Inflation is a very negative force on the economy. It can easily spiral out of control because as businesses and individuals expect prices to rise, they do rise.

"I want a raise."

"Well, then I have to raise prices to my customers to pay for your raise."

"Well, then I need another raise to pay for higher prices."

And so on.

According to Investopedia.com, there are three main causes of inflation:

1. Demand-pull inflation. Production (supply of goods and services) does not keep up with demand, so prices go higher.
2. Cost-push inflation. When production costs such as labor and raw materials rise, businesses must increase their prices to consumers.
3. Built-in inflation (also known as wage-price spiral). When workers demand higher wages to keep up with higher prices they must pay for goods and services, businesses increase their prices to consumers to offset their increased labor cost, so goods cost more to consumers, of course, including the workers who got higher wages in the first place. This is the upward spiral.

RECESSION

For purposes of understanding the consequences possible from FED actions, it would be helpful to understand what a recession is. It's a terribly scary word that everyone knows is bad for them, but few can define it, other than to say, "it's when the whole economy turns to shit." Actually, that's a pretty good definition.

Classically, a recession is defined as two consecutive quarters in which the Gross Domestic Product (GDP) goes down. This means that the US economy is not growing—it's doing worse than it had been doing. The common results of this negative trend are factors that feed a downward trend on other parts of the economy in a very circular way. US consumer demand (accounting for 70 percent of the US economy) slows down, causing business production and sales to slow, which causes layoffs, which causes lower consumer demand, etc., etc. Recessions can last just a few months or several years depending on the severity of the cause or causes for the downtrend. The bad stuff tends to feed on itself and continues to get worse—like quicksand.

Interestingly, the US economy actually experiences some level of recession about every five years. Recession seems to be something of a relief valve that throws some water on the US economy periodically to keep it from spiraling too hot and too high. If it's that built into our system, does it have to hurt so many people so badly? No. Keep reading.

THE PROBLEM

The Federal Reserve is tasked with achieving two main objectives: to keep inflation under control and to positively enhance employment. To do this, the Fed uses its two main tools: raising and lowering interest rates and buying and selling securities. One of the biggest arguments against the Fed is that it devises its policies as a reaction to what has already been happening. It evaluates data that may be from a week to several months old. Many observe that they are always looking in the rearview mirror. Conversely, the Fed's moves usually take many months for the data to show the effects of its actions, referred to as a lag. It's quite common for the Fed to keep its foot on either the gas pedal (lower interest rates) or brake pedal (higher interest rates) for too long.

The FED Tool #1—Raising and lowering of interest rates

1. When the FED raises rates, borrowing costs more. Things like houses with higher interest rate mortgages or cars with high interest rate leases or loans simply cost more. This causes fewer consumers to buy. **Importantly, consumer purchasing is 70 percent of the US economy.** At that point, all hell can break loose. Houses and cars don't sell, fewer are built, construction and factory workers are laid off, and salespeople are laid off. To sell their products, those builders and car dealers have to lose money. Eventually, the interest rate increases cause prices throughout the economy to drop. So, this is how raising interest rates lowers inflation—by hurting the economy (a.k.a. lots of people). The balance equilibrium is hard to maneuver. It's like playing teeter-totter and each side alternates against the fat kid.

2. When the FED lowers rates, it often means that inflation is back under control so it can lower interest rates to hopefully allow the economy to grow along with the FED's acceptable inflation rate, currently targeted at 2 percent per year. It can also mean that the economy is in trouble and has to be kick-started with lower interest rates, like during the Great Recession of 2008.

The FED Tool #2—Buying and selling securities

This is quite a bit more esoteric, so we won't go into much brain damage to fully flush this one out. The FED seems to have unlimited resources (money) to buy and sell securities. If the FED buys securities, it is putting money into the US economy. This is often referred to as "loose money" because all the extra cash out in the country tends to make debt more easily available for banks, businesses, and even consumers. Conversely, when the FED sells securities, it is reigning in cash called "tightening the money supply" to make cash less available for borrowing.

During recent recessions and economically negative times for the US, the FED employed massive programs for purchasing securities, including mortgage-backed securities. These programs, called "Quantitative Easing," had the FED purchasing incredible sums, tens of billions of dollars per month in securities for years, to get cash flooding into the US economy. According to Richmondfed.org, in 2022, the FED had approximately $9 TRILLION of these assets on its books. Coupled with the FED's raising of interest rates to stave off inflation in 2022, it also did a turnaround on this program to begin actively selling its securities under a program called "Quantitative Tightening," conversely to squeeze money back out of the system.

While difficult to get your arms around, this is an enormous tool wielded by the FED. How effectively does this work? Who the hell knows?

Here we go, buckle up:

Imagine your home has extreme damage from an earthquake (I live in California). You call your contractor and he shows up with his only tools being a hand drill and a toilet plunger. That's the FED.

Imagine a firefighter leaping out of his fire truck and racing to the edge of a huge forest fire. In his hand is a wrench. Great tool, but not for this job. That's the FED. You get the idea.

The early 1970s saw a particularly tumultuous time in US economics. There was long-term 10-ish percent inflation, and at the same time, high unemployment rates and stagnant demand for goods and services (called stagflation). Several US presidential administrations, beginning with Nixon, then Ford, then Carter, simply could not fix the problem. Of course, ridding the US of the plague of inflation fell to the Federal Reserve. Fed Chairman Arthur Burns did the usual raising of interest rates until the inflation numbers began to

lower. Burns then took his foot off the interest rate brake pedal to reduce interest rates and to normalize and relieve the economy. Inflation roared back quickly. The inflation scourge was built into the economy, and as soon as prices could be raised again, they were.

Along came Darth Vader, the new FED Chairman, Paul Volcker. He was a physically large man with a smug smile and confidence seeping from his pores. Right, a creepy-ass dude. The grim reaper. However, in Volcker's case, this was accurate. He proclaimed he would raise interest rates fast and high, then leave them there until the sin of inflation was literally beaten out of the economy. He didn't give a damn who died financially or was left homeless and penniless in his wake. For those of you who don't know what American citizens had to endure, Volcker raised the federal funds rate (the FED rate charged to banks, the lowest rate in the system), which had averaged an already very high 11.2 percent in 1979, to a peak of 20 percent in June 1981.

This raised other rates to the point that mortgages hit 22 percent. No joke. This was for real—and that lasted a long time. The number of home builders, manufacturers, businesses, individuals, and laid off workers who were financially killed by this nuclear blast was truly war-like. In war, a pyrrhic victory is one where you win, but at far too great a cost. This was a terrible war, and Americans were left bleeding in the streets.

Volcker's inflation war worked, regardless of the devastating human cost. Inflation was beaten down into submission. Was he right and our savior? Did he go too far, and should he be labeled a financial psychopathic serial killer? Many credit Volcker with curing inflation from the US economy for the forty years after that gruesome period. Bullshit!

The following forty years still had all of the same forces of supply and demand and greed in the US economic system. So, to the economist smartasses, why was inflation not a problem for four decades?

That same period witnessed two extremely impactful new factors into the US economy. The first was a massive shift from producing goods in the US with its high labor and materials costs to offshore production in Japan, China, India, and others with cheap costs. The US enjoyed a long period of cheaper goods flooding in constantly, keeping inflation in check. The second factor was the quick and ubiquitous infiltration, acceptance, and utilization of computers. Computers made work and workers in the US enormously more efficient, thus keeping prices down as technological advances continued to increase production. Not Volcker!

Regardless, the most frightening aspect of this is that the current Fed Chairman, Jerome Powell, who was tasked with stopping the first real bout of inflation the US has experienced in forty years, claimed to be a disciple of Paul Volcker! You should be scared to death. Powell repeated many times that there will be pain. Lots of pain. He said this as if he were just waving at a fly buzzing around his ear. He clearly doesn't understand nor give a damn that his actions were devastating to most Americans.

Powell repeated his vow that he wouldn't relax interest rates until the unemployment rates go higher and wage growth went lower. Again, this heartless asshole couldn't care less that his theories do real damage to people. Can you actually believe that a US government official wants Americans to be laid off and get lower wages? Where were the protests? Why were Americans not marching in the streets demanding his head on a platter? Holy crap; we've become lazy, stupid lemmings.

Moving on . . .

The definition of inflation above sets forth its normal causes. BUT THAT'S NOT WHAT HAPPENED TO CAUSE INFLATION IN 2022! HOLY SHIT! Until 2020, the US was enjoying its healthy and powerful economy as the global economic leader. So, what happened to bring the inflation wicked witch back from the dead? These are the causes of the 2022 inflation:

1. Covid, Covid, Covid
2. Russia's invasion of Ukraine
3. Oil, Oil, Oil
4. Supply chain problems
5. Government spending TRILLIONS of dollars in handouts to businesses and individuals
6. China's Covid lockdown, which stopped production and shipment of goods

Let's look more closely:

1. Covid, Covid, Covid

Okay, you know all too well about this one, so let's not beat it to death. But remember: Covid scared everyone. In the beginning, we didn't know if we would actually die. People were dying—lots of them—there was no cure and there weren't enough ventilators. Most who were put on a ventilator died without their loved ones able to be with them. Horrible, sad, and very scary.

Governments had no idea what to do, including the US. They acted as if they knew because they had whole governmental departments to deal with things like this: The Centers for Disease Control (CDC), The National Institutes of Health (NIH), and the World Health Organization (WHO) for a global view.

Oh, and don't forget the US had Dr. Anthony Fauci, Director of the National Institute of Allergy and Infectious Diseases; the guy with the great resume who advised each of the last five US presidents. He had a hand in solving AIDS and could be the calm face of knowledge and reason to assure Americans that we would be okay. "You don't even have to wear masks."

"Oh, now you do have to wear masks."

"Covid is transmitted on surfaces."

"No, Covid is transmitted through the air."

The other talking heads from these esteemed institutions were no better. They just didn't know (and really, how could they?), but they didn't say they didn't know. They just continued to be wrong. It added to our fear and stress instead of allaying them.

The US government always thinks its citizens can't handle the truth. They hide the truth, treating citizens like children. Most just go along in a numb state. Maybe we are just children.

Americans and the people of the world stayed bewildered and scared. People continued to die. On March 14, 2020, the entire US went into a lockdown to stop the spread of Covid. To really bring home the point, all resorts, casinos, restaurants, and entertainment closed in Las Vegas. "Holy crap, Mabel, this thing must be the real deal!"

Covid caused part of the inflation because with the US closed for business and its populous stuck in their homes, shortages of everything in demand ensued. Toilet paper, food, all antibacterial cleaning products, computers, televisions, sofas, and at-home exercise equipment, especially the critically must-have Covid item: a Peloton stationary bike. Of course, it was impossible to get sterile gloves, masks, and Covid home tests. As with all shortages, prices go up to meet the demand. Classic inflation, but not a classic cause. These prices went up from scarcity due to a major world catastrophic event, and not from something like Colgate-Palmolive deciding it could raise the price of toothpaste by 20 cents per tube because it gave its workers a 10 cent per hour raise.

2. Russia's invasion of Ukraine

What are we missing? Why aren't we just one, big happy planet? Ain't gonna happen. There's good, there's evil. Unfortunately, everyone always thinks they're right and good. Really, humans are just a step out of the trees. A small step at that.

Okay, this will be in the history books. Regardless of your feelings about Trump, the undisputed truth is that when Biden took over on January 20, 2021, the US was energy independent. We produced enough oil and gas right here for all of our energy needs, with a bit left over for export. Great for us. Arguably bad for the environment. Enter Joe.

Per CNBC, on his first day as president, Joe Biden revoked the permit for the Keystone XL oil pipeline and canceled other Trump administration energy rules. Over the next few days, Biden signed a series of executive orders that prioritized climate change and included the halting of new oil and natural gas leases on public lands and waters and began a thorough review of existing permits for fossil fuel development.

After all, the US has to stop burning coal, gas, and oil to clean up the planet and stop global warming in its tracks. Don't mention that most every other industrialized country was already way behind US environmental progress, with the really big polluters, China and

India, barely ready to admit that there's an environmental problem at all, let alone do something about it. They spew black smoke into the atmosphere like the stuff is actually great for their citizens' health. Yes, Big Bad-Ass Joe Biden is here to clean up the planet, starting with America.

Joe's attack on US oil production left America short of oil and gas for its own needs. Paradoxically, it was okay with Biden that other countries produce the stuff and just sell it to us. He had to go begging for oil. He sucked up to so many of our enemies to get oil that he can no longer walk upright.

Who's really benefiting here? Right, Mother Russia. The West's dependence on Putin's oil put enormous riches into his coffers. Putin hatched a brilliant idea: (Use a deep-voice Russian accent) "That rich land with pesky peasants in Ukraine, which just few decades ago was part of USSR, should come back home to us. We have so much oil money and the world is so off balance from Covid, let's invade. We be back in week or two, then I be at my dacha for summer, swim and ride horse with no shirt."

Of course, the invasion happened, which somehow seemed to catch the US by surprise even though Putin had been telling everyone he was going to invade for months. Anyway, he did. The US and other Western countries didn't stock Ukraine with abundant food and weapon supplies during the months Putin was threatening. Things looked pretty good for Russia in the beginning, then the Ukrainians got their wind back along with Western supplies and amazing US weapons.

Showing the kind of astonishing heroism and determination that only comes from defending your own homes and families, the Ukrainians pushed back hard. There wasn't much scoring from either side until the Ukrainians became expert with the shockingly powerful small American weapons that are able to take out a Russian tank miles away with just the push of a few buttons by a soldier who didn't get past the second grade. This incredible American weapon technology is discussed in the chapter Military and Wars.

From the beginning of the war, the world panicked that there wouldn't be enough oil and gas. The price of oil almost instantly doubled, from about $65 per barrel to as high as $130 per barrel. The oil-producing countries and companies are notorious for taking advantage of these types of situations. For decades, these bastards have exhibited insatiable greed and shameful indifference to the suffering that their price-gouging causes. Of course, this oil pricing was a very significant component of the sudden return of inflation.

This was about when Joe Biden realized that we desperately needed more oil and was seen fist-pumping the Saudi Crown Prince of Darkness to get a few more million barrels of their oil. The television news audience could perceive the smirk on Darkness's face. Joe's shameless begging even went on to the other US enemies: the terrible Venezuelan regime; then the Iranian Vampires; and finally, the good ole assholes of OPEC, who have never been friends to the US. Joe could have just gone to American oil producers, said he was sorry, and told them to get us and our allies the oil and gas we need. He refused. This was just stupid, childish, and dangerous behavior from our president. Honestly, this isn't a Democrat/Republican thing. It's an American thing and we were just being unbelievably stupid.

The huge increase in the price of oil and gas resulted in significant inflation in the US and throughout the world. We all know that oil is used in every corner of the economy: transportation, manufacturing, farming, materials. It was largely our own doing. Once again, this was not a normal cause of inflation in the US economy. It was the result of a war, global panic, oil producer greed, and bad US leadership that caused energy prices to explode higher.

OKAY, OKAY, OKAY. So, you may be thinking that this guy is just a biased, conservative Fox mouthpiece because the US eventually began producing more oil than ever while Biden was president (in early 2024). The aforementioned may appear biased, but it was the truth during the time discussed. And, it WAS one of the major causes of the inflation experienced during that time, which was the topic of the section.

Yes, moving forward in time, The U.S. Energy Information Administration reported in March, 2024 that, "Following sustained productivity increases at new wells, . . . US crude oil production increased to record highs. These record highs have come despite declining US drilling activity because the new wells are more efficient." Further, they reported that new technologies in horizontal drilling and hydraulic fracturing increased both legacy and new well production, which yielded more crude oil. Don't kill the messenger—the US did not begin producing record levels of crude oil because of Biden. It was because of technological advances and US oil producers increasing production from both new and legacy wells.

Of course, as they have always done, the oil producers kept prices higher and longer than they needed to. This contributant to inflation and misery is often called "greedflation."

3. Oil, Oil, Oil

We just included this with Russia's invasion of Ukraine. See number 2 unless you want me to repeat the whole thing. Go get something to drink with your extra time.

4. Supply chain problems

The following are the factors that made up the supply chain problem:

1. China's slowdown of production and shipping of goods destined for the US.

    a. Several things happened as China began to wake up to Covid (as they tried to disavow responsibility for starting it in the first place). They shut down entire cities along with everything around them. As this spread, the gargantuan Chinese production of goods for the rest of the world slowed to a trickle. They had difficulty getting products to ports and loaded onto ships. Later, as we'll see, ships stuck in US ports were not making the round trip back to China for reloading with more goods for shipment back to the US and elsewhere. Everything from China moved slowly and was piecemeal.

2. Hundreds to thousands of enormous cargo container ships were stranded at US ports, particularly at Los Angeles.

a. Remember, the US was under lockdown for months and everyone feared getting Covid and even dying. The ports didn't have longshoremen to unload all the ships. There was something fishy going on with their union that was never brought to light. Containers that were actually able to be removed from ships were stacked to the sky at the ports, unable to be moved.

b. Why were they stuck? There weren't anywhere close to enough truck drivers to transport the individual containers across the US. Eventually, there wasn't any place to put more containers, so the containers sat on ships. Businesses throughout the US could not get their goods.

c. The entire system was at a standstill. Goods couldn't be produced, shipped, unloaded, or delivered. Those were all the broken links in the supply chain.

d. US retailers panicked because they couldn't get merchandise and equipment such as computer chips off the damn boats and out of the harbors. Both during and after the shutdown, sellers, manufacturers, and consumers were angry and scared because they couldn't buy the things they wanted, but worse, they couldn't get the things they needed. All businesses and therefore all consumers were stuck.

Anyone with the good fortune and great timing to be at Costco when they got a toilet paper shipment stocked up for the next ten years. The stores had to begin rationing these items. Thank the heavens I know of no one who had to use leaves or the garden hose as a bidet. Maybe I'm just sheltered.

As always, when goods are in demand and supply is scarce, prices go up. Inflation. However, once again, the supply chain cause of inflation was completely abnormal and didn't fit the FED's extremely limited toolbox. Raising interest rates will not and did not solve the supply chain problem. There will be a multiple-choice test on this later.

5. Government handouts to businesses and individuals

It may sound as if I think everything is wrong or terrible with the US government. FAR from it! Don't you want to leap to your feet in the aftermath of every major disaster that befalls our fellow citizens when the US government shows up to help? I do. Thank goodness for this country and the many kind, generous people in it.

Virtually everyone was out of work from the shutdown, or worse, long-term because the companies they worked for closed. As usual, our fantastic US government rallied to help Americans who were in great need. The US government moved uncharacteristically fast to help people and even businesses. Money was provided to both as quickly as possible, often making wrong decisions because there just wasn't time for the normal slowness of government to ponder and debate. APPLAUD AND THANK THE US GOVERNMENT! They were outstanding and truly helped millions upon millions get through. I'm honestly "verklempt." The actions by the US government saved Americans and perhaps even the country.

Unfortunately, the assistance came with unheard-of price tags, in the trillions of dollars. The government spent it anyway. Also, as stated, some of the programs were just too generous and too long. The government spent it anyway. APPLAUD AND THANK THE US GOVERNMENT!

Many businesses got Payroll Protection Program (PPP) forgivable loans to stay open so they could retain their workers. Some had to close anyway because of the longer-than-expected Covid experience and dramatic changes in their business environments during that time, such as not being able to get their goods to sell or parts for manufacturing.

Employees were given much larger and longer than normal unemployment benefits. This was truly generous and wonderful. However, because of the speed to make these programs happen, many employees actually received more money from these programs than they had made from their jobs.

Millions of workers did not return to their former jobs when they could have. Reportedly, they either had more benefits coming to them without having to work; found joy in less costly kinds of financial/living structures, such as living with relatives or friends; and they had the luxury of time to find better jobs than they previously had. Many people have remained completely out of the job market, which is reflected in a somewhat falsely low unemployment rate. The larger, longer history is that there were too many companies having to fill positions with too few Americans wanting to take those jobs. This phenomenon clearly confused the Federal Reserve, who insisted on raising interest rates for longer until the unemployment rate rises. So dumb.

Trillions of dollars injected directly by the government into the economy has a very powerful multiplier effect. It works like this: a person gets money and pays for something from another business/person and that business/person buys something, and that business/person buys something, etc., etc. The huge amount of additional money multiplying in the system is inflationary. More people have more money to pay more for goods and services at higher prices due to scarcity. Inflation.

Hate to be repetitive, but once again, this cause of the 2022 inflation was abnormal and not suited for the FED's little toolbox.

If it's so easy to see that the 2022 causes of inflation were abnormal and more importantly would not be resolved by raising interest rates, why did Powell and the FED do this? We were being bulldozed, and in Powell's own words, "it will hurt." What an understatement. He actually said he would not stop until there is more unemployment and wage deflation. He didn't seem to understand—or care—that he was talking about real pain to real Americans whom he WANTED to lose their jobs, then their homes. Why were Americans not protesting? I just don't get that we Americans just don't get it.

Then, something happened. During most of 2023, inflation went down, without unemployment having to go way up and wages having to go way down. The economy remained extremely strong, yet inflation went down to about 3 percent by the end of 2023. Why? How can this be?

Well, think about the fact that **all of the causes for the 2022 inflation listed above have basically self-corrected, WITHOUT interest rate manipulation by the Federal Reserve!** Oil prices stabilized and went almost all the way back down. The supply chain issues simply went away over a bit of time and supply shortages were replenished. Covid remained a nuisance, but not a major threat, so Americans went to work and spent lots of money. This unusual bout of inflation was resolved—but not by the Federal Reserve. Hallelujah!

Here's an interesting illustration about the US economy having built-in mechanisms to correct itself: it is like what you do with your computer when you click the "print" icon and nothing happens, then you keep clicking it as if the computer didn't believe you. You end up sending the same print command to your printer thirty times. After a while, you hear a fan start to whirl and you get fifteen copies before you can pull out the plug.

When manufacturers and retailers couldn't get their shipments, they kept pushing the "buy" button. In the end, they overbought Covid items. Stores like Target and Walmart were stocked full of TVs and workout clothes (millennium-speak: athleisure), delivered at just the wrong time, when Covid began to calm and people started to think about going back to work. Now they needed nicer clothes. They had already bought computers, big TVs, and Pelotons. Target and Walmart lowered the prices of these overstocked goods. LOWER PRICES is ANTI-INFLATIONARY! This is how the economy fixes itself! Classic oversupply that caused prices to drop.

Yes, the FED used their old interest rate hiking trick to offset damn inflation like Don Quixote charging at windmills. They did NOTHING but bring economic suffering to many Americans. They're hoping no one notices that this inflation was caused by abnormal influences and that their shotgun blast of raising interest rates was unnecessary and caused enormous unnecessary pain.

The US capitalist system featuring good ol' Supply & Demand works. It just needs some help now and then. Just don't kill us all in the process.

BACK TO THE PROBLEMS OF THE FEDERAL RESERVE THAT MUST BE FIXED.

At this writing in the first quarter of 2024, the Federal Reserve has not yet begun to lower interest rates back down, even though inflation has fallen from a high of approximately 9 percent down to about 3 percent.

Sorry, but this has to be repeated: Jay Powell said two horrifying things (**loosely quoted**) to Americans as he brought out his big tool (I mean interest rates, sicko):

1. I plan to model this anti-inflation fight after my hero. Paul Volcker, who successfully drove inflation from the land for the last forty years. He was glassy-eyed and probably thinking of Saint Patrick ridding Ireland of snakes.

2. This fight will raise interest rates higher than actually needed and they'll remain high for a long time. We'll keep raising until we see inflation wither back down into its hiding place. Then, we'll keep interest rates high for a long time to be sure inflation is tamed and dead. There will be lots of pain.

I don't know about you, but I nearly fell out of my La-Z-Boy. Volcker? That asshole tried as hard as he could to financially kill me and almost every other American with the most Draconian measures possible. Can you even imagine 22 percent interest rates on home mortgages? Look it up. These idiots want inflation whipped and they will steamroll over every business and individual to get there. This is not satire. They just don't care that people will be in pain and suffer terribly, losing businesses, homes, jobs, savings, stock market values, and hope. Volcker surely didn't care. It's hard to imagine that old, avuncular Jerome Powell, who looks like your corner pharmacist, could be a stone-cold killer. He is.

And just when you thought it couldn't get any worse, it will. Powell and the other misguided Federal Reserve governors and twelve Federal Reserve Bank presidents literally didn't know what they were fighting. They still think they're fighting 1960s- and 1970s-style inflation. NO! They needed to fight 2022 actual inflation causes. Fix Covid. Fix China. Fix the supply chain. Fix Russia. Fix oil. In the words of tennis player John McEnroe, "Are you serious? Are you serious?"

Yes, they are. And they've been amazingly wrong.

How much money did you lose on your retirement funds during 2022 most of 2023 while the FED played its interest rate game? Why

aren't you screaming at them? **We don't have to take this!** Have you been aware of the daily Federal Reserve guessing game played by all of the stock market smart asses and pundits? Will they raise rates? Will they lower rates? Will they hold rates steady? How many interest rate decreases will there be this year and next? When will rate decreases begin? What did Powell say today? What will he say tomorrow? What Federal Reserve Bank president got three minutes of airtime today to give their worthless opinion? THIS IS TOTAL BULLSHIT! Only the smartass stock traders (bettors) care about financial news every minute of every day so they can continue to use the stock market as the biggest casino in the world. Stocks go up and down every day based on what these gamers think about what the goddamn Federal Reserve will do today, tomorrow, or next year. Worse yet, the vast majority of stock trades are made by computers.

Meanwhile, all of us normal Americans who have our retirement money in the stock market are not traders. We don't sell any stock because the Federal Reserve raised interest rates a quarter of a point this month. We're in for the long run and wouldn't know what to do about a tiny interest rate change anyway. We only hope we have some money growing to fund our retirement in the future.

The Federal Reserve assholes and US securities assholes really MUST stop playing games with our retirement money. It's a terrible shame and leaving millions of Americans without enough to retire well, even though they worked hard and saved what they could. We deserve much better.

The US was founded upon some pretty amazing principles, including checks and balances and rule with representation. No one in the US ever voted for a Federal Reserve chairman, or the governors, or the Fed Reserve Bank presidents. Chairmen are appointed by the president after the previous chairman's four-year term expires. The appointment is then ratified by the US Senate. There is a pitiful show of a check and balance system when the chairman reads a report to each house of Congress quarterly, then answers really idiotic questions from congresspeople who want some TV face time. Of course, the senators and representatives hold no power to remove the chairman or affect anything he/she does. Total Sham Show.

The Open Market Committee includes the chairman, the seven governors, and the twelve Federal Reserve bank presidents, with most being able to vote on policy in some closed back room that massively affects every single person in the US, and even the world. This is just not how this country was supposed to work. Ask Jefferson.

These people all sound intelligent. They're probably all great economists in their own right and speak well. After announcing the current interest rate move, the chairman does a press conference shit show, and the Fed governors and bank presidents all manage their way onto financial news shows and sometimes even network TV. They all want to play bigshot. The reality is that these people should not be affecting us so much. They wield massive power without having any mandate from "the people."

Importantly, economics is not a science. Economists are not scientists. I doubt if they know anything about working a real job or producing goods and services that answer the needs of people. There is no scientific process or proof to justify what they do with their two tricks. They want to sound like they know what they're doing so they can keep doing it. They are dangerous. We need a new way.

Do we need a Central Bank? Do we need a Federal Reserve? Do we need to fight inflation? Do we need this show run by dictators who no one elected? Damn! I wish the answer was no, but it's actually yes and no. Yes, the complex economy of the US needs real analysis, care, and assistance. No, we don't need a few unelected people acting like they know what they're doing manipulating the US economy with limited and wrong tools.

BAD-ASS SOLUTION

Okay, let's set the groundwork that the US actually needs a Federal Reserve. I'm cringing, aren't you?

- **RESTRUCTURE THE FEDERAL RESERVE AS A NEW FED BOARD, APPOINTED BY CONGRESS, WITH BROAD NEW POWERS AND REAL TOOLS FOR PRECISION SOLUTIONS.**

- **ELECT THE FED CHAIRMAN IN NATIONAL ELECTIONS.**

The NEW Federal Reserve is to be made up of a FED BOARD and structured as follows:

1. One elected chairperson and nineteen appointed directors
   a. The FED Board must have highly skilled, diversified individuals with expertise and at least 50 percent of their working life involved in their specialty area in the private sector. (Not just professors of economics.)
   b. b. Areas of expertise must include: manufacturing, healthcare, oil and gas, housing, retail, finance, automotive, food service, technology, entertainment, aerospace, medicine, labor, education, works, government, and international business.
2. Directors to be nominated/appointed by a group of qualified elected congresspeople, having an equal number of Democrats and Republicans, with directors finally being approved by the House of Representatives and the president having veto power.
3. This congressional appointment and oversight group will be called CON-FED. Individuals will be nominated and approved utilizing the same system as oulined in the previous item.
4. Chairperson and directors will have staggard six-year terms (like senators) and limited to two terms.
5. The FED Board will have a consultation staff of economists, finance, accounting, and legal experts. They will also have the latest technologies available for analysis including the best computer systems and artificial intelligence. The US has this stuff—hell, we invented this stuff.
6. The FED Board will have a board of advisors made up of the CEOs, CFOs, COOs, and CTOs from all 500 best companies making up the Standard and Poor's 500. Providing this service to the FED (and to the US) is to be considered an obligation under SEC rules and an honor to serve—at no pay.

7. The FED Board to hold closed (non-public) meetings and seek consultation from its expert board members and advisors.

8. All actions made by the FED require a 60 percent majority vote of the FED Board directors, including the chairperson, who has five votes. Any tie vote will be decided by a vote from the US President.

9. All actions voted approved by the FED Board must be approved by the CON-FED.

10. Recognizing that time is often of the essence, all FED Board directors and CON-FED members must vote within forty-eight hours or their vote will be considered to be in favor of the policy. If they miss three votes, they will be removed.

11. The FED Board will have new tools at its disposal (see below).

12. The Fed Board will have great power at its disposal (see below).

NEW ABILITIES OF THE FED BOARD

As opposed to the current FED system, why raise interest rates on the entire economy when manipulating just a few components in specific industries and labor will likely solve the problem?

The FED Board will need new precision tools and strong powers. In addition to the ability to manipulate interest rates, the Fed Board may, but not be limited to:

1. Price Freeze and Roll-Back

The FED Board can require immediate, but temporary, targeted price freezes and price roll-backs to stop price-gouging in cases of emergency shortages, such as: the price of oil during a war, the price of food during a drought, the price of bottled water following a natural disaster, or the price of baby formula during a shortage due to a factory problem.

2. Wage Freeze and Roll-Back

The FED Board can require immediate, but temporary, targeted wage freezes and wage roll-backs as necessary.

3. National Guard/Military

In instances such as the supply chain problem, where workers aren't available to unload ships and drive trucks, as a matter of national security, the FED Board could direct the military to answer the need, utilizing the National Guard or other military as required on a temporary basis.

4. Force Production

If the FED Board identifies specific causes of inflation, such as the price of oil moving higher because supply is short of demand, it can force that industry to produce more supply.

5. Override Government Regulation

In a situation calling for businesses to provide more production of goods such as oil or pandemic supplies, the FED Board can temporarily reverse government regulations such as allowing fracking and new drilling for oil.

As illustrated, the US just doesn't have to continue to use the old Paul Volcker and now Jerome Powell's Draconian answers to inflation. We're smarter than that. We don't have to use radiation on the patient's entire body when the cancer is just located on his left kidney. Fix the exact problem by creating a new Federal Reserve with the intelligence and precision tools now available to maintain a healthy US economy and prosperous employment for Americans.

CHAPTER 8
LIKE HERPES—IT'S NEVER RESOLVED

ABORTION

Immediate resolution for all sides that applies to more than 94 percent of all current abortions

"I've noticed that everyone who is for abortion has already been born."

—RONALD REAGAN

"How come when it's us, it's an abortion, and when it's a chicken, it's an omelet?"

—GEORGE CARLIN

"All you Trump fans are gonna be really pissed off when your condom breaks and your sister can't get an abortion."

—OLIVER MARKUS MALLOY

"I regret my abortion."

—SIGN HELD BY UNIDENTIFIED MALE ANTI-ABORTION PROTESTER

THE PROBLEM

Abortion has been the biggest single hot-button issue in the US for the government and the American people for more than fifty years. For many, their entire political agenda is always the one issue. Forget voting for a candidate who will pursue enacting legislation that helps Americans in dozens of ways other than the abortion matter. Instead, they only vote for candidates who will vote for abortion issues consistent with their own beliefs. This one-topic criteria has exacerbated the polarization of the US government, its political parties, and its people. The US simply must resolve the abortion issue once and for all so it can continue moving forward on other important matters and support a much happier populous.

Fanatics of anything are a problem. By definition, they are extreme and intensely devoted to their cause. They have a mindset and will pursue that direction until their dying breath. In the case of abortion, we have two polar opposite fanatical sides who believe their position to be so sacrosanct that any compromise would be a violation of their core beliefs and possibly their religious faith. No wonder the US has remained stuck in the mud on this topic for well over half a century.

Fanatical pro-choice people believe that every stage of a pregnancy is within a woman's body and that she, and she alone, has the sole rights and control over what she chooses to do with her body and a pregnancy inside that body. They demand total dominion over the unborn right up to the point of delivery and a baby takes its first breath, at which point the new life is actually a real human.

Fanatical pro-life people believe that the instant a sperm and egg are fused together, there is a new, separate life inside the mother and that life is protected by law and God. Along the same thought process, many people, including the entire Catholic faith, believe the same thing, and that this act of God cannot be interfered with by contraception, let alone abortion. The unborn human life is so sacred that these fanatics deem abortion to be murder and are opposed to abortion even in cases of incest and rape.

The pro-choice position of "abortion on demand" is often countered using horrifying videos that show the literal killing and mutilation of a baby just as it's about to be born—or even in the process of being born. Very powerful.

Generally, the adamant pro-life side has its focus on the unborn baby, not the mother. An unwanted pregnancy doesn't matter to them. Actually, an unwanted child doesn't matter to them either. Of course, they profess to want a good life for the mother and the child, but leave that part of the equation to fate, family, charity, and government agencies. They always default that the best solution for an unwanted pregnancy is to have the child and have it adopted by a family who desperately wants it. Maybe. Sure. Maybe.

Some pro-life people have less severe positions that actually accept abortions based on their personal belief about when a life begins during the human gestation period. How many weeks until a human life becomes viable? What is viable? Is it when there is a heartbeat? When can it feel pain? When can a fetus be delivered and live?

There are several areas of legal precedence that support compromise against both intractable positions on this subject.

A woman's legal right to choose what happens with her own body and a pregnancy inside that body sounds correct until one realizes that there are actually several areas in which the government has established laws and protocols that remove some rights that a woman has with regard to her own body. Prostitution is illegal in every state (except some counties in Nevada), denying a woman the right to earn money from selling sexual uses of her body. Self-mutilation and suicide are other things that a woman does not have a legal right to inflict upon herself.

Religious rules and faith are impossible to legislate away. Regardless, US courts decided long ago that schools had to teach evolution instead of the biblical version of creation over seven days. More recent court rulings have supported laws that permit same-sex marriage, which was against many religious objections. Governments certainly have the right to enact laws that are counter to, and even violate, people's religious beliefs.

Choose:
Israel or Pro-Palestinian terrorist groups like Hamas and Hezbollah?
Hawaii or Caribbean?
Catholic or Protestant?
Yankees or Red Sox?
Chiefs or 49ers?
Try to change someone's core beliefs. Forget it.

The question is, how does the US get past this problem that won't go away? How does everyone walk away bruised but accepting that the matter is resolved?

The Supreme Court overturned Roe v. Wade and explained their position that abortion is not included in the Constitution under the various Amendments that create the right to privacy, which was the basis for Roe v. Wade. The Court did not say abortion is forbidden by the Constitution. They could have done that, and some of the six conservative justices probably wanted to do that. Good thing they didn't, because the US just didn't need a bloody civil war over abortion rights.

Interestingly, the ruling interprets to: you don't have a right to abortions on a federal level as a given right under the Constitution. BUT, individual states can pass laws regarding their own position on abortion, thus making abortion something that citizens can effectively vote on, either directly by ballot or indirectly by voting for their governmental representatives. The door is also open for Congress and the president to create a federal law to have a national law on abortion.

BAD-ASS SOLUTION

It may be that I exist in a small cocoon, isolated from the masses of my fellow Americans, but the vast majority of the people within my cocoon from both pro-life and pro-choice camps feel that abortions should be allowed in the US, subject to some reasonable time period from conception. If that's an accurate representation of most Americans, then reaching a conclusion to this massive problem seems promising.

Does this whole damn thing really come down to the fanatical extremes on both sides? Yup, and they keep us stuck in quicksand. The fanatics are holding up a resolution on this problem that has polarized and paralyzed the US. It just might be that simple.

The best we can do is to have agreement among Americans that involves compromise; that wonderful word to promote harmony that we have forgotten long ago. Remember, the golden rule in negotiations: a successful resolution is when neither party is happy. We need to agree that we won't have abortions on demand up to the baby being free of the birth canal, nor a total ban on abortions for any reason whatsoever. We all have to meet somewhere between those opposite goalposts.

Pro-choicers need to be empathetic to pro-lifers who honestly believe that a pregnancy holds a real life and that even the mother has no right to terminate it. Pro-lifers need to be empathetic to pro-choicers who believe that the pregnancy is within the mother's body and that only she has the right to make decisions that best suit her and her family. No one really wants to bend, but it's time. Bend over.

As reported by Mariam Zuhaib of the Associated Press, Senator Lindsey Graham (R-S.C.) (presumed pro-lifer) recently proposed a shocking nationwide abortion ban after fifteen weeks, meaning abortion would be legal up to fifteen weeks. The proposal was based on the premise that fetuses can feel pain at fifteen weeks—a belief rejected by the American College of Obstetricians and Gynecologists.

The bill is called: Protecting Pain-Capable Unborn Children from Late-Term Abortions Act.

Unsurprisingly, neither side is happy with this proposal.

Pro-choicers argue that fifteen weeks is arbitrary and has been suggested without proof that a fetus can feel pain at that point. Further, they cite that determining pregnancy problems for the mother or the fetus requires more time. They want a new federal law to permit abortion without time restriction.

Note that Graham's bill amazingly allows for exceptions for rape and for incest against minors (provided they've met the requirements for counseling and legal reporting), and also permitted in cases when the pregnant woman's life or the fetus is endangered.

Pro-lifers' response has been difficult to find, however, the following is an astounding letter from an equally astounding source. Archbishop William E. Lori, chairman of the Committee of Pro-Life Activities, sent a letter to Senator Graham which included the following:

"I write to thank you for introducing the Protecting Pain-Capable Unborn Children from Late Term Abortions Act" protecting the right to life of unborn children beginning at fifteen weeks after fertilization."

He continued, "Since the Supreme Court's decision in Dobbs v. Jackson Women's Health Org., overturning Roe v. Wade and returning the issue of abortion to the people to decide through their elected representatives, the country has been in tremendous turmoil over the tragic and divisive issue of abortion. Although we will never cease working for laws that protect human life from its beginning and supporting mothers in need, we think that this proposed legislation is a place to begin uniting Americans regardless of their views on abortion. Further, we strongly agree that there is a federal role for protecting unborn human life."

Archbishop Lori concluded, "I support your efforts with the Protecting Pain-Capable Unborn Children from Late-Term Abortions Act to protect the right to life of unborn babies from fifteen weeks' gestation. All elected officials, including federally elected members of Congress, now have the opportunity to protect unborn human life and should rise to the occasion. We strongly encourage your colleagues in Congress to cosponsor this legislation."

TWO MAJOR PRO-LIFE INFLUENCERS CAN AGREE TO 15 WEEKS! This is an example of incredible compromise. One could argue that Senator Graham and Archbishop Lori could be trying to cut their losses because of a possible federal law that would permit most abortions. Possibly, but the real likelihood of such a law is extremely uncertain and the process would be fraught with public and governmental fighting.

THIS IS INCREDIBLE: The Charlotte Lozier Institute reports incredible information, that **"the Centers for Disease Control and Prevention (CDC) abortion data indicate that overall, approximately 6 percent of all reported abortions take place at or AFTER fifteen weeks of gestation."** This translates to approximately 55,800 of the approximately 930,000 abortions nationwide in 2020. How many of the 6 percent were due to rape or incest, which would have been allowable anyway? **AT LEAST 94 PERCENT OF ABORTIONS OCCUR DURING THE FIRST FIFTEEN WEEKS OF GESTATION. PRO-CHOICERS SHOULD JUMP ABOARD TOO!**

Fifteen weeks, just over the first trimester, clearly gives the vast majority of women adequate time to find out they're pregnant, be able to decide about the pregnancy, and terminate if they choose. Typically, abortions for rape and incest should fall within fifteen weeks but must be permissible later, given extenuating circumstances. An abortion to save the mother or if there is a serious fetal problem must be permitted at any time during the pregnancy.

So, we're basically waging this massive fifty-year fight over just 6 percent of all abortions that currently occur after fifteen weeks? The US is in perpetual chaos over 6 percent of all abortions???? This is RIDICULOUS! We can accommodate more than 94 percent of all abortion needs within those fifteen weeks! I'm utterly baffled. This is so damn obvious—and simple. Okay, can the vast majority of Americans agree to this? Right now? Just forget about the fanatics on both sides. They'll simply never be satisfied, and America has to move past this issue.

Bad joke: Negotiations that involve a King Solomon type of compromise is called: SPLIT THE BABY.

- **COMPROMISE TO ALLOW ABORTIONS ON DEMAND UP TO FIFTEEN WEEKS AFTER CONCEPTION.**
- **ABORTIONS TO BE ALLOWED ANY TIME IF THE HEALTH OF THE MOTHER OR IF THE BABY IS AT RISK.**

The other very hotly debated abortion topic now comes into play. What if the woman is a minor? Can she get an abortion without parental consent, or even notice? This is a very tough question for all sides. A minor literally has no legal rights. Can she walk in by herself for an abortion the same as walking into a salon to have her hair cut? Legally speaking, probably not.

Hold on, the ride gets bumpy again.

If a minor is sexually active, she does so with or without her parents' consent. Logic time here: if the minor has parental consent or even knowledge of her being sexually active, it may be construed that the parents have given approval for the minor to make her own decisions in sexual matters that could include contraception, having a child, and even abortion.

The situation in which the parents are unaware of their daughter's sexual behavior is much more complicated. The minor in this case is sexually active without the parents' knowledge or approval. The fact that the minor is not being supervised by the parent to the point that the parent is unaware of the minor's activities is reason to ascribe tacet approval of the minor's sexual independence by the parents. Admittedly thin premise here, but that's all I've got.

Therefore, in both instances, a minor who is pregnant should be able to obtain an abortion under the law (within the permitted time period), without parental knowledge or approval.

Obviously, the minor can involve her parents if she wants or needs their support and counsel. Being forced to involve the parents would likely just serve to make the situation much worse for all involved, probably with nothing to gain. Please don't send nasty texts, emails, letters, or billboards.

Including parents in the abortion decision sounds sensible, but in reality probably does nothing for them or the minor. The inevitable anxiety and anger just aren't worth a requirement of approval or disclosure. In a weird way, it's a case of ignorance is bliss.

- **MINORS TO BE ABLE TO OBTAIN ABORTIONS ON DEMAND WITHIN THE TIME PERIOD—WITHOUT PARENTAL APPROVAL.**

Is it crazy-ass to hope that we heal our abortion differences, respect each other, and move on together as a peaceful nation? We really do need to stop the endless fighting. It's enough already. Let's move the hell on.

CHAPTER 9
BEND OVER

HEALTHCARE

Provide great healthcare to all

"Eat dessert first—life is uncertain."
—ERNESTINE ULMER

"Life's journey is not to arrive at the grave safely
in a well-preserved body, but rather to skid in sideways,
totally worn out, shouting, '. . . holy smokes . . . what a ride!"
—HUNTER S. THOMPSON

"Everyone wants to go to heaven,
but no one wants to die."
—TEXAS SAYING

"Good health is merely the slowest
possible rate at which one can die."
—UNKNOWN

THE PROBLEM

According to cms.gov, the national health expenditure grew 2.7 percent to $4.3 trillion in 2021, or $12,914 per person, and accounted for 18.3 percent of the Gross Domestic Product (GDP).

Healthcare is probably the most difficult issue for Americans and the government. Lots of Americans feel that healthcare is a right. The other side feels that healthcare is something that individuals have to buy, the quality of which is subject to their ability to pay. Everyone wants great healthcare. Honestly, I think all Americans would be happy to have all other Americans receive great healthcare. So how do we do that?

Healthcare in America is a mess. Americans love being proud that we have the best healthcare in the world. We have the best this, we have the best that. The problem is that the best healthcare in the world is bloated, expensive, and unequally available. The truth is that no one is very happy—not patients, not elderly, not people with preexisting conditions, not sick people, not healthy people, and not even the medical professionals.

The medical structure is very difficult to navigate. What kind of treatment do I need for my problem? What doctor specialty? Will I get better? How long will it take? Where can I go? How much will it cost? How much will I actually have to pay? These questions are hard to answer.

They echo more questions right back: Do you have insurance? What kind of coverage do you have? Can you pay the deductible and coinsurance? Many sick or even healthy people just aren't equipped to address the medical monster by themselves. They need help, like an advocate. Other than family members, advocates are rarely available.

Old-Style Medical Insurance

The US has had medical insurance companies for eons. They advertised, you made a few calls and then signed up for a policy. There were no HMO and PPO distinctions of benefits. You got healthcare. You got sick, you went to your doctor, they submitted the bill to your insurance company, and you may have been billed later by your insurance company if there were uncovered or shared charges. Kind of simple.

HMO/PPO

As healthcare costs kept climbing, insurance companies got cute. What quality of care do you want to buy with your policy? If you buy HMO, you're part of a managed care organization that tells you what doctors you can see, under what circumstances, and effectively limits access to your healthcare. If you buy PPO, you're more like the old system where you can have more choice of your doctors and hospitals, but some very expensive hospitals and doctors can still be excluded or cost you more money.

Medicare

At age sixty-five, Americans get the basic two parts of Medicare, A and B. This is for hospitals and doctors. If you can pay for private insurance above Medicare, called a supplemental plan, you can get a bit better coverage limits, lower deductibles, lower copays, and prescription drug coverage. Medicare is not accepted by all doctors but is at most hospitals. One great thing is that there are no denials for pre-existing conditions.

Most seniors seem to think that Medicare is acceptable. The cost is variable, based on your income and supplemental plans. With good quality excess coverage one buys from outside companies, figure about $500 to $1,500+ per month, including what Social Security deducts for your monthly check for Medicare. Like I said, good but not cheap.

Universal Healthcare—Also Called Socialized Medicine

Medicare is universal care for seniors. It's kind of an experiment for judging if the whole country should go to this kind of universal system. It might work because the system can powerfully negotiate against drug companies, hospitals, and doctors.

Socialized medicine is like all other socialized things. Under this system, doctors for example make the same income, whether they work their asses off seeing forty patients a day or just cruise and see fifteen. Countries that have socialized medicine typically have extremely long waits for medical care even including heart and cancer surgeries. But it's free! But you're dead! I know many Canadians who have medical insurance policies in the US and come here for healthcare. "Free Healthcare" doesn't mean good or timely healthcare.

The extraordinary, innovative doctors don't make more than the mediocre or lazy. If doctors don't make a great living after going through all that school, study, and intern/residency work, will people still become doctors? If one believes in the profit motive and incentive, socialized medicine doesn't make sense to you. Worse, it probably won't work as well as what you're used to.

Obamacare—the Affordable Care Act

Does anyone really know how this thing is working? It's okay for preexisting conditions. Costs are high. Deductibles are high. Coinsurance payments are high. Most people think of this as bottom rung and really only catastrophic coverage. If you're really sick or need surgery, you get coverage after quite a lot of payment from you. A hot mess. Dump it. Actually, replace it.

So, how can America distribute medical care fairly, with quality, care, affordability, and compassion for patients and the medical community?

The problem with the whole damn thing is that it all costs too much. Something everyone must have, but the costs are insane.

Break down the costs.

PROBLEMS

1. Doctors

Doctors in private practice have large operating costs like any business. They have office rent, staff, nursing, licensing, phones, website, copier, and INSURANCE. These costs are quite a lot when viewed on a per-patient cost basis, plus the doctor's fee and test costs.

Most don't know that doctors usually receive just a fraction of what they've billed. Do you look at your statements from your insurance company? Of course not. The doctors and hospitals jack up their bills as high as possible, such as $2,000 for a given test to get the insurance company to pay $400. The doctors and hospitals accept the reduced payment and you pay little or nothing, although the statement always says you may be billed. This game is silly and probably explains part of the larger problem.

This practice of massive overbilling to get something more from the insurance companies gets draconian for people who don't have insurance. They're billed the inflated price for medical care and are never offered the same price that insurance companies pay for the same service.

2. Hospitals

There are nonprofit and for-profit hospitals. These buildings must house lots of patients with services like a high-end resort, plus they need all the other areas such as surgical operatories, food service, administration, patient receiving, emergency room, etc., etc., etc. The costs to run these empires is staggering. Lots of real estate, people, administration, cleaning, drugs, lawyers, and INSURANCE. No wonder they charge $50 for an Advil. Again, patients without insurance are billed at the rack rate. These people may be sued by the hospital and then forced to pay all they have and even file bankruptcy.

3. Malpractice Insurance and Claims

The legal profession is doing its best to kill the medical profession, or so it seems. As noted elsewhere in this book, there are too many lawyers. The surfeit lawyers do everything they can to make a living. A very large number of lawyers take on marginal cases on a contingency basis to keep food on their tables. They file a malpractice case against a doctor or hospital at no cost to the patient, then try to make the other side spend so much money on defending themselves that they settle. The lawyer typically gets 30 percent to 40 percent of the settlement. A good case can put food on the table for months or even years without the lawyer breaking a sweat.

Of course, the doctors and hospitals have to maintain malpractice insurance for nuisance claims and also for real claims of harm to patients. Since 1975, California has capped pain and suffering awards to $250,000. That number rose to $350,000 on January 1, 2023, and over ten years goes to $750,000. The effect of the cap for California and most other states is that this brought the cost of insurance down, but still typically costs a doctor tens of thousands of dollars per year. This is a very major component of the high cost of medical care and the deep frustration of doctors in the practice of medicine. The joy of helping people got seriously diluted. Many want out. The constant aggravation is just not what they signed up for.

4. Prescription Drugs

The late-night TV guys have a never-ending source of jokes about the high cost of prescription drugs. These drugs are insanely expensive and because the US doesn't regulate drug prices or negotiate with strength against the drug producers, US drug costs are the highest in the world. The US also has a middleman structure for prescription drugs that keeps prices high. The geniuses at GoodRx (and others) figured out how to beat that system and have been able to save Americans huge amounts of money on drugs—in many cases, even lower than just the coinsurance that would be charged after insurance covers their portion.

5. Competitive Health Insurance Companies

Do you detest watching network television because of auto insurance company commercials? Geico, Liberty Mutual, State Farm, and Farmers are driving Americans to alcoholism. These companies advertise like crazy to sell a car insurance policy that costs about $1,500 per year. How do they afford the cost? There must be massive profits. Really? They not only pay to advertise, but they also compete for your business.

Call us. Give us fifteen minutes, we'll save you 15 percent. It works. Annoying as hell, but it works. They protect their policy customers, they make money, and we pay less because of competition.

The point here is that insurance companies can be profitable and actually compete for your business! That's why the US economy works in the first place, remember? COMPETITION!

Health insurance companies are among the most profitable and valuable companies in the US:

1. United Health—$484.4 billion market capitalization (company's value)
2. Humana—$64 billion market cap
3. Anthem (Elevance)—$5.12 billion market cap
4. Cigna—$4.48 billion market cap

They make money and are worth billions!!!!

BAD-ASS SOLUTION

- **CITIZENS UNDER SIXTY-FIVE HAVE PRIVATE, COMPETITIVE HEALTHCARE POLICIES TO PROVIDE EXCELLENT PATIENT CARE AND PROVIDE REASONABLE DOCTOR, HOSPITAL, AND DRUG COMPANY COMPENSATION.**
- **THOSE WHO CANNOT PAY FOR A PRIVATE POLICY GET GOVERNMENT HMO-STYLE HEALTHCARE.**

The specifics:

1. Those not on Medicare buy coverage from competitive health insurance companies.
2. Like auto and home insurance, all healthcare insurance must provide the same coverage. There are no additional levels of coverage. They can compete on price and service.
3. No more HMO from private health insurance. Everyone gets PPO. That horrid game has gone on long enough.
4. All procedures cost an amount determined by a new Health Cost Board (HCB) and adjusted to different regional costs and prices.
5. Doctors in private practice receive 15 percent more than the Health Cost Board price.
6. No exclusions for preexisting conditions are allowed. All people must be accepted.
7. All doctor billings as set by HCB are paid by insurance companies within thirty days of the procedure. The doctors get paid quickly.
8. Deductibles are limited to $2,000 per year.
9. Individuals must also pay 10 percent coinsurance on all charges up to $5,000 per year, then nothing further.
10. Prescription drug prices are negotiated by the HCB and apply to all hospitals and pharmacies. All drug middlemen are removed from the entire process. Drugs cannot be marked up more than 500 percent above production cost. Sounds like a lot but consider that most manufactured goods have a 300 percent markup over cost from manufacture price to wholesale price to retail price. Also, consider the incredible cost to develop the drugs that save your life or make it better. The pharmaceutical companies deserve and need a good profit to continue innovating new medicines.

11. Each hospital to have a treatment approval board. They must approve all non-standard procedures for cost-benefit analysis. For example, the system cannot justify a heart transplant on an eighty-year-old. The costs are just too exorbitant compared to the amount and quality of time it buys. I know, harsh-ass, but reality.
12. Lawsuits against doctors and hospitals to be severely curtailed. Only suits that are approved by a new Legal Suit Board (LSB) as having legitimate damages can move forward.
13. Individual doctors' malpractice insurance to be subsidized by the government. This will help keep doctor charges low and make doctors happier.
14. Employers must provide healthcare for their employees under the same criteria as Obamacare. Not great, but at least some structure has been established and seems to have been begrudgingly accepted and already built into the US systems.
15. Americans who can't pay for health insurance get a government funded HMO system.

For the people who can't afford to buy the health insurance outlined above, the government will have to supply healthcare in an HMO type of model that is simply not as good as what private health insurance buys. Government HMO (GHMO) healthcare will look like the following:

1. There will be no cost to the patients.
2. There will be no exclusions for preexisting conditions.
3. Patients will have no choice of doctors, all of whom will be part of the GHMO.
4. GHMOs will be staffed by doctors and nurses who choose a good, stable salary rather than competitive private practice.
5. There will be local clinics for minor health problems, such as those provided by urgent care.
6. GHMO hospitals will have no private rooms.

7. GHMO will limit surgeries and levels of care based on age, likelihood of improvement, and cost. The GHMO simply cannot afford to provide heart transplants or perhaps even hip replacements for ninety-year-olds. This is against most of what Americans believe in, that we are entitled to be treated for any ailments, by any means available—whether or not we pay for all or part ourselves.

So sorry, but this is just reality. The costs for some procedures versus the possible benefit are just too enormous to justify. It's certainly a repugnant thought to put a dollar value on extending someone's life or quality of life, even if it's just for short a time and may not work at all.

Unfortunately, we have no choice. Those who can pay for health insurance and copays can buy better healthcare. Those who can't, don't.

This is America. Pay to play. I know, I know. Now I'm a capitalist-asshole. But seriously, the notion of the best medical care for free to those who can't afford to pay is just something the US cannot do. Basic healthcare, yes, which will still be a massive burden on the country.

As with most things in the US, competition usually delivers the best products at the lowest prices. Healthcare is no exception.

CHAPTER 10
CALL IN THE TROOPS

CRIME

Stop crime and protect citizens immediately

"If a person is a thief, they think everyone else is."
—PROVERB

"What you allow is what will continue."
—UNKNOWN

"Nothing is more dangerous than a man who has nothing to lose."
—JAMES BALDWIN

"Every society gets the kind of criminal it deserves. What is equally true is that every community gets the kind of law enforcement it insists on."
—ROBERT KENNEDY

THE PROBLEM

The problem of crime, and particularly violent crime, is at epic proportions in the US. Americans aren't safe anymore. If you think you are, you're either an idiot or you're an idiot.

If you're over fifty, you likely remember hearing about the Saint Valentine's Day Massacre. You may not have even known what it was, but you've heard of it. For many decades, it was in the American lexicon because of the unheard-of violence on that day.

According to History.com, on February 14, 1929, seven men were lined up against a wall in Chicago and shot to death by weapons that included Thompson machine guns (the assault rifles of the day). This was the result of a gang war that included Al Capone's gang.

This terrible killing was so heinous that it stayed in Americans' psyche for nearly a century. The event was revisited in many movies, including *Al Capone*, *Seven Against the Wall*, *The St. Valentine's Day Massacre*, *Capone*, *The Untouchables*, *The Making of the Mob: Chicago*, and *Gangster Land*.

Contrast this terrible event in American history about seven gang members who were gunned down by other gang members in Chicago against an average weekend currently in Chicago, where fifty to seventy-five people are shot due to gang violence. What the hell has happened to us and our country? One-tenth of the violence we now have in Chicago every weekend was remembered for almost a hundred years. We have become accustomed to shootings and killings. Who are we? Take a look in a mirror, America. It's ugly.

Many horrific things are happening in the US:

1. A shocking number of young people in the US place no value on human life.
2. They have no respect for other people's right to their possessions. It feels like most Americans would probably steal something if they wouldn't get caught. What a shame.
3. America has epidemic gang violence.
4. America is suffering two mass-shootings (four or more victims)

every day. There are so many dead that we're all starting to know someone or love someone who has been killed randomly. Americans are being killed in theaters, at concerts, at parades, in businesses, everywhere. Nowhere is safe.

5. Gang members killing each other along with innocent bystanders. Fifty to seventy-five people shot every weekend in Chicago has been going on for years now. Los Angeles isn't very far behind. More gang shootings occur all over America. What are these people thinking? See #1. They don't give a damn about anyone's life—even their own.

6. Criminals are armed with military-style assault weapons.

   See Chapter 4—GUNS for more detailed discussion and bad-ass solutions.

7. Crimes and mass shootings are often by mentally ill people who may or may not be under medical care, yet they can still get their hands on assault rifles. Who's crazy in this scenario?

8. Young, socially awkward boys are obtaining military assault rifles and wantonly killing everyone they can during a grandstand episode. Maybe they think they're still inside the video game they play twenty hours per day, where killing equals winning.

9. People are being robbed on the streets and often beaten, seemingly just for the extra thrill of it.

10. Criminals are following people home who look wealthy from stores and restaurants to gain access inside to steal everything they can carry. The victims are often beaten or killed. These crimes are euphemistically referred to as home invasions. They apparently wanted a sugar-coated name for following someone home for robbery and murder.

11. The slightest provocation can touch off mass destruction of commercial areas and large-scale looting.

    a. Many protests have recently devolved into riots and

looting. Destroy everything in sight. Burn stores (after looting them), burn cars, and beat people. Much of it was during "defund the police" rallies, where those idiots simply proved the need for police to the other idiots who tried to support it as a good idea.

  b. There are daily mass "smash-and-grabs" where a few to dozens of young thugs invade a store, smash the display cases, and grab everything they can carry as they run out. No one stops them, and even if caught, they are let back onto the streets almost immediately. There is no penalty to pay, so why not play this game?

The old saying, "don't do the crime if you can't do the time," applies here in reverse:

DO THE CRIME IF YOU DON'T HAVE TO DO TIME.

1. According to Forbes.com, there are at least 20 million assault rifles in the US. This is really hard to believe. We might as well invade Canada
2. Citizens are scared.

3. Citizens are arming themselves in their homes and carrying concealed weapons without permits because they can't get the permits. This is ghastly but isn't it reasonable to want to protect yourself and your family if necessary?
4. Some liberals have been demanding that police be defunded. That is, until their cities become havens for criminals. Dumb asses. Even dumber-ass politicians who jumped on that bandwagon to get votes have had to jump off.
5. Many police are demoralized and quitting their jobs. Can you blame them? They're driving for Uber—another sometimes dangerous job.
6. The remaining officers should be thanked out loud and their meals in restaurants paid for by grateful citizens.
7. Many police departments are terribly understaffed. Not many want the dangerous, largely under-appreciated job anymore.
8. The US government either doesn't know what to do about the crime problem or won't do what they can do.
9. The US is being torn apart by crime.
10. Even our Amazon delivery packages are being constantly stolen. These "porch pirates" are such asshole cowards. They don't even know what's inside the packages. Some steal so many miscellaneous items that they set up stands to sell the crap at flea markets, or even sell them back on Amazon! Great business plan, right?

When a person is desperate, he will do anything. If a person has no way to feed and shelter himself and his family, he'll steal. Stealing to feed your family is at least understandable. Anyone in that position will rationalize that they have to steal because nothing is more important than taking care of their children. They further rationalize that the people being robbed probably have too much anyway.

There are masses of people in the US who are simply chronically unemployed. For some, it's multi-generational. They're under-educated, unskilled, and often unemployable. At some point, they're so frustrated that they become unmotivated and angry.

They see so many other people who are succeeding, who have homes, jobs, and children with bright futures. That must hurt beyond description. What a terrible existence. What do people do? They do very little and try very hard just to get by. Many turn to all that's left: crime, gangs, drug dealing, or theft.

It's difficult to blame them. In that position, I might be tempted to do the same, and maybe even push very hard for revolution in the streets. Perhaps the massive dissatisfaction and anger will result in the seeds of revolution. The summer of 2020 saw factions of both the extreme left and the extreme right fighting in the streets, including destruction of property and mass looting. In some liberal cities, police were ordered not to fight for control. Just let it burn. Those policies didn't last long, thank goodness. It was sickening to watch.

When whole communities are in despair, crime becomes a viable answer. That's where we are right now in large segments of the US. It seems that the US government is turning away from addressing this massive problem. They are doing next to nothing. They can't even stop twenty-year-old mentally ill boys from obtaining military assault weapons along with hundreds of rounds of ammunition.

What are these morons thinking? The dumb-ass congress people keep arguing about controlling assault weapons but can't agree on what to do, mostly because of adhering to "party lines." They just keep fighting each other, then do NOTHING. Most of the things they even try to accomplish won't help much like ten-day waiting periods to buy enough fire power to take out Guam. Do they think these boys are going deer hunting to shoot each animal 500 times in ten seconds?

The reality is that the NRA has been so far up many politicians' asses that they can no longer think clearly. Even if you think the NRA has a reason for existence, to protect the Second Amendment, don't you think they should join in the call against assault weapons? It would be the best thing they could do for their own validity—and for the safety of the country.

Actually, the NRA's fanatical power may finally be waning as they face serious corruption charges and their long-time leader had to step down after accusations of misappropriating funds of the non-profit entity. This could portend a real opportunity for a breakthrough. Sure. Maybe. Nah. Hope springs eternal . . .

BAD-ASS SOLUTIONS

As illustrated, the crime problem in the US has many causes with many manifestations.

1. No value of human life

Young boys playing cops and robbers or cowboys and Indians is nothing new. What is relatively new is video games. Boys from ten to twenty and beyond commonly spend every waking moment locked in their rooms (dungeons) playing video games. Some video games are based on driving fast cars in races. Some video games entail developing whole cities and worlds. Some video games play sports.

Unfortunately, the majority of games involve killing. Lots of killing. Massive amounts of killing that includes maiming and loss of limbs, heads, and bodies, with as much blood and gore as the game designers can imagine. Of course, the amazing technology continues to improve to look, sound, and seem as real as possible. The next generation of virtual reality headsets will put the player literally inside the "game" to make the killing even more realistic, with the line between fantasy and reality all the more indistinguishable.

So, what is the psychological effect on a young male who spends MANY hours every day killing as many people as he possibly can to be a winner in a game? Do we need Sigmund Freud for this one? Shooting game weapons to cause as much blood, guts, gore, and death as possible is desensitizing young males in the US. They win by killing—and by killing dozens, hundreds, even thousands. They are victorious. They are heroes. They are winners. They are trained to be unfeeling killers.

International Society for Research on Aggression

Now, look at successful movies and TV shows that target this same group. Again, they are about killing and being winners from killing virtually everyone in sight.

The US prides itself on the First Amendment. Free speech is paraded in front of many problems as a right to continue doing it. If pressed, most Americans can only name one constitutional right—The right to freedom of speech. Cool. It serves as a shield against our most despised word: censorship. We have all learned to reject censorship as the equivalent of Nazi book burning.

It is the job of government to protect citizens. If a new kind of activity is causing significant death and destruction, the government must investigate and step in. The government has all sorts of laws that limit individual freedoms. Seatbelts, helmets for motorcycle riders, license requirements of all kinds, condom requirements for sex actors, medical requirements for certain jobs, age restrictions for all kinds of things from driving to drinking to voting to being a pilot, drugs being illegal, and vaping made illegal. For obvious reasons, it is illegal to yell "fire" in a crowd.

Yes, the government has the right and even the obligation to protect Americans, even from themselves. The government certainly has the right to outlaw dangerous activities.

- **THE US MUST STOP THE PRODUCTION, SALE, AND USE OF VIOLENT VIDEO GAMES.**

Sure. But until we do, we can expect more mass killings every day from these violently programmed kids. Take your pick: censor or killings. Americans and their government need to grow up and be the adults. The parents and the government need to take charge. Tough love. Screw the game and movie producers. They've screwed up American kids long enough. Hell, we just may get these little assholes to go outside once in a while or, heaven forbid, shoot a basketball instead of a person. The right to hypnotic violent video games is not in the Constitution, and to hell with the ACLU, rights groups, and gaming companies if they say it is.

So, how do we obtain and destroy the violent games? How do we stop violent games from being played online?

Remember when you were a child and someone said, "If you do that, you'll be in trouble?" You were scared because you knew your parents or people with authority would punish you somehow. You toed the line. The fear of being "in trouble" worked. It can still work if there is a real penalty behind the threat.

Never forget. Every country can make and enforce laws. Let's start there. Make these violent games illegal. Create severe penalties for the creation and distribution of violent video games. **There will be mandatory five years in jail for everyone involved in creating and distribution of the games.** The citizens and government have to "man up" and demand that judges enforce the law—quickly and strictly.

What about the millions of games that exist already, on disk, in hard drives, and online? Again, use the government's power to make and enforce laws. All violent games must be turned over to the government for a return of the money paid within thirty days. **Any PARENT whose kids do not do this will be in jail for one year.** Every game console must be "cleaned" by the manufacturer or a service company. Every computer must be "cleaned" and certified for it to continue to operate at all. Again, mandatory jail sentences for those who don't comply immediately. Okay, so this is pretty Nazi Fascist, but how else can we unring that bell?

Look, we are either serious about making necessary changes, or just forget about all of it. We need cowboy justice: quick trials with immediate sentencing and jail. Yes, we can actually do this. Don't forget that we Americans own the country and can vote to do what needs to be done. Be sure to vote for BAD-ASS REPRESENTATIVES who work to get these things done!

- **IMMEDIATE JAIL FOR MAKING OR POSSESSING VIOLENT VIDEO GAMES.**

2. Mixed Martial Arts (MMA) and other similar entities is just a fancy name for beating the ever-loving shit out of your opponent. It should be called Mixed Martial Assassins. These men and women who are amazing athletes get into an enclosed cage and fight to the near-death of the other poor bastard.

It's Roman Gladiators without the Colosseum or lions. Who the hell have we Americans become? Our culture idealizes violence, craves blood, barbarism, and bravado. We champion these killers. How can we be surprised that we're breeding and cultivating assassins with assault rifles? When you don't feel safe in a public place, remember that you or young men you know probably watch MMA and play violent video games. You may be guilty of supporting this brain washing which is prompting whacked-out boys to use their assault rifles to murder innocent people.

- **OUTLAW MIXED MARTIAL ARTS CONTESTS IMMEDIATELY.**

3. Gang shootings

Territorial gang shootings are just about the sickest thing ever. Gang members are shooting other gang members every single weekend—dozens, even hundreds of them. Chicago alone has fifty to seventy-five gang-on-gang shootings every weekend—plus innocent bystanders.

It's not too unreasonable for non-gang US citizens to just say, "Hell, let just them kill each other. We're better off with fewer gang members on the streets."

But this is wrong thinking, which is apparently exactly the thinking of the government(s). No one is stopping this. Obviously, the government doesn't even want it stopped.

Okay, besides being obscenely callous, lots and lots of innocent people, including children, are getting shot and killed in the crossfire. Residents of these areas are justifiably scared to death. Their lives are already hard enough. It's shameful that they need to be scared of being shot outside, or even inside, their homes. **This has to stop.** Now.

The US has a cool tool. It's called the military. More specifically, the National Guard.

Per Nationalguard.mil, The Army National Guard is an organized militia force and a federal military reserve force of the United States Army. The Army National Guard may be called up for active duty by states or territorial governors to help respond to domestic emergencies and disasters such as those caused by hurricanes, floods, and earthquakes, as well as civil disorder. The president may also call up members and units of the Army National Guard, in its status as the militia of the several states, to repel invasion, suppress rebellion, or enforce federal laws.

The number one job of the government is to protect its citizens. The gang shooting problem is too large for local police departments to handle.

Everyone thinks of the military as protecting us in foreign wars and from terrorists by fighting far away from the US. However, when the citizens of any community in the US are not safe and the local government and its law enforcement agencies either cannot or will not secure the people, **we need our military to help. We pay for this service!**

Bring the National Guard to South Chicago communities and all others that are war zones. Have them protect the good citizens who need help. Have them arrest and detain the criminals. Clean up America. Stop this bullshit—because we can—and because it's the right thing to do.

- **USE THE NATIONAL GUARD TO STOP GANG SHOOTINGS AND SECURE COMMUNITIES.**

4. No respect for private property

Several times per week, we see some store invasion by a group of mostly young people (punks) who smash up the place and grab everything they can to run away with arms full of merchandise before guards or police can catch them. Shoplifting has reached such an epidemic proportion that even Advil, and practically every item of any value, is locked up at CVS. That's just the beginning. Get used to everything being locked.

Even worse, stores are closing because so much of their merchandise is stolen and their employees are not safe. There's been a near total exodus of major tenants from their stores in downtown San Francisco. This signals the beginning of the end of that magnificent city—and the remainder of major US cities will fall like dominos shortly thereafter.

It gets even more demoralizing. The few punks who actually get caught are typically booked and released right back onto the streets that same day. They pay no penalty for stealing. Under Proposition 47 in the State of California, shoplifting less than $950 is a misdemeanor, having minimal potential penalties. What do you think happened immediately with thefts up to $950? The assholes are having to add up their items to be sure to be under the limit and safe. Most idiotic idea ever. New version of *The Price is Right*.

Oh, and by the way, when many criminals are arrested and charged with a crime, they don't even have to post cash bail to be released. Revolving door.

Where are values? Who hasn't taught these young people that taking something that belongs to someone else is wrong? What happened to the idea of being a "good citizen?" Only a dinosaur still believes in those things. I'm one.

Our home was burglarized a few years ago. The police said the damage was the worst they had ever seen, yet they never found any suspects. I put a sign up in my yard to future burglars: "Don't Bother—There's

Nothing Left." My property is now lit up like Dodger Stadium and there are cameras everywhere. I'm looking into a gun turret. It's a horrible thing to not feel safe in your own home. I feel terrible for so many in our country (and the world) who know that fear much, much worse than we do. Who's up next in line to be robbed? You.

We can't say why some people have no respect for the rights of others. It's a sad evolution in our society. The rest of us have to be on guard. Those stealing from us also couldn't care less about hurting or even killing us.

The US government must protect us with laws, enforcement, and punishment. Vote for bad-ass politicians who will enact necessary legislation and appoint law enforcement who will do their jobs to protect. Vote for bad-ass district attorneys who will bring the strongest charges possible against criminals and require cash bail before release. Vote for bad-ass judges who will try cases quickly and strongly sentence convicted criminals. Demand that revolving doors for apprehended criminals are stopped from putting them right back on the streets to continue committing crimes.

- **ARREST AND JAIL CRIMINALS AND PREVENT THEM FROM COMMITTING MORE CRIMES PRIOR TO THEIR TRIAL.**

Lack of good employment opportunities

Will a person rob and steal if they are gainfully employed? Yes and no. Yes, because people are often stupid and greedy. No, because having a good job with good pay is too valuable to lose. Having something to lose is very powerful. Okay, cut to the chase. Poor, unqualified, unemployable people need to become qualified and employed. They and their families obviously benefit, but everyone else benefits, too. Converting people from dependent to contributing citizens is a game-changer. Support programs to train and place poor people and even former gang members into good jobs. Of course, this is not inexpensive or an easy task, but what could be more positive for the US?

- **PROVIDE JOB TRAINING AND PLACEMENT FOR UNEMPLOYED POOR PEOPLE, CRIMINALS, AND GANG MEMBERS.**

5. Crime and Punishment

According to the Prison Policy Initiative March 2020 publication, about 2.3 million people are incarcerated in the US. Interestingly, ACLU.org reports that the US represents about 5 percent of the world population, but houses around 20 percent of the world's prisoners. It would appear that drug crimes account for this bizarre lopsided statistic.

Regardless, Americans are fed up and scared about rampant crime. Everyone is vulnerable to it. The government has to hit the criminals very hard. Lock them up and throw away the key. No more turnstile arrests and releases. No more lengthy trials. No more endless appeals. Enough.

The people in congress had better stop debating and fighting over meaningless crap. Start right now or get new jobs. Authorize police. Use the National Guard where necessary. Get prosecutors and courts on board or kick them out.

Open as many jails as necessary. Don't make them very nice. Be tough as hell. Harsh sentences. Drive-by shooters lose their cars. Criminals go to jail and stay there. Lack of prior arrests does not affect charges and sentencing. One and done.

- **BE EXTREMELY TOUGH ON CRIMINALS: ARREST, QUICK TRIAL, AND INCARCERATE FOR A LONG TIME. MAKE PRISONS UNPLEASANT.**
- **NEVER ALLOW GANGS WITHIN PRISONS.**

Americans shouldn't live with crime and fear. The good need protection. The evil need incarceration. Simple.

CHAPTER 11
THE RICH PAY YOUR SHARE TOO

US TAXES

Enact a fair tax system that will actually yield excess funds for the US

"The government cannot give to anybody anything that the government does not first take from somebody else."
—UNKNOWN

"You cannot legislate the poor into prosperity by legislating the wealthy out of prosperity."
—ADRIAN ROGERS

"The hardest thing in the world to understand is income taxes."
—ALBERT EINSTEIN

"The taxpayer: that's someone who works for the federal government but doesn't have to take a civil service examination."
—RONALD REAGAN

THE PROBLEM

What topic could be more of a rabbit hole than taxes? Everyone hates taxes. People who pay taxes always think they pay too much. People who pay little or no taxes think the rich don't pay their fair share. Every government entity, city, county, state, and federal all think they need more tax revenue.

It's a mess.

Many horrid politicians in the US have taught the masses that the villainous rich don't pay their fair share. What an outrage for US government officials to overtly and proudly do everything possible to create a class war. These people should be voted out as soon as possible and all Americans should be appalled. They're not. Most mindlessly jump on that idiot bandwagon.

Per the National Taxpayers Union:

In the US (2021):

The top 1% of earners pay 45.78% of federal taxes (nearly HALF!).

The top 5% of earners pay 65.64% of federal taxes.

The top 10% of earners pay 75.81% of federal taxes (THREE-QUARTERS).

The top 25% of earners pay 89.23% of federal taxes (nearly 90%).

The bottom 50% of earners pay just 2.34% of federal taxes.

Who is and is not paying a fair share?

High earners currently pay the top tax tier of 37 percent of their net income in federal taxes. This equates to that person effectively working 142 days (4.75 months) per year for the federal government. Top-tier earners who live in high tax states like California pay 13.3 percent of their net in state taxes. This equates to that person working another forty-nine days (1.6 months) a year for the state of California. This sample high taxpayer works more than half of every year for the state and federal governments. Again, who is and isn't paying a fair share? 75 percent of you probably hate me for saying that.

The constant rant of rich not paying their fair share from politicians is shameful. These politicians try to be heroes to a very large poor to middle class constituency by promoting multi-billion-dollar (even trillion-dollar) program after multi-billion-dollar program to attract (buy) votes. Of course, there's no more money in the deficit-ridden coffers, so the politicians' nauseating chant is to simply tax the rich more, because they're not paying their fair share anyway. Clearly, there are fewer rich people, so politicians don't care if they piss off the smaller number of voters in favor of the much much much larger number of voters. Great system ... What a pile of crap. Come on, American public—wake up.

Everyone should contribute something to their country. Don't the people who pay little or no taxes actually owe at least some modicum of appreciation to those who foot most of the bill for the whole, bloated country? Where does the need to vilify successful people come from?

Not too long ago, success was championed. Success was something everyone wanted to attain. Now, politicians try to make success equate to evil. What a shame. Success among the population is still a positive thing for the US. Success is a great aspiration. It has kept the US at the forefront of innovation and a higher standard of living for the vast majority of Americans. Successful people should be appreciated and considered a benefit to the country. It should once again be a goal.

On the flip side, the tax code gives benefits to the upper class of Americans who own homes, make investments, and have wealth. If understood by the lower classes, many of the tax treatments and tax deductions that are given to this more successful class would certainly cause rioting in the streets. We need to get rid of all of these gifts to the wealthy, hopefully before that happens.

We must begin with a discussion about our current insane tax system that everyone in America despises. Nothing new. Everyone has hated taxes throughout history.

The US uses a fairly simple concept for taxing its citizens, a "progressive tax system." As a family's income goes up, so does the rate of tax it pays on its bottom line. AARP.org lists the seven US tax tiers for 2023 as: 10%, 12%, 22%, 24%, 32% and 37%. The top tier is for singles whose taxable income is above $539,900 and married couples above $693,750. It pays to be married. Yes, dear.

Because it cannot be repeated enough, the top 25 percent of US earners pay nearly 90 percent of US taxes—and nearly half of all tax revenue is from the top 1 percent. Thanks for the indulgence of redundancy.

BAD-ASS SOLUTION

- **CREATE A NEW HYBRID TIERED/FLAT-TAX SYSTEM THAT GENERATES MORE TAXES AND IS FAIR TO ALL.**
- **REMOVE LOOPHOLES AND SACRED COWS THAT WILL ACTUALLY PERMIT THE TAX RATES TO BE QUITE LOW.**

An old adage for successful negotiations is that when no one is happy, you have a good solution. Can that apply to taxes? Probably. And probably not.

Many political candidates have floated the idea of a flat tax, including Ted Cruz, who proposed a 10 percent flat tax rate when he ran for president in 2016. He lost. A flat tax charges the same percentage tax rate to all taxpayers. Families who make more than the minimum pay a relatively small tax (e.g., at 10 percent flat tax, $50,000 net income equals $5,000 tax and $500,000 net income equals $50,000 tax). So still, the more one earns, the more one pays. The taxman always cometh . . . but under a flat tax, he seems to cometh more fairly.

According to Thebalancemoney.com, some countries and nine US states actually have flat tax systems. These include Colorado, Illinois, Indiana, Kentucky, Massachusetts, Michigan, North Carolina, Pennsylvania, and Utah. Rates range from 3.07 percent to 4.99 percent. If you think about it, sales taxes, Medicare, and Social Security taxes impose the same flat rates to all.

The pros of a common flat tax system are that the tax code is simple—it just taxes ordinary earned income. There is no tax on dividends, interest, or capital gains. The thinking is that wealthy citizens have more money to invest which creates jobs. It tries to look fair.

The cons are that the government will likely generate less income, mostly because there is no tax on dividends, interest, or capital gains. More of the lower classes will pay some tax. Will they think this is fair? Probably not.

The bad-ass solution is a New Flat Tax (NFT) tiered system that taxes all income, not just earned income, and removes old tax benefits to the wealthy.

The main concepts are:

1. The NFT will not tax lower income citizens, probably the same bottom 50 percent of all citizens.
2. There will be three NFT flat tax tiers:
   a. $0 to $49,999—0%
   b. $50,000 to $999,999—10%
   c. $1,000,000+—15%
3. Huge change to the traditional flat tax concept: The flat tax will be imposed on all income including ordinary income, interest, dividends, and capital gains. See below.

Following are the tax topics and bad-ass solutions for each:

1. Tax income fairly

So, there's nothing new about the idea of a flat tax. What is new is applying it much more broadly than you may expect.

The New Flat Tax (NFT) will have several benefits. It is quite a bit fairer than every other tax plan. It will generate more income for the government than other tax plan because many more sources for the tax apply.

- **THIS IS A HUGE BAD-ASS SOLUTION GAME-CHANGER FOR TAXES AND SECURITIES: NO CAPITAL GAINS OR LOSSES.**

(Reprinted in the Securities—US Stock Market Chapter)

2. Stop capital gains and capital losses

Long-held doctrine is that the government encourages investment by taxing the long-term gain on investments at a lower tax rate. In reality, no lower tax motivation for investing is necessary. The only two things you can do with your excess money is either put it in a bank account, similar to putting cash under one's mattress, or invest the money to hopefully grow enough to support your retirement. No side tax deal incentive is necessary. **No lower tax rate on capital gains—there is NO CAPITAL GAINS RATE.** Under the NFT, all income from all sources are taxed at the same rate.

Further, **tax dividend income at normal NFT rates**, not the capital gains rate that is a current gift to wealthy investors who live off dividends.

At the end of every year, stock market investors sell their stocks that have losses. This is called tax-loss selling. They do this because the tax code allows the investor to offset the loss against any capital gain the investor has, even capital gains in future years. To take advantage of the losses in the current year, the investor may also sell stocks in which he/she has gains, thus offsetting the gains to effectively pay no tax in that current year.

Catch this: the government allows the investor to buy back the shares he/she took a tax loss on after thirty days. This old game clearly affects stock prices at the end of each year and often at the beginning of each year as well. As discussed in the Securities—US Stock Market chapter, investors should eschew anything that affects stock prices other than the performance of companies and economic impacts from domestic/international events.

This is just a gift from the IRS to stock investors. Why? Maybe the people who write these rules are stock market investors . . .

- **THE US GOVERNMENT CANNOT BE INVESTORS' PARTNER IN CAPITAL LOSSES.**

By allowing a deduction of capital losses against capital gains, the US is effectively paying for a portion of someone's losses—even poor business choices. If this gift is stopped and all stock gains are taxed when the shares are sold, the US coffers will overflow and all Americans will benefit by having lower tax rates. Gains will be taxed. Losses will just be lost.

When taxes are considered to be low, the efforts to avoid taxes aren't worth the time and accounting professional expense. Just pay the tax and keep doing positive things that generate more income.

3. Retain retirement plans

The best deal that the federal government gives its citizens is to allow them to put money into retirement accounts and let the investments grow untaxed until the person retires. I know I said all income is flat taxed, but this deal from our government is just too important to stop. **You need to make your kids and every other young person you know understand how important this government gift is. It would also be a good idea to school them on compound interest. This lesson could be the most valuable education they ever receive.**

Rule of 7 and 10.

This is a little ditty to start an understanding of the benefit of compound interest:

1. An investment that earns interest of 7 percent, with the interest continuing to be invested (compounded) at 7 percent, will double every ten years.
2. An investment that earns interest of 10 percent, with the interest continuing to be invested (compounded) at 10 percent, will double every 7 years.

This is how just one year's investment in an Individual Retirement Account (IRA) grows, when 10% interest compounds to double every seven years:

Age 25—$10,000 invested at 10% and compounds

Age 32—$20,000 value

Age 39—$40,000 value

Age 46—$80,000 value

Age 52—$160,000 value

Age 59—$320,000 value

Age 66—$640,000 value to retire with!

— From just an original $10,000 investment! Holy Shit!

And the best part? NO TAXES while you gain all of this wealth! It's only taxed when you make distributions to yourself when you have retired. Wow!

Now, imagine what your retirement will look like if you do this every year of your working life and add every dollar you can into your retirement account and invest those funds with care. You're easily a multi-millionaire when you retire!

The regular Individual Retirement Account (IRA) lets people contribute to their IRA and deduct that amount from their current year's income taxes. The account grows untaxed on the gains from interest or even capital appreciation! Once that person retires and withdraws funds from their IRA, those distributions are taxed, presumably at the retiree's lower tax bracket.

The Roth IRA is different in that the contributions are made with a person's funds after they've already paid the tax on the income—there's no tax deduction for the contributions. Again, the account grows untaxed. However, when the retiree takes distributions, they are NOT taxed. What a deal. It's very short-sighted not to do the Roth IRA, because none of the gain on your investments in your Roth IRA will EVER be taxed! The taxes you pay now on the amount of your contributions will be minuscule by comparison.

Please, please, please make it your mission in life to get young people started as early as possible on a Roth IRA to ensure their happy and successful retirement decades from now.

4. Stop inheritance tax benefit

"Fly first class, or you children will."
—LARRY STRAUS

"Unexpected money is a delight. The same sum is a bitterness when you expected more."
—MARK TWAIN

Warren Buffet famously told *Fortune Magazine* that he would give his children "enough money so that they would feel they could do anything, but not so much that they could do nothing."

Inheritance tax (also known as the "death tax") has been a hotly contested tax since the peasants were abused by the landed aristocracy whose lands and wealth simply passed from generation to generation. Most generations included idiot sons who abused their power and the people who were dependent on them. Not a very good system if you're a peasant.

Perhaps the biggest single tax loophole in the US tax system is that assets of the dead person are valued at the market value as of the date of death. The abuse circle is completed by having extremely large individual inheritance tax exemptions.

It works like this:

Let's look at an upper-class couple who have done well financially during their lives. They purchased the nice home they lived in for thirty years for $400,000, which is now worth $2 million. Over the years, they invested in properties and stocks, rarely selling anything because that would have triggered a capital gain tax. The properties and stocks have grown from the $1.5 million they invested over the years to $10 million. Guess what? They didn't have to pay any taxes on this gain along the way. Because they didn't sell assets to trigger taxes during their lifetimes, they did really well. Cool.

To understand how this bad inheritance structure works, let's say the couple dies within days of each other. The US government currently allows just under $13 million inheritance tax exemption for EACH person, so this lucky couple with their even luckier children would be able to leave up to $26 million to those lucky-ass kids, without paying ANY inheritance taxes. Most states follow suit with the federal government, so no federal tax typically means no state tax either. The kids get the house with a new tax basis at its current value of $2 million. They also get the investment portfolio with a new tax basis at its current value of $10 million. The kids get $12 million from their folks and don't have to pay a dime in taxes. The spoiled brats will likely be pissed at their parents for leaving them only half of the allowed $26 million tax-free exemption.

Isn't this the same as a landed aristocracy? Isn't this a significant factor in maintaining the schism between the rich and the poor in the US? Isn't this just wrong?

This lucky/smart family had a gain from their home of $1.6 million and from investments of $8.5 million. They NEVER paid tax on ANY of the gain. That's just not right! It gets worse. Note that whenever the kids sell the house or the investments, their basis is the value as of the date of their parents' deaths. They pay NO TAX except any gain in appreciated value after they received the assets.

The current inheritance structure resulting in this untaxed $8.5 million has to change or I'll join the rioters in the streets with my megaphone. The country and its citizens DESERVE to participate in that gain—just as it does with all other types of income and gain.

It's understandable for parents to want to leave assets to their children. Fine. Do that. Just pay the taxes on the increase in value of your assets and give it to the little monsters, who'll probably just piss it away anyway.

Think of how much more money would make its way into federal and state coffers if taxes were paid on these gains. Further, if a flat tax of approximately 10 percent were applied, it's not too onerous. Just paying the flat tax actually makes it all much simpler for everybody.

This whole matter always has the no-inheritance tax side ringing the bell of "what about family-owned businesses and family farms?" Okay, okay, okay.

No one thinks family-owned businesses and family farms should have to be sold to pay inheritance taxes. So, what's the bad-ass solution here?

Again, with the NFT, the roughly 10 percent tax burden is not too onerous. The government can generously give (loan) the kids twenty years to pay off the tax with a 2 percent interest rate, amortized over the twenty years. Any sale of the business or the farm would first pay off the twenty-year inheritance tax loan. It may sound harsh, but if the business or farm can't make the payments, force a sale. The taxman always gets his money.

5. Stop 1031 tax deferred exchanges

This is another shocking loophole. The government allows its citizens to exchange "like-kind" assets and "defer" the tax on any gain from the original asset. The new asset has to be equal to or greater than the value of the original asset. If the new asset is lower value, then a capital gain tax is applied to the difference.

Here's an example:

A person buys a retail building for $1 million. Rents go up every five years, and after ten years (two rent hikes), the property is worth $2 million (coincidentally, 7 percent compounded). The person now sells the property for $2 million and exchanges it into another property for $2 million. The tax on the $1 million gain is deferred until the person ultimately sells, without doing another exchange. After another ten years, the person sells and exchanges for a $4 million property. Again, the tax on the now $3 million gain is deferred and the person's basis is still the original $1 million.

Now, go back to the discussion on inheritance tax. If the person above leaves the final property to his/her heirs and the total of his/her estate is less than $13 million, the estate pays no taxes on the gains from the succession of exchanged properties—and never will because their basis is now the value of the property as of the date of the person's death.

Unbelievable! If poor people get wind of this, gun sales will skyrocket, and you had better have a bunker. This loophole clearly needs to be plugged up.

Again, just pay the tax—a reasonable flat tax. Think about it—the time and brain damage aren't worth messing with the exchange if the tax is reasonable to begin with. And the US tax coffers will be full, allowing for a lower overall flat tax rate!

6. Tax deductions only for valid cash expenses

Tax deductions make sense—but only some. Tax deductions should be limited to the actual expenses that a business or individual incurs to generate income. These are obvious things such as business rent, payroll expenses, and advertising. Simple.

It gets complicated when the government allows tax deductions of things such as depreciation, which is non-cash, and other items such as interest paid on business loans.

The bad-ass solution here is to only allow actual cash expenses that could not be avoided:

1. Interest could be avoided if the business had no debt—no tax deduction.
2. Depreciation is a non-cash concept—no tax deduction.
3. Rent, payroll, legal, accounting, property taxes are not avoidable—they get tax deductions.
4. Research is avoidable but required for a business to grow or even continue—gets a tax deduction.
5. Charitable deductions will continue to be deductible just so the people will hopefully continue to donate to worthy causes. Flat tax makes the deduction less valuable to the donor and also less costly to the government because the deduction is worth less. However, it's also worth noting that when people have more money (because they pay less in taxes), they give more to charity.
6. **Mortgage interest will continue to be deductible** because the entire housing industry is dependent on this gift from the US government to encourage and support home ownership. The current limit for the deduction is the interest on a $750,000 loan (married couple). This must be revised to reflect geographic differences in housing costs. The new limit should be equal to 70 percent of the median price for homes in the taxpayer's home's geographic area.

7. Corporate tax at flat rates on all net income not paid out as dividends.

Corporations are supposed to make money—profit. They can do several things with that profit:

1. They can pay some or all of the profit as dividends to its shareholders (owners).
2. They can use some of the profit to buy back their own shares. This benefits shareholders because the percentage of the company they own is greater after the share buyback. There are fewer shares, so their shareholders' same number of shares is a bit larger percentage of the smaller pie.
3. They can expand the business, create new stores, factories, increase employee rolls, etc.
4. They can keep some money for reserve.
5. Taxes paid by corporations:
6. Any money that goes to shareholders should not be taxed at the company level. The shareholders will pay taxes on their dividend income at the same level proposed here as flat tax. It makes no sense to tax the income twice—by the corporation and then by the shareholders.
7. All profits not used for dividends should be paid at the flat tax rate. Profits must be calculated as income less cash expenses. Again, depreciation and interest are not deductibles.
    a. **Use of private jets cannot be a tax deduction. While cool as hell, they are unreasonably extravagant and generate insane pollution. There is simply no way to justify the public's subsidy of this in the form of tax deductions. Commercial air travel for business purposes can retain deductibility. Yes, even first class . . .**

8. The New Flat Tax will generate much more revenue for the US and tax returns are much simpler.

The NFT will generate much more revenue because all sources of income will be taxed, without the old tax benefits for the wealthy and corporations.

The NFT will greatly simplify tax returns. This will result in much easier and cheaper tax return preparation costs. Accountants will hate it. (Probably a good sign.) Individuals should be able to prepare their tax returns in about fifteen minutes every year.

The NFT will significantly reduce the audit functions of the IRS, saving enormous costs for the US.

BAD-ASS SIDE THOUGHT ON TAXES

Could it be said that if a person is past a certain age and doesn't pay any income taxes, they should not be allowed to have a say (vote) on the way the government spends the tax money from other people? Although there's a reasonable argument there, NO, that's just not what the US is about.

Could it also be said that a person who pays no taxes doesn't feel like it's really their government? It's something like Freud, who said that unless a person pays for their own therapy, they won't get anything out of it.

American citizens should have a say in their government. They should be taxpayers. We don't tax the poor—nor should we. Wouldn't the poor feel like the country is more theirs if they pay SOMETHING? Just $10 per month from a family? Let all Americans have the pleasure of paying for their government and call themselves taxpayers. The psychology is strong.

What if some people really can't pay even $10 per month? Would it be callous to suggest that every adult who can't pay tax of $10 per month work two hours per month for community service? Remember, high earners work more than four months a year for the federal government. Can't poor people work two hours a month for the public good? Won't they feel like they're contributing?

Just askin'...

CHAPTER 12
WATCH YOUR ASS

LAWSUITS
Stop the pain and waste in the current legal system

"If you want to make crime pay, go to law school."

—WHITEY BULGER

A lawyer died. At the pearly gates, he told Saint Peter that there
has been a terrible mistake. He was too young to die.
Saint Peter looked in his large golden scrolls and said,
"Not really, it says right here that you're eighty-seven."
The lawyer (relieved), said, "No, that's wrong! I'm just fifty-seven."
Saint Peter looked a bit deeper into the page and said,
"Oh, I see. We calculated using your billed hours."

"If a man belittles a woman, it could become a lawsuit.
If women belittle men, it's a Hallmark card."

—WARREN FARRELL

"A good lawyer knows the law;
a clever one takes the judge to lunch."

—MARK TWAIN

> "A lawyer is a person who writes a 10,000-word document and calls it a brief."
>
> —FRANZ KAFKA

THE PROBLEM

The US has too many lawyers. The very best lawyers, who graduate from top schools, at or near the top of their classes, work at the best legal firms. They kill themselves to make partner by working eighty-plus billable hours per week for years on end.

All of the other lawyers trickle down through the pinball bumpers until they find their place in the legal hierarchy. Many end up working as lawyers with very few clients knocking on their doors. They have to go out and get clients. Are you familiar with the term "ambulance chaser?"

The top lawyers get hired by the rich and powerful to both protect them and enforce their rights. These modern-day medieval knights go forth and try very hard to vanquish everyone in their path. Their strategy is often to batter their opponents into capitulation. Their first line of attack is to make the other side spend a lot of money. The lawyer doesn't care. In fact, they love it because it means they're also racking up billable hours to get paid from their clients. They get the other side to spend money, time, and aggravation doing lots of depositions, interrogatories (answering questions), and procedural hearings.

When the two sides are equally matched in client money and lawyer quality, the gladiators wage truly magnificent warfare. Take no prisoners. Get the courts tied up for years. Get millions from the clients. Forget what you're fighting about. The whole thing is designed to keep lawyers working for years and raking in millions. Never mind that the clients are bloody, broke, and worn out. After a while, they hardly care about winning anymore.

The lower-level lawyers take on cases that often have little or no merit. They convince a client to let them fight and maybe win some money for them. When the client doesn't have the money to hire them, the lawyer frequently offers to take the case on contingency, meaning they only get paid if they win the case. They usually get 30 to 40 percent of the award or settlement. The lawyer already has the basic legal documents needed in the computer. Just a few edits and the case can be filed.

Speaking of settlement, many cases only get a lawyer on contingency because the other side has insurance coverage for the claims of the lawsuit. This could be a car accident with real or imagined injuries. It could be a doctor who performed surgery that didn't yield an excellent result, which would be a suit for malpractice that goes after the insurance. It could be a suit against a company whose employee thinks they were wrongfully terminated, and the insurance coverage is pursued.

Very often, after depositions and interrogatories, the insurance company will determine that they are going to spend quite a bit of money defending their client, then may or may not lose additional sums from a verdict. They decide to offer settlement roughly equal to the amount they would have to pay just for their defense lawyers and limit their losses. Catch this: the client has virtually no say about the insurance company settling the case. The insurance company has the right to limit their exposure and offer settlement. If the client doesn't agree, they can pursue the case—but at their own risk. None do.

Have you ever been sued? You get served with official papers from the court that set forth who is suing, why, and usually the size of the "damages." Even if the lawsuit is totally frivolous, it's a terrible pain, and no matter how innocent you are, it's frightening. It's meant to be that way. You have to get your own lawyer to answer, pay them a bunch of money, and work with them to establish your defense. Often, you counter-sue because you may have real or potential claims against the other side, and well, why should they not also suffer?

Too many lawyers with their financial need to file suits to try to get settlements has become a pain to Americans and gummed up the court systems throughout the country.

BAD-ASS SOLUTION

The time and money wasted on lawsuits is a shame. Even the suits that involve real damages take too much time, cost too much, and are needlessly difficult on everyone but the lawyers.

The US needs new rules for lawsuits:

- **NO FRIVOLOUS LAWSUITS**

Some lawyers file cases either as a nuisance or to just take a shot at being such an irritant that it's worth a few thousand dollars to make them go away. All cases must be reviewed for merit and actual damages by a new pre-court judge system in order to move forward as a valid lawsuit. If not, the case is thrown out.

- **STREAMLINE CASES**

New rules must be created to permit only very specific discovery that is determined by the pre-court judge to be necessary and acceptable.

- **NO INSURANCE SETTLEMENTS**

Insurance settlements actually cause more lawsuits. On an individual case basis, it may be more cost-efficient and expeditious for the insurance company to settle and walk away, but the practice encourages lawyers to file suits with the goal of getting an insurance settlement. It feeds on itself. Insurance companies cannot settle any cases. They must go through the entire trial and have the court decide a verdict. The court will have the ability to accept a settlement between the parties after a trial but before a verdict is reached.

- **THE COURT SYSTEM TO BE REVISED AND STREAMLINED**

    Cases take way too long and are far too expensive to be of much use—other than to lawyers. Most cases should be ordered to binding arbitration with very limited appeals.

    Aside:

    Don't you get frustrated when you have judges on your ballots? Who knows any of these people? First, there's virtually no information about them included in the voting packet, and second, who has the time to review as many as twenty judges? The electorate is just not qualified to vote on judges. All state judges should be appointed by a **non-partisan** judicial panel made up of state representatives with final approval by the governor. Judges should be able to be recalled immediately by a no-confidence vote by the judicial panel. Terms should be four years.

    On the federal court, including the US Supreme Court, judges should not be appointed for life. The original purpose was to keep judges non-political. The solution was to not require reappointment. That's just ridiculous. They should serve six-year terms and be ineligible to serve past their seventy-fifth birthday.

- **NO JUDGES OLDER THAN SEVENTY-FIVE YEARS**

    Maybe I'll feel differently about this when I'm seventy-four.

CHAPTER 13
DRUGS COST A LOT MORE IN PRISON

DRUGS

Immediately dismantle the entire criminal drug world

"A prohibition law strikes a blow at the very principles upon which our government was founded."

—ABRAHAM LINCOLN

"Don't do drugs because if you do drugs you'll go to prison, and drugs are really expensive in prison."

—JOHN HARDWICK

"The prestige of government has undoubtedly been lowered considerably by the prohibition law. For nothing is more destructive of respect for the government and the law of the land than passing laws which cannot be enforced. It is an open secret that the dangerous increase of crime in this country is closely connected with this."

—ALBERT EINSTEIN

> "The war on drugs is wrong, both tactically and morally. It assumes that people are too stupid, too reckless, and too irresponsible to decide whether and under what conditions to consume drugs. The war on drugs is morally bankrupt."
>
> —LARRY ELDER

THE PROBLEM

According to Open.lib.umn.edu, mind-altering drugs (including alcohol) have been used since ancient times. Virtually every society for thousands of years used drugs of some kind that were derived from plants, including alcohol, opium, and marijuana.

Drugs have always been used in the US. Before and after the Civil War, opium was extremely common and used to feel good, as a painkiller, and a cough suppressant. It was doctor-recommended for everything from depression to toothaches. It is estimated that 500,000 Americans were addicted to opium by the end of the nineteenth century.

Cocaine was another widely used drug beginning in the late 1800s. Again, it was used to feel good and as a remedy for virtually every ailment. Dr. Sigmond Freud was a cocaine addict. Catch this—cocaine was a major ingredient in Coca-Cola, introduced in 1886. Coca meant cocaine??? No wonder it became so popular so quickly. "It's the real thing!"

Marijuana (cannabis, weed) also became popular in the late nineteenth century and was used in many medications. That said, marijuana has been used in the US virtually since the nation began. Marijuana has been a widely-used recreational drug in the US for more than a hundred years, and likely thousands of years globally. Nope, it wasn't discovered by hippies in the 1960s. "Everything old is new again."

Most people don't think of alcohol as a drug, but it is. No need to waste your time with facts about how deeply integrated alcohol is seated into American culture and habits. We can use the legal alcohol business as a potential model for dealing with legal drugs.

Do you want illegal drugs? You can get anything you want in minutes in any urban area in the US. Beyond horrifying, right? Now realize that this is just as true for teens and even pre-teens. Every drug you can name is readily available. Cannabis, cocaine, mushrooms, LSD, meth, hashish, ecstasy, heroine, etc., and every kind of prescription drug is on the menu. Step right up . . . the line forms to the right.

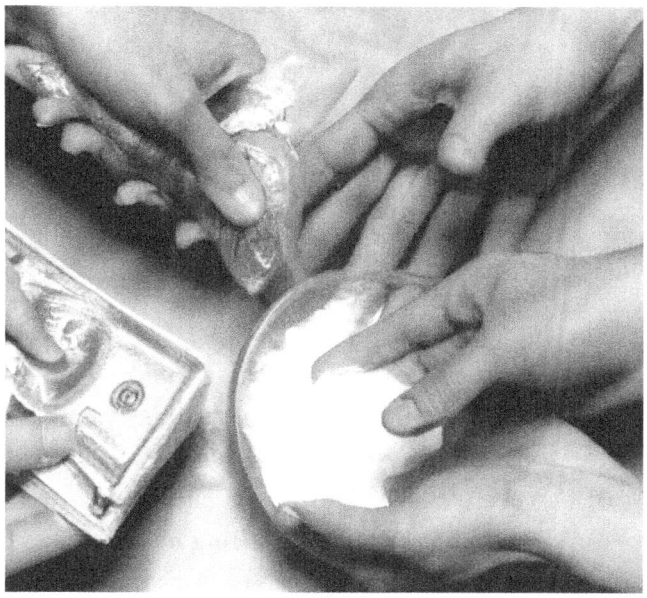

I don't understand the attraction of prescription drugs, particularly the category of opioids such as painkillers like OxyContin and Percocet. These kinds of drugs are downers. They dull you into not feeling pain, or much of anything else. I just don't seem to have the capacity to understand why teens are taking these drugs like they're candy. I understand the good feelings one gets from most illegal drugs, but taking enough painkillers that would dull an elephant's toothache? Sorry, I must be much more ancient in my thinking than I thought because I just don't get this.

Now add an even bigger nightmare to the prescription drug mess. Fentanyl. The Department of Justice and Drug Enforcement Administration define Fentanyl as a potent synthetic opioid drug approved by the Food and Drug Administration for use as an analgesic (pain relief) and anesthetic. It is approximately one hundred times more potent than morphine and fifty times more potent than heroin as an analgesic. So, who could possibly need that much?

Illegal Fentanyl is being produced as an inexpensive filler for other drugs like cocaine, heroin, and opioids. The chemicals necessary for illegal fentanyl are made in China and flooding into the US via Mexico because it is a very inexpensive yet incredibly powerful drug. Colored pills that look like candy are making their way into the US, generating fear that children will take them and die from the drug overdose almost immediately.

DEA.gov reports that: "Fentanyl remains the deadliest drug threat facing this country. It is a highly addictive synthetic opioid. Just two milligrams of fentanyl, the small amount that fits on the tip of a pencil, is considered a potentially deadly dose."

Unintentional overdose deaths in the US from Fentanyl are approaching 100,000 per year and climbing fast. A shocking number of deaths are teens and people younger than forty.

A shot of perspective: **The American death toll from the entire Vietnam War was 58,200. Fentanyl is killing nearly twice that many Americans—every year. SO FAR, WE'VE LOST APPROXIMATELY FIVE VIETNAMS OF AMERICANS TO FENTANYL.**

Per US Department of Justice, Bureau of Justice Statistics: A drug-related crime: it is a crime to possess, manufacture, or distribute drugs classified as having a potential for abuse (such as cocaine, heroin, morphine, and amphetamines). Drugs are also related to crime, as drug trafficking and drug production are often controlled by drug cartels, organized crime, and gangs.

DRUGS AND CRIME
(THIS IS GOING TO BE WORSE
THAN YOU EVER THOUGHT.)

Following are statistics of crime related to drugs compiled by the National Center for Drug Abuse Statistics:
1. 80% of prison inmates abuse drugs or alcohol.
2. 244,000 Americans are sent to prison annually for drug related crimes.
3. 26% of all arrests in America are related to drug offenses.
4. 46% of all prisoners in federal prison are there for drug related crimes.
5. 59% of all women sentenced to federal prison are serving time for drug offenses.
6. Nearly 60% of Hispanic federal prisoners are in prison for drug-related offenses.

The following regarding gangs and drugs in America is from the National Drug Intelligence Center:
1. Street gangs, outlaw motorcycle gangs, and prison gangs are the primary distributors of illegal drugs on the streets of the US. Gangs also smuggle drugs into the US and produce and transport drugs within the country.
2. Large, nationally affiliated street gangs pose the greatest threat because they smuggle, produce, transport, and distribute large quantities of illicit drugs throughout the country and are extremely violent.
3. Some (smaller) gangs collect millions of dollars per month selling illegal drugs, trafficking weapons, operating prostitution rings, and selling stolen property.
4. **There are at least 21,500 gangs with more than 731,000 active gang members in the US.**

*****Authorities throughout the country report that gangs are responsible for most of the serious violent crime in the major cities of the US. Gangs engage in an array of criminal activities including assault, burglary, drive-by shootings, extortion, homicide,**

identification fraud, money laundering, prostitution operations, robbery, sale of stolen property, and weapons trafficking.

Nothing has worked to stop the use of illegal drugs in the US.

According to CNBC.com, President Nixon declared a "WAR ON DRUGS" in 1971. It was directed toward eradication, interdiction, and incarceration. The tough-on-crime policy agenda continues to produce disastrous results today.

By 2022, it was estimated that the United States spends **$41 billion annually** on these initiatives, and after fifty years of the drug war, it is estimated that the US has spent a cumulative $1 trillion on it. By all measures, this long war failed. Drug use remains high. Crime related to drug use is skyrocketing.

Incarceration for drug-related crimes has had virtually no impact on drug use or public safety in the US. Incarceration of drug related offenders costs the US tens of billions of dollars per year.

In the 1980s, First Lady Nancy Reagan had a campaign to stop drug use by young people in the US. Television ads were everywhere with the slogan, "JUST SAY NO to drugs." Snappy, right? This was supposed to be the plan that every young person could use when offered drugs. Just say no. Sure.

The US had a fifty-year war on drugs, but never went to war. We never invaded the Latin American countries and China where the drugs were being made and imported into the US. We never had US military use its might against the drug lords, cartels, and gangs who brought drugs into the US and made us junkies. We never fought a guerilla war within our borders to wipe out the mafia and gangs who made fortunes while they ruined people's lives and killed thousands by overdose.

Of late, both China and Mexico are the sources of Fentanyl that is killing up to 100,000 Americans PER YEAR. Isn't that a war? Why has the US not declared war on the drug manufacturing and distribution networks in China and Mexico? Right now, you should feel faint with anger and frustration. Take a minute.

Of course the war on drugs failed. They mostly utilized law enforcement against drug users and the idiots who were last in line to sell the drugs. A trillion-dollar, fifty-year wasted effort. Let's not go into why the government didn't fight this war as a war. Did they not really want to win? They didn't seem to. It's a real conundrum that we will probably never get a good answer to. Some people believe it was a component of the "school to prison pipeline," referring to the theory that the government wants to shift potentially dangerous kids from the classroom to the juvenile and criminal justice systems to control them.

Short of going to a real war on drugs, we simply cannot stop drugs. People can get any drug they want in a matter of minutes. It's barely more effort than getting a pizza. We're making criminals of drug users who have to steal to pay for expensive street drugs while they break the law for using the drugs.

We're greatly enriching the cartels, gangs, and thugs to provide the poison to our people. We're spending billions and billions of dollars per year to arrest and incarcerate people who just go back to the illegal activity when they get out. The number of people in prisons for drugs (as listed above) is staggering—in some cases, roughly half of all inmates and more than 65 percent of women are in for drugs. The violent crimes from gangs has made the US unsafe. It's like a killing zone. This is the biggest blight on the US imaginable. STOP IT! IT CAN BE STOPPED OVERNIGHT.

BAD-ASS SOLUTION

Everyone heard the theory that legalizing marijuana would be enough for people to stop using harder drugs. We did that. It didn't.

- **LEGALIZE ALL DRUGS IN THE US.**
- **INSTANTLY PUT THE CARTELS, GANGS AND CRIMINALS OUT OF BUSINESS.**
- **REDUCE ADDICTION AND HELP ADDICTS REHABILITATE.**

A fascinating experiment recently played out in Oregon, where they decriminalized small amounts of virtually all illicit drugs. It was a terrible failure because drugs continued to be illegal, thereby keeping the entire criminal drug structure in place, feasting on an even larger marketplace. Right idea, but not even going halfway doomed the program from the start.

The US has no choice. Legalization is the only way to get control of this ruination of our country.

Legalizing drugs will bring massive benefits to the US and its citizens including saving thousands if not millions of lives.

1. Legalize all drugs except:
   a. Fentanyl, because if real prescription drugs are available, unmercifully deadly Fentanyl will not be desired or even present, as it is currently utilized by drug dealers as a cheap filler included in other street drugs.
   b. Crystal methamphetamine, because this cheap, extremely addictive drug can be replaced with other drugs such as cocaine that are arguably less dangerous.

Remember, right now, all drugs are available to anyone, including children, within minutes. It's a dirty, dangerous business. Legalization cleans the entire process. It ensures safe drugs, stops most gang crime, lowers the cost of drugs, saves billions of dollars, controls drug use by minors, frees up law enforcement to pursue real violent criminals, generates revenue, and helps addicts recover.

2. Millions of Americans will no longer be criminals. People won't be criminals subject to arrest and jail for using drugs. People will not have to steal to pay for drugs because they will cost much less. Lower drug costs stops crime and hopefully does not increase usage. Legalization of marijuana does not appear to have materially increased use.

Rehabilitated addicts will be able to apply for jobs without having to admit to being convicted of felonies.

3. Drugs will go from back alleys to storefronts where they can be controlled.

4. Allow US companies to produce and sell drugs. Do not allow marketing or advertising to entice usage. Provide clean drugs at a lower price.

5. Overnight, the entire illegal drug machine is out of business. Can you imagine taking the entire drug business away from gangs? Can you imagine drug users not having to steal to support their habits? The Mexican drug cartels will have to find something new to do. How about something productive? Not happening. They'll probably continue killing each other because that's all they know. That too has to change.

6. Crime, including violent crime, will be reduced dramatically in the US.

7. Control drugs to minors the way alcohol is controlled. This presents the greatest benefit of legalization. There won't be thugs on every corner trying to entice kids. Police will have to be extremely vigilant on this.

8. As with other criminal matters reviewed in this book, providing drugs to minors will necessitate immediate harsh penalties with cooperation from law enforcement and courts. Again, bring back the movies' hangin' judge.

9. We don't have to worry about fentanyl. There will be no need for it, and it won't be imported illegally. 100,000 Americans, including children, per year will be saved from this alone. Huge!

10. Drug addiction will no longer be a police matter. Addicts can get help under this new program to stop using and get help to improve their lives.

11. The entire legal system will be greatly relieved with as much as 50 percent fewer criminal cases. America can become safe again. Seriously, this is a big-ass deal.

12. Generate sales tax income from drug sales to pay for education and treatment programs.

13. Generate income taxes from drug manufacturers to pay for education and treatment programs.

14. The US will save at least $50 billion per year that can be used for drug treatment, retraining, and job placement.

15. The US will have funds to train former criminals and gang members to get good jobs and have better lives. Will they take the opportunity? They'll need to find some way to make a living. Hopefully, they can be persuaded to come from the dark side to the good side. The US will have the money to help make that happen.

16. Inmates whose crime was possession of illegal drugs can be given an opportunity to be released to halfway houses for education, job training, and job placement. This will save billions of dollars and hopefully turn criminals into productive citizens.

17. Have controlled venues (drug consumption sites) for people to use hard drugs without affecting or endangering the public. There could be private businesses that supply a bar-type

atmosphere for drug use. All customers will be required to spend enough time in the facilities (that will include bedrooms) until they are certified sober. Alternatively, they can be driven home by the facility.

USE THE MONEY

With the billions of dollars per year saved on drug crime and the billions of dollars per year of income from drug taxes, federal and state governments will have massive resources to help people with their drug abuse. **Money will be available for rehab, treatment, education, and job placement. We just need the will—and guts.**

CHAPTER 14
PAY TO PLAY

ELECTIONS

Take special interests out of election funding immediately

"I am not a member of any organized political party.
I'm a Democrat."

—WILL ROGERS.

"A government which robs Peter to pay Paul
can always depend on the support of Paul."

—GEORGE BERNARD SHAW

"There go the people. I must follow them, for I am their leader."

—ALEXANDRE AUGUSTE LEDRU-ROLLIN,
ONE OF THE LEADERS OF THE FRENCH REVOLUTION OF 1848

"In America, anyone can become president. That's the problem."

—GEORGE CARLIN

A WORD ON POLITICAL PARTIES
(REPRINTED FROM THE INTRODUCTION)

I (perhaps like you) have become extremely critical of both parties and their intractable "party positions" that just serve to feed on our differences and only exacerbate hate and distrust of each other. I am also sick of the red-state / blue-state categories that try to succinctly define an entire US state and its population of millions of diverse Americans as if there is only one issue involved, as there was for the Civil War. Is that what they're trying to duplicate? Feels like it. This political polarization is dangerous stuff. We need to be brought together, not separated for the benefit of political parties and the convenience of the press.

In the real world, apart from the party-line politicians, aren't we all actually liberal on some issues and conservative on others? It seems everyone I talk to is this way. This thoughtfulness and flexibility I find in real Americans gives me hope. We need to bypass the intractable loyalty to rigid party positions to actually accomplish something.

That said, the remainder of this chapter addresses ELECTIONS.

THE PROBLEM

It is almost laughable that at the election night celebration parties, the winning candidates for the House of Representatives actually kick off their campaigns for the next election two years away. These people spend virtually all of their time campaigning, which is short for fundraising. When the hell do these people actually govern? They barely do.

Senators are a bit better because they only have to face elections every six years. So what's their excuse for the poor performance and slowness to accomplish anything of much value to the country?

Presidents fall in between senators and representatives. They run every four years, so they have to campaign about 50 percent of the time during their first term, then none if they're elected to a second term because of the two-term limit. They do spend a great deal of time campaigning for their hopeful successor, from their own party of course.

This merry-go-round is repeated on state and local levels in every nook and hamlet in the US. Our government doesn't govern, it raises money for annoying political ad campaigns to get the American consumer to buy their product. The politicians are professional actor/campaigners. This just has to change.

Elections also include a numbing number of local propositions, measures, and bond approvals that few voters spend time to evaluate. The most ridiculous items to vote on are the myriad judges and education trustees. Who spends time evaluating all of these people? The materials sent to voters rarely include any information on them so it's virtually impossible to be an informed, well-considered voter on these matters. I doubt many people take the time to read the materials anyway. This makes an even greater joke of our elections, but it's not at all funny.

For many months prior to elections, Americans are subjected to an endless barrage of ads, billboards, phone calls, mail, texts, and even knocking on their doors. We have a populous who is sick and tired of the entire Hollywood production. And they are slick, conman-style productions. Americans are sold politicians the same way advertisers sell retail products. The similarity is nauseating. The two opposing campaigners look like type-cast actors and the messages appear virtually the same, "I believe in goodness and growth and all Americans deserve a great life—and I'm going to see that they get it. And by the way, the other side is responsible for why you don't already have those things."

Note that the sales pitch never explains exactly how the campaigner is going to deliver this stuff, just that he/she will work hard to get the job done FOR YOU. Yeah, we've all heard that crap way too many times. It's gotten to be as useless and infuriating as the constant barrage of car insurance commercials where each promises the lowest rates.

There's another disturbing issue about all of this. Candidates are spending insane amounts of money to get elected. The two candidates competing for the US Senate seat from Georgia in 2022 spent $380 MILLION between them. The job only pays $174,000! Isn't something terribly wrong here? Sure, there were huge implications about which political party would control the US Senate, but this just smells bad. Campaigns of much less importance still cost tens of millions of dollars.

Here's how this happens: individuals and political committees have relatively low limitations on how much they are allowed to donate to candidates for their campaigns. It is horrifying that a mechanism called a Super PACc (Political Action Committee) can accept unlimited contributions, then effectively run a separate campaign for their favorite candidate, including the funding and producing of all the television commercials we are bombarded with. They have a tag at the end of the commercial usually saying that they paid for the ad and there is often another voiceover from the actual candidate saying that he/she approved the message.

The *Los Angeles Times* reported that even before the actual primary voting for the California Senate seat in 2024, "Super PACs spent more than $21 million and have at least $71 million more at their disposal." They further detail that many very rich people and even labor unions have contributed up to several million dollars to different Super PACs. This just stinks.

The cynic wonders, "What makes a relatively low-paying job worth tens or even hundreds of millions of dollars to get?"

Good question. You just have to wonder if it's an indication of very deep and hidden corruption.

Campaigning has become a much-too-frequent Super Bowl of competing players. The country shouldn't spend its time on this hyped circus popularity contest.

The political parties themselves contribute massive amounts of money to their candidates through the impressive-sounding monikers Democratic National Committee (DNC) and Republican National Committee (RNC). There are serious problems with this practice:

1. Donors give money to the candidate and also to the party. The party then gives money to the candidate, so the per-person contribution limits are effectively non-existent.

2. In return for the large contributions, the parties demand strict party-line adherence on voting issues from the candidates they

back. This is a prime reason for the terrible lack of compromise in our government. If an elected official compromises, or worse, votes for a measure outside of the party platform, he/she risks being denied funds from the party for their next election. This is mafia-style payment for allegiance and should have no place in the US government.

Beyond the campaign finance problems, the press has become an insidious barrier for Americans to want to serve as an elected servant for their country.

Sometime around the advent of Ted Turner's CNN delivery of twenty-four-hour news, the US news industry began a rapid devolution from a valuable, objective freedom of the press engine into a non-stop, intrusive, opinionated, sensational, feeding-frenzy parasite. They have to fill twenty-four hours per day of news, seven days a week. They have endless competition from other news outlets including television, radio, online, podcasts, X (Twitter), Facebook, etc., etc. These "reporters" stop at nothing to get on air with a report. Everything is fair game. This is particularly true of everything to do with celebrities, criminals, mass shootings, car chases, and politicians. The old saying attributable to the requirement for a successful academic career seems to be the credo for all media today: publish or perish.

Politicians and their families are subjected to constant intrusions into their personal lives. Political reporters are no better than paparazzi chasing down current teen pop stars for a picture of their tongue down another pop star's throat. The political press waives the First Amendment in the air like a sacred pass to justify doing anything they choose to get the goods on politicians and their families. This just isn't what Jefferson, Madison, and the other boys had in mind.

It's not as if a good reporter stumbles upon something seedy about a politician and feels compelled to report it. These hyenas target and dig for dirt. They want to find bad things about public people. They want to ruin lives in the name of their career advancement. Sensationalism sells. News is a business, and their product is scandal, sex, infidelity, and divorce. Back in the day of newspapers, the mantra was, "if it bleeds, it leads." Now, the media mantra appears to be, "if it's sleaze, it leads." Who is more at fault: the people who provide the sleaze and make us think it's important, or we who watch and read the sleaze? Can you say boycott?

Here's the problem. What really good, well-qualified people would want to subject themselves and their families to this endless attempt at character assassination? We get that unfortunate answer often. It seems that only people who are narcissistic and self-aggrandizing would be interested. The remaining 99 percent of truly qualified people who could contribute tremendously to the country would never subject themselves and their families to the abuse. Sad. America is not being led by the best and brightest. Instead, we get who we have—a very unimpressive group of narcissistic career politicians, most of whom do a very poor job.

The US needs to completely overhaul its election systems. The actual restructuring of the government is addressed in another chapter. Let's just keep to the issue at hand: elections.

The entire campaign and election process revolves around money. With very few exceptions, the campaigner who raises more money to buy more advertising usually wins. Also, with few exceptions, campaigns are funded by the political parties (DNC and RNC), special action committees (PACS), special interests, organizations, businesses, unions, individuals, and even foreign governments.

Campaign contributions range from a few dollars from hard-working people to millions from big wigs and special interests.

Don't you cringe when you hear that someone running for president is staging a dinner at a Hollywood celebrity's house where the guests pay something like $100,000 per plate? My skin crawls. This just reeks of influence and cronyism. The wealthy get to influence our public servants while the poor and middle classes just don't have access. The law of the jungle shouldn't be the law of the US. Equal access should always be the rule.

The need for politicians to constantly raise money gets in the way of our government officials actually doing the job that needs to get done. Worst of all, what do major donors expect from their donations? At the very least, it gives them access to the politician once in office. At the very worst, it influences the politician toward the donor's interests instead of the best interests of the public. This smells bad at every turn.

BAD-ASS SOLUTION

- **ALL CAMPAIGNS ARE TO BE FUNDED BY THE GOVERNMENT.**
- **THERE ARE NO PRIVATE, PAC, OR PARTY CONTRIBUTIONS.**
- **CAMPAIGN TIME IS LIMITED.**
- **ABANDON THE ELECTORAL COLLEGE.**
    1. **Limit Time for Campaigns.** All campaigns for office are limited to nine months prior to the general election.
        a. To qualify as a campaigner, all candidates must meet age and residence requirements. Additionally, prior to commencing a political career, all candidates must have a minimum of five years' experience working in the private sector or in the US military. No career politicians.
        b. Level One—During the first three months, nine through seven months prior to the election, a candidate lets it be known they are running for the office.
        c. To move to the next level, they must obtain a number of signatures from within their representation area equal to at least 5 percent of the average number of votes cast for that specific office.
        d. No funding is needed during the first level.
        e. No advertising or fund raising is allowed during this period. Only meeting with potential constituents (voters) is permitted.
        f. Candidates who obtain the minimum number of signatures move on to level two.
        g. Level Two—During months six through four prior to the election, all candidates for a given office are provided a marketing budget equal to two times the annual salary for the office, or other amount which may be determined

       by the relevant state or federal government as necessary to have an informed public.

    h. Throughout the campaign, the public funds for marketing may be used by the candidate for marketing as they choose, except cannot be used for personal expenses for the campaigner or his/her family.

    i. The primary election is held at the end of level two, three months prior to the election. Winners of the primary election are now in the final phase.

    j. Level Three—The final three months. Each candidate is provided with a budget equal to five times the annual salary for the office, or other amount which may be determined by the relevant state or federal government as necessary to have an informed public.

    k. The general election is held at the end of the ninth month of campaigning.

2. **The Government as Sole Source of Funds.** The funds for all campaigns are split appropriately between the local, state, and federal government, relative to the office. No other donations are permitted.

3. **Maintain Candidate Privacy.** The problem of an intrusive press must be addressed for elections and also during and after a person is in office. The press has a very strong shield to ensure that it can continue to pursue and report anything it wants—the First Amendment to the Constitution.

The First Amendment: *Congress shall make no law respecting an establishment of religion or prohibiting the free exercise thereof; or abridging the freedom of speech, or of the press; or the right of the people peaceably to assemble, and to petition the Government for a redress of grievances.*

All Americans should highly value the First Amendment. It can be regarded as the cornerstone of our freedom. But what if it's abused as previously discussed? Although sacred, most rights granted under the

Bill of Rights (the first ten Amendments of the Constitution) have had some laws that serve to define or restrict those rights to fit into the current needs of the US.

These alterations even include the First Amendment. Peaceful assembly requires permits and restrictions as to where and when such assemblies take place. Rules restricting the exercise of religion in places like airports and schools are common. There have been laws and rules surrounding the Second Amendment for years, calling for the registration of firearms, concealed carry laws, background checks, etc.

We should institute laws to protect the right to privacy for candidates and elected officials from predatory press actions. Our law makers and courts should agree that personal information about a person's day-to-day life is off-limits to the press. Worth a try.

Beyond laws, it's important to remember that the press is a business. Americans have the powers of boycott and ownership control.

Americans tend to like to jump on board of popular and trendy causes like pollution, human rights, civil rights, LGBTQ, pro-choice, pro-life, #MeToo, etc. If boycotting news outlets who report on private, personal matters and hound politicians becomes trendy, things will change.

Also, if shareholders demand that officers of news outlets utilize a more responsible criteria for its reporting, those businesses will change. They are businesses and its shareholders' (owner's) demands are powerful.

4. **No Public Candidate Tax Returns or Financials.** Perhaps there can be a strictly confidential review of candidates' financials and tax returns by the IRS (who already have the returns) to certify the absence of illegal activities. After that review, an individual's finances are simply none of the voting public's business. Again, we want good, successful people to run for office without their private lives being laid bare to the public. It's important that even government officials retain their right to privacy.

The US desperately needs to make serving the country by running for office be considered an honor. These people should be appreciated and protected.

5. **Abandon the Electoral College.** The Founding Fathers struggled during the Constitutional Convention and wrote extensively in the Federalist Papers about choosing a process for electing a president. The problems mostly centered around states' rights and the difficulty in the 1700s of imagining how everyone (white men) in the US could vote for president in any efficient manner. Trust me, the arguments are boring and irrelevant today. I can just picture those guys laughing their asses off that we retained the clearly obsolete Electoral College given current technologies. After all, they wrote this stuff with a feather!

I believe that most Americans are frustrated by this topic that effectively translates to the fact that they do not vote directly for president, but instead a somewhat representative, archaic process is utilized. Many times, the Electoral College has elected a president who actually did not win the popular vote, including Trump's 2016 win over Clinton. A part of Trump's winning strategy was to pursue electoral votes rather than the popular vote. Hillary Clinton has been criticized for not paying enough attention to those critical electoral votes.

The US should firmly stand in this century and commit that voting be as meaningful as possible. Abandon the obsolete Electoral College bureaucracy and have all future presidents elected by the popular vote. Make each American's vote for president actually count.

6. **Prohibit Union Endorsements.** Let's not debate the value of unions but just agree that the political power and undue influence wielded by some of the largest unions seems way beyond their purpose of collective bargaining. The current pandering to unions by many politicians gets in the way of enacting laws for the greater good. Union members should vote their conscience, not blindly as their union bosses direct.

It's really time to clean up this political campaign and influence peddling mess. The US and Americans must demand these changes.

CHAPTER 15
NOT TO DIE FOR

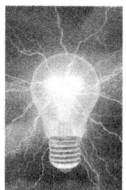

MILITARY AND WARS

Never lose another US soldier on the battlefield

"In preparing for battle, I have always found that plans are useless but planning is indispensable."

—DWIGHT EISENHOWER

"You don't make peace with your friend, you make peace with your enemy."

—YITZHAK RABIN

"The object of war is not to die for your country, but to make the other bastard die for his."

—GENERAL GEORGE PATTON

THE PROBLEM

The Art of War by Sun Tzu (fifth century BC) has been the military strategy, tactics, and philosophy manual for generals and governments for more than 2,000 years! The book goes into great detail about how military units should strategize a win under every kind of situation: when the opponent controls the hill, when you control the hill, when the opponent is starving and surrounded, when your army is starving and surrounded—you get the idea.

In addition to strategies for field battles, *The Art of War* provides dozens of axioms for battle of all kinds. "Victorious warriors win first and then go to war, while defeated warriors go to war first and then seek to win."

In 1987, the book became a widely known inspiration for business generals to aggressively attack and defeat their enemies. Michael Douglas's character, Gordon Gecko, taught the tactics to wage war as applied to manipulating securities in the film *Wall Street*. Sun Tzu's *The Art of War* has inspired western military, legal, business, sports, and political strategy.

The Art of War has been incredibly valuable because throughout history, wars were fought on battlefields. The book addresses virtually every type of situation that can exist in such battles. Of course, there's no specific information about what to do while your enemy is bombarding your positions with long-range ballistic cruise missiles or endless sorties of its jets bombing everything in sight.

In the past eighty years, wars have evolved to include nuclear weapons, cold war stand-offs, and a devastating evolution of war tactics that initially took shape in the Vietnam War against the US military. The two warring sides did not meet on sprawling battlefields. The war was fought in villages, cities, and rice patties. The North Vietnamese fought the US along with a guerilla fighting group called the Vietcong, who dug tunnels throughout the South. They escaped bombings and silently infiltrated US military locations to bomb and shoot American soldiers by popping up literally inside US controlled areas. The US lost the war.

The US wars that followed, particularly in Afghanistan, greatly expanded the military strategy for fighting against the Americans. The enemy soldiers realized two extremely important things about the US military. First, if enemy soldiers hid among the resident population, especially among women, children, and the elderly, the US would not attack. Second, the massive technological weaponry advantage held by the US is effectively useless in a guerilla war.

It is abundantly clear to enemies that the US can be suckered into guerilla warfare. Enemy soldiers hide within the general population, which draws US soldiers out into the streets. Our brave soldiers are sitting ducks to be shot at by enemy snipers. The enormous military technological advantage of the US is thus reduced to disadvantaged fighting units being shot at. No wonder Afghanistan was the longest war in US history and we had to leave in the most terrible, embarrassing way possible. We couldn't win that war. In fact, we can't win any guerilla war.

The last time the US really fought a war without being hog-tied as described previously was in World War II. The US decided that it had to win that war—and stop that war—no matter what. The US was willing to kill military and civilians to such a massive degree that the enemy would be forced to surrender.

That opportunity came with the development of the atom bomb. The US and its allies had already won the war in Europe. Hitler was dead. The US finally had a weapon that could win the war in the Pacific. The bomb was dropped on Hiroshima. Then, with no surrender from the Japanese, another bomb was dropped a few days later on Nagasaki. The Japanese surrendered and World War II was over.

It has been postulated that if the war had continued, many more US soldiers and Japanese people would have been killed than the numbers lost from the two atomic bombs. The US has never been willing to kill civilians on a mass level like that again. And we have never won a war again since.

BAD-ASS SOLUTION

- **IMPLEMENT NEW RULES FOR THE US TO DETERMINE WHETHER OR NOT TO PARTICIPATE IN A WAR.**
    1. **Never fight in a guerilla war.** The US military is super high-tech. When suckered into a guerilla war, the technological advantage disappears. We can't win. US servicepeople walking down the street carrying an assault rifle makes them targets for enemy snipers. The enemy hides among women and children and just waits for US soldiers to pass by. Many Americans have been killed and wounded in this manner and other examples of guerilla warfare. US involvement in guerilla warfare should never be repeated.
    2. **Realize that the US will never win a war in which the US is not prepared to kill its enemy's civilians who are being used as shields by enemy soldiers.** The US can take out military targets using its weaponry, but not defeat an army hiding among women and children. Unfortunately, the decision to fight to win must include the willingness to have civilian casualties in order to win battles. If that decision is unacceptable, then winning will be impossible.
    3. **Never put a single US soldier in harm's way due to disadvantage.** Beyond defending the US homeland from within the US, no cause is worth losing a single American soldier. The job of fighting can be done exclusively by utilizing the US military's technology. American soldiers waging war on the ground where they can be killed or wounded must be a relic of the past and never again used.

"Never bring a knife to a gunfight."

—THE UNTOUCHABLES (MOVIE, 1987)

4. **Only fight wars that can utilize the incredible US technological advantages—exclusively.** Again, if the kind of destruction that is accomplished via US military technology is not utilized, the fight simply is not worth fighting. Sun Tzu and I agree wholeheartedly on this.

We may be willing to die for a cause, but unless we're willing to kill for that cause, we cannot subject our beloved service people to lethal danger.

At the time of this writing, the country of Ukraine is doing surprisingly well fighting off a horrific unprovoked military invasion by Russia. Russian tanks, soldiers, rockets, and aircraft have pummeled Ukraine. The Ukrainian people have responded with almost unimaginable courage and heroism—the way you get when you're defending your homes and your families. To the death.

After more than two years, the Ukrainians have taken back some of their lost territories and pushed the Russians back. The media shows

Russian tanks and materials burned-out and left behind. We may be seeing only a one-sided version, but the Russians have at least been spanked and embarrassed by Ukraine. The war continues. Damnit!

Besides courage and heroism, the Ukrainians have had another shockingly successful ingredient. US technological weapons. The world has witnessed the unbelievable accuracy and effectiveness of American weapons; in particular, Sidewinder and Phoenix missiles. These shoulder-mounted tubes send a rocket into the sky with a video camera along with its bomb. The camera sends real-time video footage back to the soldiers who launched it so they can effectively fly the rocket directly into a tank or other target, up to THREE MILES AWAY! Think real-life video game. This US technology has been seriously damaging the Russian effort. Wow. And there's lots more the US technological weaponry can do—both offensively and defensively.

- **THE US MUST MAINTAIN CONTROL OVER ITS MILITARY TECHNOLOGIES.**

    So, with this capability:

    1. **The US can never have its soldiers walk down a street in a third-world country like Afghanistan to be shot at.** That would be criminal of the US against its own soldiers.

    2. **The US can never give up this superiority. The US must be extremely careful when selling the technologies to other countries.**

    3. **The US must prevent its enemies as much as possible from developing these technologies for themselves.** The US must continue to develop technologies that can defend against these rockets and suicide drones that Iran is now selling to Russia to be used against Ukraine, and to the Houthis against the US and shipping in the Red Sea. It came out that these drones use American technology. Shit . . . We MUST be smarter than this.

CRITICALLY IMPORTANT: The US must develop technologies to stop nuclear weapons once they've been fired at the US or its allies. Remember Reagan's Star Wars? We must make this happen to get rid of the nuclear missile threat once and for all. This includes long-range nuclear missiles that can destroy cities and also the kind Putin has been threatening to use against Ukraine, called tactical nuclear weapons. These terrible things destroy a much smaller area than conventional nuclear weapons. With tactical nuclear weapons, you can destroy city blocks instead of the whole city. How about putting one under Putin's chair in the Kremlin?

Veterans

My wife contributes to veteran charities. Without exaggeration, we receive at least ten solicitations from veteran causes per week. This is shameful. Not that the veterans are asking for help, but that they have to beg US citizens for it. This is perhaps the biggest single failing of the US government—that we don't adequately take care of our veterans and their families.

The US government has an obligation to its veterans and their families to help them in every way they need. If a veteran was injured, their wounds, psychology, housing, job training, and employment must be provided as needed. If a soldier is killed, his/her family who was dependent on them must be supported with the same benefits as needed. This simply must be accomplished immediately. We citizens pay our taxes and must demand that our government resolve this shameful situation right now.

All Americans suffer because of the senseless deaths and mutilations of our valiant hero soldiers. We can never make up for the unbearable losses to them and their families. That said, we must see that this mission is accomplished.

Mandatory Service

The US has had many periods of military draft. Service to the country was viewed as an honor, not an obligation. During World War II, thousands of men and many women volunteered immediately after the bombing of Pearl Harbor. The draft took every able-bodied man to serve. Service always began with boot camp. The military, and particularly boot camp, was one of the great equalizers of our citizens. Guys got to know other guys from every walk of American life. Although shameful bigotry and segregation existed, the shared enemies, Hitler, Mussolini, and Hiro Hito, brought them together. They all fought valiantly and most gained knowledge and appreciation of all Americans.

It would be a very positive development if the US adopted a mandatory service requirement of its citizens. All young people, either after high school graduation or if not in school, at the age of eighteen, would be required to serve their country. Think of the massive, inexpensive, non-union workforce of young people to do good for the US. The service options could be broad: actual military; caring for elderly; assisting in schools; assisting in the construction of public works; cleaning parks, streets and highways; driving elderly to medical appointments; cooking and delivering food for the needy; etc.

This service could assist the US with its problem of the gap between rich and poor. The Service would integrate the masses while they're young and impressionable and hopefully open to learning from each other. A much stronger country could result in myriad ways, including better, more caring young people. It would give them a stake in our country and make them feel like they are a part of something greater than themselves.

The Service could be twelve months for military service and eighteen months for non-military service. Everyone serves in whatever way they are physically and mentally able. People who don't cooperate and disrupt the good intentions of The Service spend their time working in jails.

Conclusion

The US has the ability, equipment, technology, and personnel to win every battle IF IT WANTS TO. Never again can a single US soldier be sacrificed instead of using our technological weapons advantage that can secure the objective without risking Americans.

It's difficult to voice, but unless the US is willing to kill civilians who the enemy is hiding among, a war cannot be won. Some wars are actually worth such horrifying pursuit. Remember that the atomic bombing of Hiroshima and Nagasaki probably saved many more lives, especially American lives, than those who perished.

Wouldn't the best answer be no more wars? Wouldn't it be fantastic if an institution such as the United Nations actually had the commitment and the power to resolve international matters so that war would become obsolete? It's a dream that this one planet could have peace among its inhabitants.

Isn't that how we think other planets would be? Don't we automatically think other planets must speak one language and have a peaceful existence among their inhabitants? Yeah, well let's hope no other advanced civilization on a distant planet is looking at the third spinning blue rock from this star and decide that Earth is not worth keeping with its constant warring and killing.

CHAPTER 16
PLACE YOUR BETS

SECURITIES—THE STOCK MARKET

Close the casino

"I'm not concerned about return on my principal . . .
I'm concerned about return of my principal."

—WILL ROGERS

"You can't save your way into prosperity.
You have to invest your way into prosperity."

—TIM COOK, APPLE CEO

"The first rule of an investment is don't lose [money].
And the second rule of an investment is don't forget the first rule.
And that's all the rules there are."

—WARREN BUFFETT

"Money doesn't buy happiness unless you don't have any."

—MITCH

Investing in the stock market is: "Place Your Bets."

—NORMAN FEIRSTEIN (MITCH'S LAWYER AND FRIEND)

THE PROBLEM

I have a recurring dream. I'm parachuting for the first time. I'm standing near the open door, next in line to jump with the deafening wind rushing inside the small plane. I creep nervously toward the opening. I'm surprised that in this hurricane wind I feel sweat forming on my forehead. I leap. It then occurs to me that I don't know where I'm going. Wait! I don't know how to open the chute! I don't even know if I have a chute! I pull a cord. I look up. Instead of a parachute unfurling from my backpack, millions of dollar bills are streaming upward in a vortex. I wake up in a pool of sweat, grateful to be in my own bed, in my own house, on land. I'm still shaking from the dream. I gasp. I wasn't parachuting at all. I was "investing" in the stock market.

Buying securities is supposed to be a place to put your excess, hard-earned, and overly taxed money to grow for you. The goal is to purchase shares of companies that are doing well financially and appear to be able to continue to do well. Simple concept. Sorry guys, the game is rigged. Worse, this shouldn't be a game in the first place. This is your money that should grow and take care of you in your old age. The stock market should be relatively safe. It should be regulated by the US government via the Securities and Exchange Commission (SEC) to ensure that the whole investing environment is safe and that if you lose money, it's because you made poor choices of which companies you wanted to own by purchasing their shares.

This is just not the way it is. In fact, it is a game. And the smart-asses who play it as a game are making the money. We "investors" play into their game plans. We're truly jumping out of that plane with our money parachutes being blown about by the smart-asses. The smart-asses are the market-makers, hedge funds, private equity funds, stock analysts, stock pickers, financial show hosts, investment banks, and brokers. They know "the game." They're making money when stocks go up and when stocks go down. We're just supplying the cash.

Remarkably, the Securities and Exchange Commission supports this game. They routinely don't even enforce their own rules for the game. Worse, they turn their heads to the abuses of the system by the smart-asses. They even ignored several warnings from qualified sources that Bernie Madoff was running a Ponzi scheme while people continued to "invest" tens of billions more dollars with him. The Securities and Exchange Commission acts as if their name and duty is actually The Risk and Bet Commission. The Nevada Gaming Control Board actually does a much better job at protecting the public than the SEC.

The Great Recession of 2008? Most remember it as a housing crisis. It was, but there are some surprising factors. Administrations took up the good-sounding rally of making home ownership easy for the masses to accomplish. They encouraged lenders to furnish financing to people with almost no down payment and ultimately to those who were wholly unqualified buyers. Everyone who could breathe bought a home with virtually no cash and a mortgage featuring payments they couldn't afford.

The lenders knew they would be stuck with thousands of terrible loans on their books, with massive future foreclosures that would likely bankrupt them. Voila! Here's the answer. The lenders pooled their loans together in nice little bundles of mortgages that were mostly very poor investment grade, such as "D." Cute trick: the lenders purchased mortgage insurance from companies like AIG so they could get falsely re-graded from garbage up to grade "A." Hey, they were insured against loss ... The investment banks sold these bundles as mortgage-backed securities with a false A rating. Of course, this was blessed by the Securities and Exchange Commission, either overtly or tacitly. Well, we all know what happened. Thousands of people lost their homes that they weren't qualified to buy in the first place. The mortgages were nearly worthless. What a fraud.

The individuals, companies, and countries who had purchased the bundled loan securities foreclosed and got next to nothing because the homes were barely worth the debt. They lost most of their investments. The greatest mystery in this terrible chapter is that it doesn't seem that anyone got money from AIG for the insurance that was supposed to be paid on these mortgages. Incredibly, AIG was bailed out by the federal government in 2008 and is still in business. How is that possible? This burst housing bubble was the root cause of the greatest recession in US history, second only to the Great Depression. It took approximately twelve years for the S&P 500 to return to value. The Securities and Exchange Commission still reigns and heads never rolled. Poor investors don't seem to have a chance against these games of abuse by the smart-asses and our government who doesn't protect investors.

Buying stock simply means that one is buying a bit of ownership of a given company. Note that the money from an investor in a stock trade goes to a seller of that stock—not to the company itself (unless the transaction is an offering direct to the public by the company to raise capital). The pure transaction for the shares is what makes a "market value," a price that a seller agrees to sell and a buyer agrees to buy. Should be a perfect marketplace. It's not.

Warren Buffet has always recommended that investors should buy stocks of companies that the investor actually knows their products and determined that they prefer those products over competitors. Mr. Buffet

liked drinking Coca-Colas and eating See's Candies. He bought those stocks and, in the case of See's, bought the whole company. Besides drinks and sweets, he made a shit-ton of money with this investment philosophy. Importantly, Mr. Buffet is almost always a long-term owner of the companies he invests in and recommends that others do the same. Owning companies for the long term is referred to as "being long" on a given company. This is exactly what INVESTING should be.

The biggest casino in the world isn't owned by MGM or Wynn. The United States stock market is the biggest casino in the world. What a shame on our country. What an abuse of regular Americans' investments. The stock market needs to be a bastion of safety for regular people to grow their money. Instead, it's a craps table (not an exaggeration). This sham is a knife in the side of the US. Americans deserve and need better.

BUYING STOCKS

Once a company goes public, its shares are traded on an exchange. The two main US exchanges are the New York Stock Exchange and the NASDAQ. Although the lines have become blurred over the years, the New York Stock Exchange usually is the marketplace for the shares of old, large, well-established companies that include the largest industrial companies in the US. The NASDAQ usually is the marketplace for the shares of newer technology companies. There is also a large group of typically smaller companies whose stocks trade on several small exchanges called "over-the-counter."

To facilitate a smooth marketplace, every stock has market makers (employees of brokerage companies) who price shares to manage the sell orders and buy orders.

When an investor owns shares of a company, he/she gets the benefit of ownership of the percentage of the company represented by the number of shares owned. Simply, if a company issues one hundred shares and an investor buys five shares, he/she owns 5 percent of the company. The owner of the shares gets to vote those shares at the annual shareholder meeting on topics such as board members and auditors. If the company receives an offer from a buyer, the shareholders vote to accept or reject the sale. Shareholders also get their share of dividends (profit distributions) if the company pays them.

S&P 500 Side Note

The Standard and Poor's 500 is an index that measures stock price movement of the top 500 companies in the US stock markets. At any moment during the trading session, the S&P 500 provides an instant snapshot of how all of these top stocks as a whole are doing. They may be up thirty points or down fifty points from the prior day's closing price. Typically, when someone says the market is up or down, they are mostly referring to the S&P 500.

Real stock investors typically want two main things from their investment. First, they want dividends if the company pays them. Second, they want the stock to increase in value over time. It's pretty simple. Companies that focus on business fundamentals typically make more profit over time that should result in their stock price increasing. An investor decides when, for various reasons, it's time to sell. Of course, companies who make less profit or actually lose money usually see their share price drop.

This rather simple view of stocks is really how the whole thing should work. A wise and lucky investor should be able to make money from share appreciation and possibly dividends over time. Unfortunately, there are many factors that can make the shares lose value. These are decreased profits, competition, product obsolescence, and economy forces such as interest rate fluctuations and recession. There is another: market speculation.

Derivatives

There's buying stocks and there's selling stocks. All of the other things you can do with stocks are called derivatives. These other things have goofy names like puts and calls. **The smart-ass corps made up this game to make the rise and fall of shares of stock something to BET on.**

Here's how the simplest form of derivatives called options work:

(Note that we are calling the stock smart-asses "bettors," and the market makers who establish the price to be paid for their bets, "bookies." These terms are meant to be disparaging.)

The following details how a call (option) works—A bet the stock price will go up:

Bettor #1: "I bet that XYZ stock, which currently sells for $25 per share, will sell for at least $3 per share MORE (at least $28) in the next twenty days."

1. This type of bet is named a "CALL." The bettor pays the price for that specific bet as established by the bookie.
2. In this case, the bookie says that the price for this bet will cost the bettor $1 per share. The bettor has to buy this bet in one hundred share blocks called a contract.
3. The bettor buys ten contracts for $1,000 (10 contracts x 100 shares, or 1,000 shares x $1).
4. The bettor now has the option (right) to buy 1,000 shares of XYZ anytime up to twenty days. He will have to pay $25 + $3 per share, so $28 per share.
5. Remember, the bettor already paid $1 per share for the calls (options), so his break-even point is $29 per share.
6. Here's where the gambling excitement gets this guy all slushy.
7. What if the stock price goes up $10 per share during those twenty days? The bettor is wetting his pants.
8. The bettor's profit: XYZ stock is worth $25 + $10 = $35 per share, less his cost of $29 leaves a profit of $6 per share, times 1,000 shares equal $6,000. Again, he invested $1,000, got that back, plus $6,000 profit. The guy is now being obnoxious to his brother-in-law.
9. Stay with me, it gets a little difficult now.
10. Instead of the bettor coming up with $35,000 to exercise his option, he simply sells the shares as if he owned them.

192   BAD-ASS SOLUTIONS

11. The only money this amazingly brilliant gambler put up was the original $1,000 to buy the one hundred contracts.
12. This titan of men made six times his money in less than twenty days!
13. Where do we sign up for this? Get outta my way ...
14. Not so fast ...
15. What if the twenty days went by and the shares of XYZ never got above the bettor's break-even point of $29 per share?
16. Not much. The options expire, the contracts are canceled, and the bettor lost his $1,000. He avoids his brother-in-law who told him not to do it.

The following details how a PUT (option) works—a bet the stock price will go down. It works exactly the same as a call, only betting the other direction. This is a bit more difficult to grasp, so here are the steps:

Bettor #2: "I bet that XYZ stock, which currently sells for $25 per share, will sell for at least $3 LESS per share ($22) in the next twenty days."

1. This type of bet is named a "PUT." The bettor pays the price for that specific bet as established by the bookie.
2. In this case, the bookie says that the price for this bet will cost the bettor $1 per share. The bettor has to buy this bet in one hundred share blocks called a contract.
3. The bettor buys ten contracts for $1,000 (10 contract x 100 shares or 1,000 shares x $1).
4. The bettor now has the option (right) to buy 1,000 shares of XYZ anytime within the twenty days. He will have to pay $25: $3 per share, so $22 per share, actually less than the shares sell for today.
5. Remember, the bettor already paid $1 per share, so his break-even point is $21 per share.
6. What if the stock goes down $10 per share during those

twenty days? The bettor is headed to the new car showroom.

7. The bettor's profit: XYZ stock is worth $25—$10 = $15 per share, plus his cost of $21, leaves a profit of $6 per share, times 1,000 shares equals $6,000.

8. Instead of the bettor coming up with cash to exercise his option, he simply sells the shares as if he owned them.

9. The only money this gambler put up was the original $1,000 to buy the one hundred contracts.

10. He made six times his money in less than twenty days!

11. Again, if the twenty days went by and the shares of XYZ never got below the bettor's break-even point of $21 per share, the options expire, the contracts are canceled, and the bettor lost his $1,000.

It seems that the smart-ass corps try to keep these gimmicks secretive, difficult, and esoteric from mainstream investors. They want the game they created to themselves.

Shorting

Simple definition: Shorting is betting that the price of a company's shares will go down. Real easy concept, much like a put, except the bettor actually buys the shares at the lower price. The way it actually works is daunting.

Here's an example of how it works:

1. A shorter-bettor believes that the share price of XYZ Company will go down in the near future. This can be for several reasons, such as rising interest rates that may cause decreased sales for a home builder company or a report that consumer spending may be lower this Christmas, which may cause decreased holiday sales at Macy's.

2. The shorter-bettor decides to take advantage of his beliefs, so he will short Macy's.

3. A stock brokerage lends the shorter-bettor 1,000 shares of Macy's and then the brokerage sells them in the market at the current price.
4. Say the current price for Macy's stock is $50 per share.
5. The term of the short in this example is 60 days, meaning the shorter-bettor has to return new shares he buys to the brokerage by that date, regardless of the price the shorter-bettor has to pay for the replacement shares. Note that the broker charges a fee for doing the short, which is not included in this analysis.
6. Again, the shorter-bettor is betting that he can buy the shares back in the marketplace at a lower price than he already received by selling the shares at $50. Any amount less than $50 would represent profit.
7. Let's say in 50 days, the shares are trading for $40.
8. The shorter-bettor decides to purchase the shares at $40 per share, so it costs him $40,000 to return the shares to the broker.
9. The shorter-bettor pockets the difference of the $50,000 initial stock sale and the $40,000 final stock purchase for a profit of $10,000. He's calling his real estate broker to rent a house on the beach.
10. But what if the shares actually rise instead of fall?
11. Let's say the Macy's share price rises for several days because new reports reverse the earlier reports of a bad holiday sales season.
12. The stock goes up to $60 per share.
13. The shorter-bettor panics. He's upside down because he has to return 1,000 shares to the brokerage, and remember that the shorter got $50,000, but now has to buy the shares for $60,000, and maybe more if the stock price keeps going up! The shorter-bettor is tearing his hair out.
14. He buys the shares at $60,000 to fix his loss at $10,000. This is called short-covering. When there have been many shorters

of that stock and the price moves up, the rats run to the exits. They'll pay any price for the shares to get out and stop their losses from escalating. This is a delightful occurrence if you happen to own the shares of this company in your portfolio and is called a "short-squeeze."

Note that when you short a stock, the maximum profit is 100 percent, which is equal to the short price because the stock price cannot go below zero. However, the amount you can lose is unlimited because the stock price can just keep rising. Limited upside, unlimited downside. Not for sissies. Now, just think if you could influence the stock to go down . . .

Major players who routinely short stocks are often quite public about their activities. They frequently issue their own press releases that disparage the company and its management. They point to the reasons for their beliefs that the company's financials will decrease. The age-old problem with this entire practice is: do the shorters actually cause the share values to drop? Certainly, the shorter benefits greatly by getting other stockholders to dump their shares and cause the price to drop. The more the price drops, the more the shorter makes.

How would you feel if you owned shares in this company that you researched and believe in, with good fundamentals, but the value was dropping hard because some big shot stock smart-ass was campaigning against the company? Not a good situation. Your loss of value had nothing to do with the performance of the company, but rather from a stock market gambler affecting the price. Is this illegal? No! However, the SEC, exchanges, and brokerages all allow the stock market to act like a casino. Of course, all of them benefit. As usual, "screw the average investors."

Machine Trades / Algorithmic Trades / Automatic Trading

This relatively new phenomenon is just too weird to believe. We all have a sense of the capabilities of computers and artificial intelligence. Computers now drive approximately 70 percent of all stock trades. Computers are programmed to execute buying and selling of stocks in nanoseconds so that large stock companies can purchase or sell large numbers of shares without causing the price to change dramatically as they buy/sell. Of course, we poor slobs don't have that ability. Further, computers execute preprogrammed orders that operate without human emotion. Machines can even be programmed to seek arbitrage opportunities, which are situations to yield just a fraction of a percent gain in seconds, or even fractions of seconds, resulting in huge annualized returns.

Before we wake in the morning, machines have been trading millions if not billions of shares of stock. These computer trading methods have exponentially increased the trading volume of stocks. Logic dictates that these volumes must have an effect on share prices. If you follow stocks daily, you see that the aftermarket (overnight trading) has already established the initial direction for every day's trading before the actual market even opens. We often see the market fluctuate wildly from the opening through closing, which may be attributed to some degree to machine trading.

Machine trading just has to be wrong. This is not investing. It changes share prices. It's gaming the system by computer algorithms. Let me off! Let us all out of the casino.

Event Market Betting

There are many events that have an effect on the stock market rising or falling as a whole. Stock bettors develop hunches about the outcome of a given event and if that outcome will cause the market as a whole (usually the market refers to the S&P 500 index) to rise or fall. They bet on this by buying individual stocks or one of the exchange-traded funds (ETFs) that owns all the companies in the S&P 500 (called SPY), or another that owns the top one hundred companies listed on NASDAQ (called the QQQ). These betting events include:

1. **Quarterly financial reporting.** All public companies are required to report their financial results every quarter. In addition to reporting each quarter and once-a-year annual reports, on the same day of the report, the CEO and CFO

typically do a conference call where they answer shareholder questions, but most callers are stock analysts who ask questions.

The CEO and CFO discuss the quarter's performance and often provide a glimpse of how they expect the next quarter or even the entire year will perform. Event bettors try to anticipate whether the individual company will report good or bad results every quarter.

If bettors guess the report will be good, which will cause the share price to rise, they'll buy shares or call options before the actual report is issued. Conversely, if they think the report will show bad results, which will cause the share price to drop, they'll sell their shares or buy put options.

There is another terrible aspect of this quarterly results game. The company is judged to a very large degree on whether its performance beat or failed to beat the results estimated by stock analysts. See the section further below about analysts and be prepared to be massively pissed off.

Event betting can include the entire market. Quarterly reporting is a big event that takes about two to three weeks for all companies to report. The overall performance of "The Market," coupled with the interpretation of overall future outlook, can cause the entire market to rise or fall so that bettors will buy shares, sell shares, or buy call and put options.

2. **Federal Reserve reporting.** The Federal Reserve Open Market Committee (FOMC) has eight meetings per year to determine the need for it to manipulate the economy via its two main tools: raise or lower interest rates and buy or sell securities. When the FED is seen as loosening the money supply and/or lowering interest rates, the stock market generally goes up. When the FED is seen as tightening the money supply and/or raising interest rates, the stock market generally goes down.

Bettors who have a feeling about which way the FED will move want to buy or sell shares, calls, and puts based on what they think will happen.

How much money did you lose on your stocks and retirement funds during 2022 while the FED and the stock market played their interest rate games? We shouldn't have to take this!

3. **Elections.** Elections generally sway the market one way or the other depending on which party wins and the effect the new political reality will have on the economy.

Once again, bettors buy or sell securities based on their prediction of the outcome and market impact.

4. **Wars and their effects on commodities such as oil.** Fears of wars and changes in the supply of commodities because of a war can cause the market to fluctuate.

Predictions of outcomes and shortages are fodder for stock options bets.

5. **Disasters such as Covid or a major hurricane can cause the economy or certain commodities or goods to falter so the stock market responds by going down.** Same betting opportunities.

6. **Causes of reversal of a down market.** Things stabilizing from a down market such as Covid receding, more oil supplies, or the FED lowering interest rates. Same betting opportunities.

Stock Market Craps Table: place your bets.

Stock Analysts

This has become the strangest, most ridiculous occurrence in the stock market. And that's really saying something. All large public companies are followed by stock analysts who usually work for big brokerage companies. These analysts pour over recent company reports (based on the past quarter or year) and try to gather all the information they can about the current economic trends for that business. They then apply their best estimates to the company they follow and issue a report that includes their best guess, called an estimate of the company's next quarter or even annual performance. They estimate the business's sales, revenue, expenses, and profit. They issue this report to their brokerage company's clients and to the public.

It is important to note that the analyst cannot have any more information than the general public. They cannot have what is referred to as Material Nonpublic Information (MNPI). No one outside the given company is permitted to have this MNPI, which is also called insider information.

Here's where this gets crazier-ass than anything I could dream up. When a company actually issues its quarterly or annual report, the stock goes up or down based on whether or not the company beat ANALYST ESTIMATES. Again, someone from outside the company, with no direct company information, comes up with GUESSES for the company's revenue and profit. If the company's actual numbers come in better than the stock analyst estimates, the stock price goes up from buyer demand. If the company's actual numbers comes in lower than the analyst estimates, the stock price goes down due to sell orders. What the fuck???? What the hell kind of game is this? Beat the estimator? What is the point of that? If the company's reported numbers reflect an increase in its business, the stock should go up. If not, it should go down. Period. Simple. No analysts. No games.

Hedge Funds

Hedge funds are limited partnerships that wealthy "accredited" individual investors and companies invest into, whose many different types of investments include stocks, stock derivatives, real estate, and currencies. These are termed risky, but the success of the hedge fund really depends on the talents of the hedge fund manager. These funds are different in many ways from mutual funds, but the big difference is that hedge funds are not strictly regulated by the Securities and Exchange Commission.

Hedge fund managers are extremely highly paid, typically receiving 2 percent of the funds they manage annually plus 20 percent of the profit they generate.

There are three important requirements to be a hedge fund manager:

1. You have to think you're the smartest guy in every room you enter.
2. You aren't. And everyone knows it but you.
3. Your parents had to spoil you beyond reason. They couldn't say no to you. They had to tell you constantly how incredibly great you were, no matter what an average kid you were. Your poop smelled like roses.

The US government has been particularly (and suspiciously) generous to hedge funds by using very limited scrutiny and allowing extreme tax benefits, including the movement of profits to offshore places like the Bahamas to avoid US tax. Further, the US taxes the hedge fund manager's fees at lower long-term capital gain rates rather than ordinary income tax rates. What a scam.

These largely unregulated hedge funds get deeply involved in the stock market, and their activities can effectively affect share pricing. Some hedge funds actively short stocks and routinely publicize what they think is wrong with the given company. Whether or not they're correct, the marketplace usually responds by dropping demand for the shares, causing a lower share price. How would you like to own shares of that company?

Hedge funds also often take an activist position in a company and its shares. (See the next section on Activist Shareholders). Again, these largely-unregulated hedge funds can affect the share prices of companies. Unfortunately, these players are typically some of the most odious smart-asses, who figured out how to take advantage of laws, companies, and shareholders.

Activist Shareholders (Corporate Raiders)

These are the guys who really figured out how the game is played. Of course, they're the problem, not the solution. They come in many disguises. Some as hedge funds, some as individuals, and some actually call themselves "activist shareholders." They have staff who pour over company reports until the bells start ringing that they found a company that is either undervalued for some reason or they think could cut expenses, like they may have too many employees or factories or stores or product lines that don't sell as well anymore. They reason that if the company could make their changes, net income would rise, the stock would rise, and they can cash out. They make their move.

Cockroaches send in a scout before infesting the whole area. That's what activist shareholders do. They start buying stock in the target company. They don't have to report their presence until they reach 5 percent ownership. Some stay below, some go higher and report themselves.

Suddenly, management of the company gets a letter or a call that one of their major shareholders would like to meet with them. Management will usually take a meeting with a major shareholder. With smiles on their faces, the activist explains that he loves the company and would really like to help make it even better. They suggest that the company cut staff or get better software or close 20 percent of their stores. Oh, and they'd also like to be on the board of directors. Management always says they'll get back to them.

The company requests some basic information, such as the background of the activist and their fellow raider associates. Usually, the activist has stock trading knowledge and perhaps some business schooling, but literally NO education or experience in any of the subject company's actual business. This can include the company's products, software, marketing, staffing requirements, and sales. The activist probably just found a company that they got excited about, thinking if the company could cut some expenses or grow more locations or whatever, the stock price would rise. The activist and his investors would get a nice profit, then scatter away like all cockroaches do when you turn on a light. They really couldn't care less about actually helping the company or its shareholders.

After a while, the company's corporate counsel writes a letter to the activist thanking him/her for their interest and suggestions for the company. The letter continues, noting that management has things well under control, based on its analysis of a great deal of information that the corporate raider is not permitted to have. They state that the company needs to remain unchanged and oh, by the way, the board is currently full and doing a great job. So thanks, but no thanks.

Of course, it doesn't matter to the activist. They begin a press release campaign against the company's management and eventually file the documentation to obtain seats on the board of directors at the next annual shareholder meeting or, in some cases, they may try to replace the entire board. This is called a proxy fight for a corporate takeover. The amount of time and expense the company's management spends on their side of the proxy fight can cripple the company. The activist fights hard. They often threaten or even file lawsuits, with or without cause. Again, the company's management time and legal costs are a big fat loser.

Frequently, to get rid of the activist, a negotiation takes place for the company to buy the shares back from the activist and his/her investors—at a big profit of course. This is called greenmail—a euphemism for blackmail, but blackmail just the same. All of this totally screws the shareholders.

BAD-ASS SOLUTION

Quarterly Stock Reports (Form 10-Q)

Ninety days goes by very quickly. Few businesses experience any real changes in that short of a time span other than any usual seasonal fluctuations. American business is handcuffed to short-term results. Every quarter better show improvement... or else! This is just not the way to grow meaningful, profitable businesses. Long-term results are the real test of success and proof of concept. Allowing corporate officers to concentrate on the business instead of nonsense reports every couple of months would be massively more productive.

The time and cost to prepare a new financial report every ninety days is enormous. The CFO and his/her team have to write a Form 10-Q (Quarterly) report that is usually at least fifty pages for a small company and up to hundreds of pages for a large one. Of course, the financial statements are included. The entire report must be reviewed and approved by the company's auditors, legal counsel, officers, and directors. Upon approval from all of these, the report is filed with SEC; an earnings press release is issued; the report is available to the public; and the CEO and CFO have to hold a conference call to read prepared statements, then field questions from a couple shareholders and lots of stock analysts. What an incredible time suck for no real purpose other than keeping the public a tiny bit better informed—usually about nothing new.

- **IMMEDIATELY STOP QUARTERLY REPORTS (FORM 10-Q).**
- **ONLY ANNUAL REPORTS (FORM 10-K) WILL BE REQUIRED.**

Insurance on Qualified Stocks

We have insurance for everything. Everything but stock investments. Sounds impossible, but it's not. The top blue chip companies are extremely secure. Sure, they drop out of favor when their product ultimately becomes obsolete, but that's predictable far in advance. Wild swings in a top company's share price are usually the entire market reacting to the Fed or a war or something big like that. Major US companies rarely actually fail quickly on a grand scale.

A new kind of insurance could be created either by the federal government or by the private sector. In either case, the insurance company would only have to cover losses up to 12 percent of an investment because the insurance company will automatically force a sale of the shares at a 10 percent loss, which may be a bit lower due to the timing of the sale in the marketplace. Of course, they will charge an annual premium, say 2 percent of the initial share price. If the insurer is the federal government, it can be something like FDIC for your bank account. This will go a very long way toward securing Americans' investments and their futures in strong American companies.

Just pray we don't see new, endless, awful Geiko Stock Insurance -like commercials every three minutes during a ballgame.

- **CREATE INSURANCE TO SECURE INVESTMENTS IN MAJOR US COMPANIES.**

No Derivatives of Any Kind

This casino stock market has to stop right now. If you are familiar with a craps table, you can see that these bets are really like a gambler placing bets on a craps table, betting on the next roll of the dice. Bet the Pass Line, the Don't Pass Line, the hard-eight (two fours), hard-ten (two fives) and the numbers 4,5,6,8,9,12. Place your bets.

The manipulation of shares by short-term speculators who bet on calls and puts along with short sellers and all other sophisticated (casino) derivatives has to stop. The safety and security of Americans' investments should have never been a game and should not continue as one. The hard-earned investment dollars from hard-working Americans have to be treated with respect and security. Fuck the gamblers.

The shares of a company must represent an investor's ownership stake in that company because the investor has confidence in the company's business and its management. The investor also believes the company will continue to do well in the foreseeable future. The investor buys the shares with their hard-earned, after-tax money and deserves the three possible benefits associated with stock ownership. They can get dividends if that company pays them, they can sell their shares in the future if the shares rise due to the company's continued success, and they can sell their shares if the company performs poorly, or if it is merged or acquired.

- **TERMINATE ALL STOCK DERIVATIVE TRADING.**

Financial Statement Reform

For the most part, only professionals really understand what is presented in a company's financial report. Incredibly, the answer to the most basic question of "how much free cash flow did the company make" doesn't exist. There is a Statement of Cash Flows included, but many of the line items make it impossible to understand how they impact the actual cash flow and are worthless to a non-accountant without a deep understanding of the company. Accounting standards require the precise structure for financial reports and explanations.

You may not believe this, but those requirements do not include reporting free cash flow, or even a common cash flow indicator, EBITDA (Earnings Before Interest, Taxes, Depreciation and Amortization), which is actually frowned upon from even being mentioned in reports. Adjusted EBITDA, which accounts for unusual or one-time expenses, is even more discouraged. To attempt to determine the free cash flow of the company, you would have to add back to net income the depreciation, amortization, stock-based compensation, and any other non-cash expense you can find. How ridiculous. Do we need to become CPAs to invest wisely in stocks?

Financial reports must be revised to be easily understood by average investors. The actual financials need to yield real usable information rather than data only a CPA might be able to wade through. Public company financials are by accountants, for accountants—not for investors to use. Asinine.

Americans desperately need a safe place to invest their money. People should be confident that if they buy a diversified range of quality American companies, their money will be safe and secure. Business success does ebb and flow, and the value of companies reflect that fluctuation. But over time, without outside negative market influences, the values of good companies should remain stable and rise over time. We just cannot accept the smart-ass casino forces that cause the stock market to be a dangerous game with our money.

Some say shorters are necessary to balance out the market and individual stocks from becoming too hot. Bullshit. Stocks sell on bad performance of the company like they rise on good performance of the company.

- **SIMPLIFY ALL COMPANY FINANCIAL REPORTS.**

THE NEW STOCK MARKET:

1. **There are no derivatives.** No betting on the rise or fall of prices on individual stocks or the entire market.
2. **No activist shareholders as directors.** Shareholders can run for a director seat only if they submit their qualifications that demonstrate their potential value to the specific business.
3. **No outside stock analysts.** The quarterly game of beating the analyst estimates must end. **Stock prices have to rise or fall based on the company's own performance and fundamentals.** Once again, analysts are not permitted to have inside information from the company, so their estimate is of no value to anyone. Stop this nonsense.
4. **No machine trades.** This is a ridiculous practice and an unfair advantage over individual stock investors (humans). It causes share price swings that are not related to company performance. This cannot be permitted.
5. **No quarterly reports.** Companies only supply annual reports.
6. **Without quarterly reports, expand requirement for**

company press releases to immediately disclose all material developments.

7. **Standard financial reports are to become understandable by laypeople.** They must be simplified so that the average investor can easily understand how the company is doing, particularly how much real cash the company is earning or losing along with their prospects going forward.

8. **Stock insurance policies underwritten by the US like FICA.** Create and regulate private insurance company stock policies to safeguard investors of excellent quality stocks against excessive risk of loss. This will go a long way toward ensuring that Americans' futures will be much more secure.

9. **Streamline public company costs: legal, court, and insurance.** The costs for a company to be publicly traded are extreme and excessive.

   a. The ability for shareholders to bring lawsuits against a company must be limited to fraud with evidence.

   b. There must be a limitation of award to the actual loss of a given shareholder's investment.

   c. A company must be able to sue a shareholder for cause, including malicious prosecution (which it can't do now).

   d. Damage award limits will reduce the number of suits and the amount of extremely expensive insurance the company must carry. The lowest current annual premium for directors and officers insurance for even a small public company is $1 million, plus extremely high deductibles.

   e. All lawsuits to have the loser liable to pay all of the victor's legal expenses. There can be no suit filed by a lawyer on contingency. The number of cases will drop significantly.

   f. Insurance companies cannot settle lawsuits. The

settlement for less than legal costs game just causes more nuisance suits.

g. All cases between shareholders and companies must be adjudicated via binding arbitration, not in courts.

THIS IS A HUGE BAD-ASS SOLUTION GAME-CHANGER FOR TAXES AND SECURITIES:

(Reprinted in the US Taxes Chapter)

Stop Capital Gains and Capital Losses

Long-held doctrine is that the government encourages investment by taxing the long-term gain on the investment at a lower tax rate. In reality, no lower tax motivation for investing is necessary. The only two things you can do with your excess money is either put it in a bank account, similar to putting cash under one's mattress, or invest the money to hopefully grow enough to support your retirement. No side deal is necessary. **No lower tax rate on capital gains.**

At the end of every year, stock market investors sell their stocks that have losses. This is called tax-loss selling. They do this because the tax code allows the investor to offset the loss against any capital gain the investor has, even capital gains in future years. To take advantage of the losses in the current year, the investor may also sell stocks in which he/she has gains, thus offsetting the gains to effectively pay no tax.

Catch this: the government allows the investor to buy back the shares he/she took a tax loss on after thirty days. This age-old game clearly affects stock prices at the end of each year and often at the beginning of each year as well. As discussed in this chapter, investors should eschew anything that affects stock prices other than the performance of companies and economic impacts from domestic/international events.

This is just a gift from the IRS to stock investors. Why? Maybe the people who write these rules are stock investors . . .

- **THE US GOVERNMENT IS NOT AND SHOULD NOT BE INVESTORS' PARTNER ON LOSSES.**

By allowing a deduction of capital losses against capital gains, the US is effectively paying for a portion of someone's losses—even poor business choices. If this gift is stopped and all stock gains are taxed when the shares are sold, the US coffers will overflow and all Americans will benefit by having lower tax rates. When taxes are considered to be low, the games to avoid taxes aren't worth the time and accounting professional expense. Just pay the tax and keep making good investments that generate more income.

The buying and selling of shares of stock must become a pure and unmanipulated opportunity for people to prudently invest their money for the future. The stock exchanges must be a sacred place of security for people's money. Keep casinos in Vegas.

I feel dirty after all the discussion about the slimy, nefarious gamblers and smart-asses in the stock market that affect our money. I'm going for a shower.

CHAPTER 17
WTF? 22,000 GOVERNMENTS IN THE US?

STATE & LOCAL GOVERNMENT RESTRUCTURE

Bring government out of the horse and buggy era

"I don't make jokes. I just watch the government and report the facts."

—WILL ROGERS

"Suppose you were an idiot, and suppose you were a member of Congress; but I repeat myself."

—MARK TWAIN

"A government big enough to give you everything you want, is strong enough to take everything you have."

—THOMAS JEFFERSON

THE PROBLEM

The federal, state, and local governments within the US are inert. They get very few things accomplished that Americans actually need. As discussed in the Elections chapter, politicians spend a great deal of their time getting reelected. When they're not doing that, they're fighting for their party's position on any given topic, with steadfast resolution to toe that line. The US political parties have become intractable, polarizing encampments for our "leaders." Each side simply rejects anything that comes from the other side.

Along with the chronic lack of compromise to accomplish much, the size of the federal and state governments is just too big, with too many redundant functions. Stalists.com reports that 18.3 million people worked for state and local governments in 2021, and 2.85 million worked for the federal government. The business of the people is not getting done very well and the price tag is just insane.

The United States has the following number of governmental representatives, jurisdictions, and major departments:

Federal Government:

President—1

Senators—100

Representatives—435

Supreme Court Justices—9

State and Local Governments:

Governors—50

Counties and equivalents—3,142

Cities/Villages—19,495 (14,768 of these have populations below 5,000)

School Districts—14,061

Police Departments—17,985

**From USAfacts.org, Worldpopulationreview.com, andWorldatlas.com

Can you believe the enormous size and waste of the state and local bureaucracy having **22,000 separate governments in the US? WTF?**

Do you remember the first time you toured the older sections of Boston or Philadelphia? You were likely struck by how narrow the streets were. If you're not particularly good at riddles, you don't know why they would crowd everything so tightly. However, if you're fairly analytical, you quickly realize that the cities were created prior to the automobile. The streets are quite sufficiently wide enough for horses and carriages.

Similarly, it took the founding fathers enormous amounts of time and effort to travel among the colonies and even between cities and villages. There were no telephones or even telegraphs for nearly a hundred years. Mail delivery (the only communication medium) took days, even weeks.

The point here is that without the benefit of modern technologies, there was a real need for local governments to respond to the needs and emergencies of the widely dispersed American populations.

But now we have instant communications, video every few feet, and satellites. Why does the US need to pay for so many redundant governments? Every place is much closer now to every place else.

According to the New York State Department of Labor, Ballotpedia.org, Texas Tribune.org, and Comptroller.Texas.gov, New York has sixty-two counties, 1,525 municipalities, and 1,189 special districts. California has fifty-seven counties, 482 municipalities, and 2,949 special districts. Texas, for some reason, has 254 counties and more than 1,200 municipalities. Presumably, each county and each municipality has an entire government system with buildings, supervisors, mayors, councils, myriad departments, and hundreds or thousands of employees.

Repetitive local governments are simply wasteful, inefficient, and often corrupt. They are now totally obsolete and a waste of citizens' money.

BAD-ASS SOLUTION

Bring government out of the horse and buggy era.

How can the US—and particularly its taxpayers—continue to

financially support more than 22,000 governments? With the current state of communications and technology, the archaic need for so many governments is truly obsolete. The entire structure of state and local governments must be completely redesigned.

It is no longer valid to say, "That's the way we've done something for two hundred years, so we'll just keep doing it."

While all agree that regional populations have differing needs, they are due more to geographic/climate differences rather than more obsolete concepts such as religious and long-illegal racial and financial differences.

Here is a way to make all US state and local governments significantly more efficient and also save billions and billions of dollars.

- **REPLACE MOST OF THE 22,000 LOCAL GOVERNMENTS IN THE US WITH NEW CITY ZONES.**

Following is the Bad-Ass Solution for restructuring state and local governments in the US:

1. **City Zones will govern all former county areas, cities, towns, villages, and rural areas within its borders.**

a. Small cities, towns, villages, and rural communities/areas will still exist, but without their own governments. They will have representation in the City Zone governments relative to their population, akin to the US House of Representatives.

   b. Small cities, towns, villages, and rural areas will still have services like local fire, police, and schools, but those services will be administered by the government of the entire City Zone.

2. **Create City Zones for each large city containing at least 500,000 people and its surrounding region.**

   a. Limit the region controlled by large cities to a maximum radius of seventy-five miles.

   b. Where large cities and thus multiple City Zones are closer together than seventy-five miles, create demarcation lines between them to represent populations.

3. **Abolish all county governments.**

4. **Abolish all municipal governments other than in the largest city in each City Zone.**

5. **All unincorporated areas currently under county jurisdiction will be annexed into the nearest City Zone.**

6. **Rural areas outside of City Zones will be governed by the largest city in the seventy-five-mile radius.**

As with any major business, the US government, from top to bottom, must continually evolve the way it does things, particularly taking advantage of new technologies and social evolution. The monetary and efficiency benefits should yield incredible cost savings throughout the country on a continual basis.

Another example of technical and social evolution is the US Postal Service, which has become obsolete. Even though it raises postage rates constantly, it loses money every single year. How long will it take for all remaining written communications to become electronically created and delivered? It is also clear that package delivery is much more cost-efficient and with better quality when done by the private sector such as the delivery systems of Amazon, Federal Express, and UPS.

The idea of the people within the US Postal Service losing their jobs is painful. I don't know if it's just me, but I've noticed a material change in how friendly and helpful postal workers have become. Hopefully, they'll transition into other companies that can remain viable (profitable) over a longer period. Better still, they can be absorbed by private companies taking over the Postal Service functions.

Clearly, with such dramatic changes such as City Zones, it is critically important to remain mindful to design systems that provide the best services possible to every population.

CHAPTER 18
THROWAWAY PEOPLE

HOMELESS / MENTAL ILLNESS

House and treat everyone who needs it—at very low cost

"I was planning on my future as a homeless person. I had a really good spot picked out."

—LARRY DAVID

"I told my psychiatrist that everyone hates me. He said I was being ridiculous—everyone hasn't met you yet."

—RODNEY DANGERFIELD

"Freud: If it's not one thing, it's your mother."

—ROBIN WILLIAMS

"When you look at how much we spend on social programs in our country, it separates us from a lot of countries. In our country, if you're hungry, we'll feed you. If you're homeless, we'll house you. If you're too poor to be sick, we'll pay for your doctor. But all of that comes at a cost."

—JOHN KENNEDY

> "I think we love watching people that are
> flawed because we're all flawed."
>
> —BRAD GARRETT

THE PROBLEM

Ronald Reagan's presidency was marked by myriad perceived benefits to the US. Generally, the US and its people were better off from his programs to grow business, lower taxes, and strengthen the military, which essentially brought down the USSR and ended the Cold War. As a result, Ronnie is remembered as a great president. Great and not so great.

That said, Reagan's efforts to lessen the breadth and costs of the federal government left some enormous problems in the country. Perhaps the most devastating effect from the Reagan administration that has lasted over the past forty years is due to that administration effectively closing the nation's mental hospitals and forcing thousands, if not millions, of mentally impaired people onto the streets and sidewalks of the US.

They're everywhere. The hordes of homeless people line freeway exits, overpasses, doorways, sidewalks, bus benches, transit systems, and every nook and cranny that provides some shelter or safety. The lucky ones have tents. The really lucky ones live in their cars—if they have a car. These people are drug addicts, the mentally ill, and folks just failing economically for a multitude of reasons.

Most of us give a couple bucks here and there but are usually uncomfortable and threatened by homeless people. Their plight is a horror. Do you ever take a wide view to see hundreds of homeless people at a time and wonder what has happened to our country to be failing so many? This is what you see and get depressed about when traveling in Third World countries. But in the US? America? This is shameful. Shame on us.

The ACLU and many other civil and mental rights organizations have fought for years through the court system to argue that American citizens have the right to live, pander, sleep, eat, piss, and shit on public spaces including sidewalks, parks, etc.

Many local governments created laws that have taken up that same tragic banner. As a result, front-line authorities such as the police have for the most part been unable to move homeless people away from these areas and into some kind of shelter.

Unfortunately, the courts have mostly been total wimps and rule in favor of the rights groups' position, which keeps these people suffering on the streets. What's wrong with this picture?

So what? So, the streets, sidewalks, parks, freeway lands, bus stop benches, busses, and subways are populated with desperate homeless people in misery along with their stolen shopping carts, plastic bags, cardboard, tarps, tents, personal belongings, trash, and feces.

America looks like a trash dump. To make matters much worse than the visual horrors, America's public areas are filthy and crime-ridden.

Case in point:

Las Vegas is the number one tourist destination in the US. The multi-billion-dollar resorts that span the four-mile Strip are beautiful, impressive, and fun to visit. Walking the Strip has been a must-do attraction for tourists to see the resorts, discover great shopping, and enjoy a huge range of dining choices.

Unfortunately, the Strip has become a mirror of the cesspool seen throughout America. Homeless people are every few feet. They are typically unclean and often drugged out, begging, selling bottled water from ice chests, and always making a loud, scary nuisance of themselves. Many are scuzzy, unclean street beggars who badger tourists every few feet.

Employees from businesses along the Strip have to hose down the urine, vomit, and human feces every morning around their facilities from the night before. Who would want to work there?

The Las Vegas Strip has become a place to avoid instead of enjoy. What a shame. It's hard to believe that Las Vegas and its powerful resort corporations can't clean this up. How can this be? This would never have occurred in the old days when the mafia controlled Vegas. Bring Bugsy back!

Again, the rights groups have sued at every opportunity. The pusillanimous (cowardly) courts have sided with them. The sidewalks are public domain and people are permitted to use them, no matter how dangerous and filthy the sidewalks are. Of course, the worst part is all of the tragic homeless people who aren't being cared for.

Recently, on the Strip in front of the Venetian Resort, a crazed guy stabbed and killed two innocent people and stabbed six more people who survived. He was caught but was determined to be mentally incapable of assisting in his own defense, so he was remanded to an institution rather than jail. Is this what it takes for someone mentally ill to actually get the help they need? They have to maim and kill innocent people? Intolerable.

Once tourists see the frightening homeless and the filth, and understand the real dangers, who in his right mind would walk the Strip anymore? Right, no one who has heard about this. Wrong! You won't believe this, but people are still walking the Strip. Maybe Americans have simply become numb to the problem. The flip-flop fanny-packers walk past the homeless and grime, shaking their heads while they suck in their three-foot-long margaritas from straws.

If the dirt and violence get bad enough, the tourists may avoid Vegas altogether. Adele and Lady Gaga will just have to entertain them in Branson, Missouri. Poor Las Vegas, who won't see that homeless people are helped. They apparently prefer ruining their city and endangering their guests and employees.

The Las Vegas Strip is a shocking microcosm of America. While on vacation, we can easily witness how many of our fellow citizens are suffering terribly.

Another societal horror from the ACLU, other rights organizations, and even some local laws is that mentally problemed people can only be involuntarily committed for care for up to three days! Even severely diagnosed people cannot stay committed in a facility unless they, themselves choose to stay. They can leave any time after the three-day hold. Who's actually crazy in this scenario? As is common, a great many mentally ill people do not believe their diagnoses and refuse medicine, care, and shelter.

Communities and frontline workers are deeply frustrated because when they offer shelter to many of the mentally challenged or addicts, they refuse. Many of these people opt to stay on the street. Of course, in our ridiculous system, authorities cannot force people to leave the streets for free shelter. Come on, now. This is just too stupid for discussion. Who's in charge here? An old adage comes to mind: "The inmates are running the asylum."

The massive numbers of homeless constitute five basic groups, with lots of lines blurred between them: poor people, drug addicts, handicapped, veterans, and mentally ill.

The US is not a great society and will not be until it provides quality care for people who cannot take care of themselves. The "Shining City on the Hill" is no longer the global image of the US. It is now a sad, often ugly and scary place in decline and decay.

Just recently, after endless attacks by mentally ill people, the mayor of New York City decided to implement new laws to provide for the detention or commitment of the seriously mentally ill. They can be removed from the streets and cared for properly—without their consent. About damn time!

Has the problem and danger become so great that government is finally responding? California is jumping on board with new legislation called the CARE Act that provides for CARE courts with judges having the authority to order treatment plans for people with untreated severe mental illness and remove them from the streets. This is quite new and so far has inadequate funding and infrastructure. This mental health $6.4 billion bond measure was approved by California voters in March

2024 to build mental health treatment facilities and provide housing for the homeless. Great start!

Note: it is estimated that approximately 25 percent of all homeless people in the US are in California. Seems that half of them are in tents at my freeway exit.

BAD-ASS SOLUTION

- **MOVE HOMELESS PEOPLE OFF THE STREETS AND PUBLIC AREAS—WITH OR WITHOUT THEIR CONSENT.**
- **CREATE LAWS AND FUNDING TO PROVIDE ALL NECESSARY FACILITIES AND SERVICES TO TAKE GOOD CARE OF PEOPLE WHO NEED HELP.**

Can you fathom that there is some news about this that you can consider to be good? Albeit you may do so with a wince. Policyadvice.net reports that there are approximately 550,000 homeless people currently in the US. (A horrifying and depressing number.) However, if we consider that homeless people account for just 0.00164 percent (roughly 16.5 percent of 1 percent) of the 335 million US population, something actually positive comes to light.

Homelessness (now fashionably called "unhoused") actually accounts for such a tiny percentage of the US population that fixing the problem should be far less daunting than we would presume. More specifically, **if the US had to spend $25,000 per year to take care of 550,000 homeless people, the annual bill would only be about $14 billion.** That's hardly a rounding error in the US annual budget, which is basically around $4 trillion, but events like Covid added several trillion dollars more. **It would still be immaterial at double that cost—even triple that cost!** For perspective, remember that the US is spending nearly $4 BILLION PER DAY in interest on its debt.

Hey, we really can take care of these people for that surprisingly low price tag. So, what the hell is Congress doing? Virtually N.O.T.H.I.N.G. The US simply must take care of its citizens who are homeless. It is critical that the US change the policy that allows addicts and mentally ill people to remain on the streets when shelter is available for them. To get around the ridiculous rights groups' interference, new laws will need to be passed that do not permit loitering, sleeping, or living on public areas as a primary place of living. Courts must support this effort.

Further, we need laws and courts to allow authorized agencies of the government and charitable organizations to keep mentally ill people under care for as long as necessary. A legal system to protect people from being unduly committed will obviously be necessary.

When the government and support agencies have the ability to remove people from the streets, the much more difficult problem of how to care for them comes into play. The US needs to establish many different environments to place people according to their needs. These facilities must be pleasant and provide the services that each category of homeless people require, and even subcategories for people with more specialized needs.

These programs will require massive funding, real estate facilities, services, medical care, and staffing. To continue the reality of a great society, quality provisions must be made to help the people who are not able to stand on their own. The goal should be to transition as many people as possible into having productive lives and independent living.

Stop thinking *One Flew Over the Cuckoo's Nest*. We have to do better, and we can. It's about commitment (no pun intended) and money. Remember the data above? Only about 16.5 percent of 1 percent of Americans are homeless. Huge numbers, but not a huge percentage. The US has the money—we citizens provide it every April 15.

Various levels of board and care with support will dictate the kinds of facilities and staffing needed to service so many homeless people with real problems. Here are the general types of facilities and services that will address the needs of the mentally ill, drug addicted, handicapped, and poor:

- ✓ Various types of board and care facilities: institutions, communal living projects, and independent multi-tenant projects. (Make facilities as pleasant as possible.)
- ✓ Various types of care: psychiatric, medical, social work, and services.

- ✓ Various kinds of support: food, clothing, cleaning, basic medical, and entertainment.
- ✓ Skills development: independent living, human relationships, job training, and job support.
- ✓ Opportunity: empty "zombie" office and retail buildings? Buy and redevelop them into housing/shelter for people. Develop programs such as HUD's Section 8 to make it profitable for private developers to provide quality facilities.

A great goal of the entire program should be to assist all who are capable of being productive on some level. In many cases, there is no better medicine than to be busy and productive. As many residents as possible should be trained to provide the support tasks for their own facility such as cleaning, food service, laundry, and outdoor services. It is possible that some portion of the program costs could be reduced by resident labor, who are paid for their services.

Servicing all of these facilities will require an army of people. Many chapters in this book identify people who need retraining for new jobs. Service industry training can supply people needed to support all of the new facilities. What about the millions of immigrants who are in the US and desperately need employment and housing? This can be a wonderful benefit to all.

Here are two alternative living and working structures for qualified people or those who "graduate" from homelessness or are unable to thrive in a structured environment:

1. US Military

Many people who are homeless due to addiction or financial difficulties may be able to serve in the US military or other government agencies, perhaps in support types of positions rather than front-line positions. Some people just need structure and a job to do. They may thrive and serve the government quite well.

2. Kibbutz—Collective Farms

There are many people who simply do not succeed in the US capitalist economic system. The Israeli example of a communal living structure is usually based on agriculture, but can be centered around any number of enterprises such as assembly of products, manufacturing, or art. A Kibbutz may be an excellent answer for individuals who may have families and for society as a whole. Everyone contributes their labor and intellect to the Kibbutz, which is usually self-sufficient. This could be a bit of Israeli Walden, right here in the US. Everybody wins.

We probably all know someone who was brilliant as a young person, then suddenly developed a serious mental illnesses like schizophrenia. I heard about a mother whose initial reaction to finally hearing her son's diagnosis of schizophrenia was, "Why couldn't it have been cancer?" Yes, the gods can be unmercifully cruel.

Most people want to be productive and feel good about themselves. Mentally ill people may have useful skills but are overlooked when it comes to employment because they frighten fellow workers and customers.

I know a skilled accountant who is schizophrenic and yet graduated from a top university. He has been trying to get a real accounting job for more than twenty years. He is skilled but is always rejected due to his obvious problem. So damn sad.

This may be just a dream, but wouldn't it be an even better country if Americans employed people who may sound and look a little odd but can do a pretty good job anyway? Emphatic YES is the answer. Imagine it was your kid. We Americans can and should be better and do better.

CHAPTER 19
MOM'S BASEMENT HILTON

HOUSING SHORTAGE

Use the basics of US capitalism to oversupply/cheapen housing

"Owning a home is a keystone of wealth . . . . both financial affluence and emotional security."

—SUZE ORMAN

"Don't wait to buy real estate. Buy real estate and wait."

—WILL ROGERS

"Real estate cannot be lost or stolen, nor can it be carried away. Purchased with common sense, paid for in full, and managed with reasonable care, it is about the safest investment in the world."

—FRANKLIN D. ROOSEVELT

"I will forever believe that buying a home is a great investment. Why? Because you can't live on a stock certificate. You can't live in a mutual fund."

—OPRAH WINFREY

THE PROBLEM

There are drastic housing shortages in many parts of the US, including single family homes, condominiums, and rental apartments. As with all high-demand, low-supply products in a capitalist economy, prices rise. Prices to purchase homes and rent apartments are so high that many families simply cannot afford to live where they want.

Owning your own home has always been "The American Dream." While many millennials and younger people have learned the benefits of living in their parents' homes until they're nearly getting social security benefits, owning a home is still the dream for most. Homes have historically been people's largest and most valuable asset. One thing many people ignore about buying a home is that if you have a fixed, thirty-year loan, you have level housing costs for all that time—no rent increases! Of course, you also pay off the entire loan over the thirty years. Best investment ever.

Housing is one of the largest components of the US economy. The development of housing uses vast amounts of materials and employs millions of workers from construction labor to mortgage processors. Other businesses such as Home Depot, furniture stores, and pool contractors flourish from housing as well.

The US economy and its citizens thrive from housing. Shortage of housing is a significant depressant to the economy and populace. Further, this can be a classic cause of inflation.

People who live in most communities in the US suffer from an incurable disease called NIMBY. Every time some new development tries to enter the community such as more housing, a shopping center, or God forbid, some kind of a shelter, the NIMBY folks become enraged. So, what is this horrible disease? Not in my back yard. NIMBY.

Apparently, there is a universal human trait that once people get their homes, they don't want any development that would allow other people to accomplish the same thing. They attend community meetings and pound on the tables that the new development will snarl traffic, stress the infrastructure, and overpopulate the schools. Put that damn development somewhere else. NIMBY.

The local bureaucrats want to be reelected, so they hop on the idiot bandwagon and rail vociferously against any growth in their district. This is leadership by really selfish, shortsighted people who then cry and complain when their grown children have to move to a different state to afford a place to live.

Every community spends a great deal of time and money developing zoning and planning codes and ordinances. Somehow, many NIMBY communities rigged the system so that virtually all new developments, even if they comply with the existing zoning and planning ordinances, must be approved by the local community of NIMBYs and politicians who pander to them. The added time, cost, and financial risk that this abusive system brings to any development is a reason not to build in that community at all. The NIMBYs view this as a victory. This unfortunate, prevalent practice is one of the main causes of the US housing crisis.

The problem is that this same disease happens in nearly every homeowner association, community, city, and county. What's left? A housing crisis. Few new homes, few new apartments. Of course, nothing stops the demand or even the need to live in certain areas for work or family, so with low supply, prices of existing homes and apartments skyrocket and become unaffordable.

Look at this NIMBY disease at its largest and most idiotic: the San Francisco Bay area. For decades now, very few new single-family home and apartment developments have been approved. During this same time, Silicon Valley became the focal point of the new technology revolution. Major businesses such as Apple and Google grew, which ultimately exploded with real estate and staffing needs in the area. Prices of existing homes and apartments skyrocketed.

The problem is enormous. Workers have to live far away from their jobs because there's literally nothing available nearby that is affordable—even for these highly paid workers. Finally, the problem got so bad (coupled with crazy high income taxes and government overregulation in California), that many companies such as Tesla left the state for less expensive taxes and cheaper housing for its people. Texas—yeehaw!

How much will the NIMBY people complain when the businesses leave and home prices crash downward—including their own homes?

BAD-ASS SOLUTION

- **SIMPLE: JUST PUT BASIC US CAPITALISM BACK TO WORK.**
- **ENCOURAGE DEVELOPMENT OF HOUSING.**
- **STOP THE RED TAPE FROM LOCAL GROUPS AND GOVERNMENT BUREAUCRATS.**

The following is so obvious, so universally understood, that it's hard to call it bad-ass.

Every US citizen with even a minimal amount of education about the way capitalism works understands supply and demand. This is the most important ingredient in a capitalist system. This "law" of supply and demand is also responsible for maintaining reasonable prices of goods and services throughout the US economy.

To restate for all the new-wave socialists in the US who missed this whole concept in school and every day of their lives, here goes (there will be a pop-quiz on Tuesday):

1. When there is more supply of a product than the demand for it, the price goes down.

2. When there is less supply of a product than the demand for it, the price goes up.
3. When demand is higher than the supply of a product, producers make more product (meet the demand).
4. When demand is lower than the supply of a product, producers make less of the product.

You can see that supply and demand move cyclically, which totally messes with suppliers/producers/entrepreneurs. Here's an example of how it works with housing. Note that there is a long lead-time to build new housing. This example is without NIMBY.

1. A developer believes there is a demand for housing in a given community.
2. He raises capital, buys land, develops plans, gets approvals, gets financing, and builds one hundred houses.
3. If he was right that there was a demand for new housing, he sells out the project and makes money.
4. What if the demand for housing is so high that he has 500 buyers for his one hundred homes? He raises the prices of his homes and still sells out. The developer takes his family to Italy for the summer.
5. What if ten other developers had the same idea and built a total of 1,000 homes, but there are only 500 buyers for them? The developers are stuck with too much supply, and they have to lower the price of their homes to entice more buyers. They end up making much less, or even lose money. Developers move into their parents' homes. Buyers move out of their parents' homes because they can now afford the lower price.
6. In this last example, the price of housing in the immediate area dropped!
7. Why? Because the Law of Supply and Demand worked!

8. The cyclical oversupply of housing dropped the price of housing in the whole area.

The idea here is to simply let the basic capitalist structures of our entire economy work as they're supposed to. The US has to tell NIMBY residents and bureaucrats that there are professionally-created and government-approved zoning and planning codes that they can no longer change on a project-by-project basis to suit their selfish, spoiled, childish demands. The US needs housing. Millions of houses and apartments are needed.

Governments and their NIMBY populations must get out of the way and ENCOURAGE new development of homes and apartments. Developers will eventually produce too many homes and the prices will drop. We just solved the housing crisis. Oversupply of homes brings lower prices. Done.

Developers must be able to depend on professionally-created and government-approved zoning, planning, and development codes and ordinances. Local resident groups have continual opportunities to influence codes and requirements. It must be the law of the land that as long as a project conforms to current requirements, the project can proceed without delays from local NIMBY homeowners or government bureaucrats.

CHAPTER 20
FREE-FOR-ALL

IMMIGRATION

Fair laws for immigrants and US citizens

"They say there are about 12 million illegal immigrants in this country. But if you ask a Native American, that number is more like 300 million."

—DAVID LETTERMAN

"Remember, remember always, that all of us, and you and I especially, are descended from immigrants."

—FRANKLIN D. ROOSEVELT

"A nation that cannot control its borders is not a nation."

—RONALD REAGAN

"I don't want to be a member of any club who would have me as a member."

—GROUCHO MARX

THE PROBLEM

Everybody wants to come to a major event. Those with a cherished ticket are let in by the screener at the door. Some who can't get a ticket devise their own way in, such as cutting through the fence, tunnelling under the wall, or swarming their way in.

Many people in the world live lives of sheer desperation from extreme poverty and/or extremely dangerous conditions. They will do anything to escape the horrors that include extortion and persecution in their homelands to find a better life for themselves and their children by seeking asylum in the US.

Just getting into the US can be enough, regardless of whether they're in the US legally or illegally. They're willing to put up with the difficulties of being an alien in the US. Their plight is terribly sad. Every American family other than Native Americans had ancestors who came, probably with the same desperation, to find a better life. All Americans can or should be able to relate and empathize.

This book identifies many enormous problems in the US. And yet, it's impossible to find a better place to live and have dreams for your children. We can never lose sight of that, and I hope the snarkiness in this book is viewed as an effort to make this wonderful country even better. I am grateful every day that my dirt poor, frightened ancestors made their way here.

People who somehow get into the US get many privileges, no matter whether they're legal or not. It's certainly not simple to navigate getting work, a place to live, school for your children, and healthcare as needed—especially if one doesn't speak English. If Latin American migrants are lucky enough to enter through Texas, California, Arizona, or Florida, they'll find many people who speak Spanish—because they and their ancestors got here, too!

Imagine you are producing a concert at the SOFI Stadium in Los Angeles. It will be the best concert anyone in world history has ever experienced. You have tickets to sell for 60,000 seats. They sell out in seconds. Now you have a serious problem. Thousands more are dying to get into the stadium. Ten thousand people climb walls, wade through the lake, and somehow crowd past security. Nothing you can do.

The fire marshal warns that any more people and he'll have to shut down the concert and send everyone home. You are a good person and want to let everyone into the concert—even for free. But you can't. There's no more room because there just aren't enough services and places to accommodate any more people. And besides, it wouldn't be fair to those who paid to get in. Even worse, imagine that the people who bought a ticket also have to pay for a ticket for each person who made their way in past security. They're massively pissed. You have no choice but to fortify the access points and post heavy guards. No more people can get in without a ticket.

Isn't this metaphor a good representation of the situation we have at the US borders? Americans want to let poor and desperate people in, but we simply don't have the funds and infrastructure to accommodate the many millions. The number of illegal, undocumented immigrant crossings at the southwest borders is often in the tens of thousands PER DAY, totaling millions. There is almost no screening for criminals, gang members, or even drug smuggling such as Fentanyl. Border states simply can't take care of all of these people, so they have been sending multitudes to other states and cities, who are also unable to care for these masses of people. This is just not sustainable, no matter how altruistic the citizens are. Sad but true.

BAD-ASS SOLUTION

- **IMMEDIATELY CLOSE THE US BORDERS COMPLETELY.**
- **ALL IMMIGRATION AND BORDER MATTERS BECOME 100 PERCENT THE RESPONSIBILITY OF THE FEDERAL GOVERNMENT, NOT THE BORDER STATES.**
- **REQUIRE ALL UNDOCUMENTED IMMIGRANTS ALREADY IN THE US TO BE FULLY SCREENED AS SOON AS POSSIBLE.**
- **IMMEDIATELY DEPORT ALL GANG MEMBERS AND CRIMINALS.**
- **LEGALIZE ALL REMAINING ILLEGAL, UNDOCUMENTED IMMIGRANTS AND THEIR CHILDREN CURRENTLY IN THE US.**
- **STRICTLY ENFORCE IMMIGRATION LAWS AND BORDERS GOING FORWARD.**
- **CREATE MASSIVE JOB PLACEMENT AND HOUSING PROGRAMS FOR THE IMMIGRANTS ALREADY IN THE US AND THOSE WHO COME IN THE FUTURE.**

1. The more than 12 million illegal aliens currently living in the US are here because the US let them in. That is, the US did not stop them, nor did the US deport them. This is tacit approval, meaning the US has allowed the immigrants in the US.

2. As a result of the approval, it is only fair that all of these people, including their children, be allowed to stay with Green Card work permits and the ability to become citizens. They must have all the benefits of this status. This group is called "Dreamers." Let their dream come true. Not doing so would be cruel.

3. All undocumented immigrants who commit crimes or are proven to have nefarious backgrounds will not be granted the aforementioned rights. They must be deported, or if convicted of a crime, remain in prison as sentenced, then be immediately deported.

4. Going forward there must be strict laws and enforcement to not permit any illegal immigration into the US. Immigrants can enter only if they are permitted under the law.

5. Remember, the US has a process to go through to get permission to immigrate into the country. Many thousands of people seeking asylum from all over the world have applied correctly and have been waiting for years to be accepted. It is unfair to them for the US to accept or even encourage illegal immigration while all of these people sought approval legitimately. It would be fair to streamline the process for those who already applied properly and have been waiting.

6. Walls, security, technology, and deportation must be utilized as much as necessary to stop illegal immigration.

7. Illegal immigration is a federal problem and should not be passed off to the border states where masses of people are effectively allowed into the US by the feds. This is a ridiculous burden on these states and their citizens. Conditions are also unacceptably terrible for the immigrants.

8. Fentanyl is made in China and is said to get into the US through Mexico. It kills approximately 300 Americans per day; 100,000 DEAD AMERICANS PER YEAR. **This is war** and the US has to stop this immediately, both its manufacture in China and its import through Mexico. Really. War. Bring out the missiles and drones. Not kidding.

9. Immigration has of late been an unbearable financial and social burden. It is fairly easy to assume that the vast majority of immigrants want to work and build a better life for their families. Federal, state, and local governments certainly don't want to provide 100 percent of the support for them. That lack of structure is failing all concerned terribly. For immigration to work for all, there must be job and housing placement. People capable of working must be paired with jobs so they can actually be productive citizens rather than unsustainable wards of the state. New immigrants can't come in unless there is a job and housing ready for them.

For the millions of immigrants already in the US, there must be a massive effort to arrange jobs and housing for them immediately. They must transition from being totally supported to supporting themselves.

Remember all of the service people who will be needed to house and care for the homeless under that bad-ass solution? Certainly, enormous numbers of immigrants can be trained to fulfill many of these service functions. Again, everyone wins.

10. THIS IS THE MOST IMPORTANT BAD-ASS SOLUTION FOR IMMIGRATION:

Although immigrants are flooding into the US from everywhere, most have come from Latin America, where likely tens of millions, if not hundreds of millions of people would choose to emigrate to the US rather than stay in often terrible and dangerous conditions in their home countries. The US simply cannot open its doors to so many people.

The most viable and kind thing to do would be for the US to commit to an enormous effort to support the countries that need help and create real opportunities for better lives for the citizens in those countries so that their people don't need to escape.

This is not unprecedented. It could be done on the scale of the Marshal Plan that rebuilt Europe after World War II.

- **ASSIST COUNTRIES TO PROVIDE SECURE, PEACEFUL LIVES WITH OPPORTUNITIES FOR THEIR CITIZENS SO THEY DON'T NEED TO SEEK ASYLUM IN THE US.**

CHAPTER 21
NOT MY PROBLEM

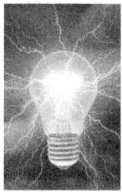

SO NOW WHAT?

Do something!

"If you cannot feed a hundred people, feed one."
—MOTHER TERESA

"I am no longer accepting the things I cannot change.
I am changing the things I cannot accept."
—ANGELA DAVIS

"Whatever you do, always give 100 percent.
Unless you're donating blood."
—BILL MURRAY

"Every person can make a difference, and every person should try."
—JOHN F. KENNEDY

"All great change in America begins at the dinner table."
—RONALD REAGAN

"Anyone who thinks that they are too small to make a difference has never tried to fall asleep with a mosquito in the room."

—THE DALAI LAMA

"The difference between involvement and commitment is like ham and eggs. The chicken is involved; the pig is committed."

—MARTINA NAVRATILOVA

"What's right about America is that although we have a mess of problems, we have great capacity—intellect and resources—to do something about them."

—HENRY FORD

"The world will not be destroyed by those who do evil, but by those who watch them without doing anything."

—ALBERT EINSTEIN

"Never doubt that a small group of thoughtful, committed, citizens can change the world. Indeed, it is the only thing that ever has."

—MARGARET MEAD

"Change will not come if we wait for some other person, or if we wait for some other time. We are the ones we've been waiting for. We are the change that we seek."

—BARACK OBAMA

"I alone cannot change the world, but I can cast a stone across the waters to create many ripples."

—MOTHER TERESA

THE PROBLEM

Thank You and congratulations! You finished twenty chapters about the biggest, most critical problems we face, along with solutions for all of them. You're much wiser now. You know how to fix everything.

As we've explored throughout this book, even the biggest problems have solutions that can be extremely effective. While I'm hopeful that you share my enthusiasm about these bad-ass solutions, you must also share my frustration with perhaps the biggest problem of all: getting the solutions implemented. After all, what good is a great solution for a terrible problem if it will never be accomplished, or even attempted?

Have any of the twenty big-ass problems been personal to you? Have any given you an electric shock because the problem is so bad—or the solution is so possible? I'm hoping the answer is yes.

You are also likely more concerned about the future and frustrated by the enormity of the problems because instituting the bad-ass solutions seems virtually impossible.

So, what do we do with this golden knowledge? Do we let it sit in a tiny corner of our brains like high school calculus (interestingly, the study of mathematical change)? Or do we act? If WE don't do something, who will?

Does anyone really want to get involved when a stranger collapses in front of us and needs CPR? If you know what to do, you simply have to jump in and save a stranger's life. You are morally bound to put your mouth over his and blow.

If someone whispered the absolute cure for cancer in your ear, what would you do? Hopefully, you'd tell everyone you know, join the American Cancer Society, and help get the word out and the cure implemented in any way you can.

Of course, you're saying, "Mitch, dude. You didn't cure cancer here. Get a grip!"

I know, I know. But many of the bad-ass solutions may save many lives and improve the lives of many more. And a writer can make a point with a metaphor, you know ...

Who wants to volunteer? That word makes us shudder and retreat. Our lives are so filled with work, family, food, shopping, healthcare, and twelve different series we're streaming on Netflix, Disney, Hulu, Prime, and HBO that we have no more time or brain power to volunteer.

So many people can be helped by implementing our bad-ass solutions. What stops us? I have to admit that I'm as guilty of not getting off my ass as everyone else.

Getting involved is frightening for many reasons. We think once we cross that imaginary line into "the cause" that the desperate people who work on the other side won't let go of us. I envision them grabbing me, tying me up, and never letting me go back to my safe, cushy world. **They'll suck up my time, my money, and my heartstrings.** The other side of that line represents a bureaucratic quagmire of darkness and unknown demands on us. Run.

Further, people don't think they have expertise to contribute. They don't want to deal with strangers. They don't want to be consumed by the massive, sad, frustrating problems. They don't want to get dirty, both figuratively and literally. Finally, it's hard for most of us to walk into a strange place, with strange people, and declare, "I'm here to help." It would be much more comfortable if we were invited.

It's so much easier to wear our blinders, do nothing, and go about our already busy lives in peace.

BAD-ASS SOLUTION

If *Bad-Ass Solutions* hasn't motivated you to act in some way, I've failed. You'll just sound brilliant at parties.

We have the solutions. Each of us needs to empower ourselves to do something. All of us are amazingly valuable. All of us have a voice. All of us can contribute.

Passion. Where does it come from? I feel passion in my gut, somewhere between pain, ache, and electricity. I get deeply interested, then obsessed. The subject is never far from my consciousness.

I'm passionate about stopping the rising oceans, while at the same time bringing fresh water to the thirsty world. I'm passionate about total reformation of the Federal Reserve before they destroy everything financial in the US. I'm passionate about stopping ubiquitous crime and assault rifles.

As an aside, I have been a founding director of two charitable organizations and remain on those boards. Though important, neither organization deals with the twenty topics addressed here.

I'm ready to act. Are you? Which one(s) of the twenty are you passionate about?

How do we harness passion and put it into action? The first step is deciding what channel can bear fruit from our selfless efforts. The second step is much harder—walking through the door. "Hi. I'm Mitch and I'm here to help your organization solve X problem. And I specifically want to propose and work on this solution."

I envision frowns, scorn, and laughter. Get over it. Walk in.

That sounds easy, but we all know it's not. Let's back up a bit. I feel a list coming on.

Following are steps we can take toward contributing to a cause:

1. **Pick a cause.** Identify a big-ass problem with a bad-ass solution that you care about. Choose something close to your heart.

2. **How much do you want to give?** Look hard at yourself. Be honest. Don't get scared. The throngs of a needy world won't be lining up at your door. Let's agree to go slow. Start with a toe in the pool. If you're unhappy, move out and try a different direction. If you found a home for your passion and altruism, stay and let it grow naturally.

    a. Time

We're all too busy. I blame the fast-paced world and Netflix. Again, start slowly. Let's say between two and six hours a month of your time.

    b. Money

If you're giving time, you don't have to give money. Of course, donations are every organization's life blood. In the going slow concept, don't agree to make any donation. Tell them that you want to start slowly, that you want to get personally involved first.

    c. Expertise

Charitable organizations have specific causes, but all of them operate like big businesses. They need virtually every skill a commercial business does.

What are you really good at that every organization needs?

        i. Accounting

        ii. Advertising

        iii. Writing

        iv. Raising money

        v. Public speaking

        vi. Interacting with other people

        vii. Handing out fliers

        viii. Making phone calls

        ix. Dealing with politicians

        x. Legal skills

        xi. Strategy

All of these are of enormous, valuable assistance to every organization. You may be the best accountant on the planet, but the last thing you want to do is more accounting. You may want to get involved doing something completely different, and that's every bit as valuable. They need you. They also need you to be fulfilled by your contributions.

Finally, have some meetings and discussions with the organization. Tell them what your interests are within their cause, what you want to see happen (bad-ass solution), and what you'd like to assist with toward that goal. See what they say. They may tell you right there that they aren't interested in pursuing the same goal. Or they may tell you they're elated by your ideas and need you to help make them happen. A lot comes from interacting with people. Hopefully, you'll land at the perfect organization that will enrich your life and let you contribute toward making the lives of countless others wonderful too.

    d. Emotions

This is a difficult part of charitable work. Even though you're in the trenches, fighting to make people's lives better, the problems weigh heavily on you. It's extremely difficult to see people suffering or that bad problems are festering.

How much of your emotions do you have to give? It may help you decide how you can be involved. Can you be on the front lines with your heart breaking for people that you assist? Or do you need to be in the background, helping in other valuable ways?

3. **Find an Organization.** You've chosen your cause. As an example, let's use Chapter 3: Global Warming / Rising Oceans.

    a. Find the organization that fits your interests. Two preliminary criteria to look for:

        i. The organization's main purpose. What is it trying to accomplish? Does it mesh with your interest and passion?

        ii. The organization's method(s) for reaching its goals. Do they address the cause of the problem, or do they address the result of the problems? For example, do they work to stop illegal drugs, or do they work to help people addicted to drugs? This is an important difference in choosing an organization to work with.

4. **Google search skills.** Refine your search to most efficiently reveal the results that most closely match your interests from the thousands of potential organizations dedicated to virtually every cause.

    a. First, define for yourself the organization you would like to find.

b. Global warming or climate change is such an enormous topic, we really need to narrow it down.

c. We want to address a single result of global warming—the rising sea levels.

d. Note that this already avoids the thousands of organizations that work on the causes of pollution and, more specifically, carbon emissions that cause global warming, which cause the ice to melt.

e. We also want to see if any organizations already deal with our bad-ass solutions.

5. **Google keyword search.**

    a. Start with the most obvious keyword.

    b. Many of the descriptive words are not needed, such as global warming, pollution, carbon emissions, fossil fuels, and melting ice caps.

    c. So, what's left? Rising sea levels. This gets the search focused on the exact result of the problem we're interested in. All the causes of the rising sea levels point to the words we're not including above, so they're unnecessary. There really is no other problematic cause of rising oceans, so we don't have to generate massive unnecessary search results to waste our time on.

    d. Just searching rising sea levels will still generate hundreds or even thousands of search results. So, we need to refine our search further.

    e. Again, we don't need the causes of the rising oceans (melting ice caps due to global warming due to carbon emissions). We also don't need the problems resulting from the rising sea levels (flooded coastal communities and submerged islands).

f. Consider exactly what we do want. We want an organization dedicated to stopping the rising sea levels that is not concerned with stopping the cause of the rising sea levels—or the result of rising sea levels. They have to be focused on stopping the sea levels from rising at all, using alternative methods such as our bad-ass solutions of diverting some rivers' massive water flows into the oceans and thousands of desalination plants. So, what do we call that for our search? Solutions? New solutions?

g. Let's try: rising sea level solutions.

h. This yielded many results for ideas to stop the sea level oceans (all ineffective), but just a few organizations came up.

i. Try: rising sea level solution organizations.

j. This gets lots of results, mostly from organizations who suggest the same old solutions that don't actually stop the oceans from rising, such as building sea walls and elevating roads.

k. Let's try for the whole enchilada: solve rising sea levels by diverting rivers.

l. Again, there are many pretty wild results, but I haven't found anything close to our bad-ass solution. Part of me is thrilled because the solution is truly new. Part of me is frustrated because it means we have to choose organizations that are trying but missing the mark. Our work is more difficult. We have to convince the organizations and the world to pursue our solutions.

Sorry to have failed finding a few perfect organizations to work with, but we certainly generated many results from which to choose a target organization to check out. Using this search methodology for your own interest is totally valid. We all have to find the best, closest organizations to our interests and work within them to pursue the Bad-Ass Solutions we need.

Another strategy is to try an opposite organization, such as if you passion is advocating for an assault weapons ban, work *within* the National Rifle Association (NRA), which seems to want an assault rifle strapped to a child as they emerge from the birth canal. The thinking is that the NRA really should be against assault rifles in favor of more reasonable firearms. Think of the great public relations and legitimacy that such a move would engender. You may convince them—give them a call! Really. Millions of us should join them and provide a reasonable, cogent argument about why stopping assault weapons would be great for the NRA and the US. Simple! Sure.

> "Better to have your enemies inside the tent pissing out, than outside the tent pissing in."
>
> — PRESIDENT LYNDON B. JOHNSON

If you want to take a smaller first step, it can be as simple as just spreading the word. Tell other people about a big-ass problem and its bad-ass solution and hope they do the same until we create a critical mass of people who want that solution put into action. Blog, tweet, Facebook, TikTok. The massive electronic outreach and its ability to spread the word is incredibly powerful. Do it.

Contacting the Congress people who represent you directly is actually quite effective. The website below allows you to input your address and then email the two Senators for your state and the member of the House of Representatives from your local district.

CONGRESS CONTACT INFORMATION

Contact Members of Congress:

https://democracy.io

Send emails to *members* of the United States House of Representatives and Senate in just a few easy steps.

We can get solutions enacted only if there are massive numbers of constituents demanding them. Write to your governmental representatives.

It's actually pretty simple. Vote for candidates who support bad-ass solutions and will do their best to make them happen. We can call them Bad-Ass as a badge of honor.

BE A BAD-ASS!

"When the people lead, the leaders will follow."

-- MAHATMA GANDHI

SOURCES

"The 17 Things Joe Biden Did on Day One." POLITICO, n.d. https://www.politico.com:443/interactives/2021/interactive_biden-first-day-executive-orders/.

Ainsley, Julia. "Migrant Border Crossings in Fiscal Year 2022 Topped 2.76 Million, Breaking Previous Record." NBCNews.com, October 22, 2022. https://www.nbcnews.com/politics/immigration/migrant-border-crossings-fiscal-year-2022-topped-276-million-breaking-rcna53517.

Amadeo, Kimberly. "What Is a Flat Tax System?" The Balance, October 13, 2022. https://www.thebalancemoney.com/flat-tax-pros-cons-examples-compared-to-fair-tax-3306329.

"Army National Guard." The National Guard—Official Website of the National Guard, n.d. https://www.nationalguard.mil/about-the-guard/army-national-guard/.

Backman, Maurie. "49% of Americans Couldn't Cover a $400 Emergency Expense Today, up from 32% in November." The Motley Fool, May 26, 2022. https://www.fool.com/the-ascent/personal-finance/articles/49-of-americans-couldnt-cover-a-400-emergency-expense-today-up-from-32-in-november/.

Barmann, Jay. "In Test of Civil Liberties Law, the Mayor of New York Announces Sweeping Program to Remove Mentally Ill from Streets." SFist, November 29, 2022. https://sfist.com/2022/11/29/in-test-of-civil-liberties-law-the-mayor-of-new-york-announces-program-to-remove-mentally-ill-from-streets/.

Black, Derek W. "America's Founders Knew Democracy Requires Public Education." Time, September 22, 2020. https://time.com/5891261/early-american-education-history/.

Brenan, Megan. "Economy Tops Voters' List of Key Election Issues." Gallup.com, October 5, 2020. https://news.gallup.com/poll/321617/economy-tops-voters-list-key-election-issues.aspx.

"CBS MORNINGS." Episode. Guns Violence in America—433.9M Civilian Firearms—Approx 100M More Than People. CBS, n.d.

"Central Arizona Project—Highlighting Key Features from the CAP System, an Engineering Marvel." Central Arizona Project, n.d. https://cap-az.com/ and https://storymaps.argis.com/stories/b7b28dd4c36a41e8d533ba540f998cb/print.

"Central Arizona Project—Part 1." American Water College, November 29, 2018. https://www.americanwatercollege.org/cap-part1/.

Chabria, Anita. "Column: These Families Are Flaming the ACLU as California Debates Mental Health Care." Los Angeles Times, August 4, 2022. https://www.latimes.com/california/story/2022-08-04/mental-health-california-newsom-proposal-care-courts-aclu.

Chen, James. "1913 Federal Reserve Act: Definition and Why It's Important." Investopedia, n.d. https://www.investopedia.com/terms/f/1913-federal-reserve-act.asp#:~:text=What%20Is%20the%201913%20Federal,bank%20to%20oversee%20monetary%20policy.

Chen, James. "What Are Stock Options? Parameters and Trading, with Examples." Investopedia, n.d. https://www.investopedia.com/terms/s/stockoption.asp.

ChinaFolio. "Population Power: China's Shifting Masses." Chinafolio, May 4, 2020. https://chinafolio.com/population-power/#:~:text=According%20to%20UN%20statistics%2C%20in,1.064%20billion%20or%2010%25%20respectively.

"Cities in California." Ballotpedia, n.d. https://ballotpedia.org/Cities_in_California.

"Cities in New York." Ballotpedia, n.d. https://ballotpedia.org/Cities_in_New_York#:~:text=City%20government,-Click%20the%20links&text=According%20to%20a%202022%20study,villages%2C%20and%201%2C189%20special%20districts.

"Convert Cubic Meters of Water to US Gallons of Water / Water Volumes. Weight Conversion." Convert to, n.d. http://convert-to.com/conversion/water-weight-volume/convert-m3-of-water-volume-to-us-gal-of-water-volume.html.

Curwen, Thomas. "State Readies Mental Illness Courts." Los Angeles Times, n.d. https://enewspaper.latimes.com/infinity/article_share.aspx?guid=51626e57-db65-4398-8572-539bc86cba88.

Dasgupta, Saibal. "Race for Semiconductors Influences Taiwan Conflict." Voice of America, August 8, 2022. https://www.voanews.com/a/race-for-semiconductors-influences-taiwan-conflict-/6696432.html.

"Desalination Plants Worldwide." Green City Times, September 17, 2022. https://www.greencitytimes.com/water-desalination-clean-water-for-a-thirsty-world/.

"Digest of Education Statistics." Digest of Education Statistics Home, n.d. https://nces.ed.gov/programs/digest/.

"Drug Related Crime Statistics." NCDAS National Center for Drug Abuse Statistics, n.d. https://drugabusestatistics.org/drug-related-crime-statistics/.

Drug Use in History, n.d. https://open.lib.umn.edu/socialproblems/chapter/7-1-drug-use-in-history/.

Drugs and Gangs Fast Facts, n.d. https://www.justice.gov/archive/ndic/pubs11/13157/13157p.pdf.

"Editorial: A National 15-Week Abortion Ban Would Be a Nightmare. Voters Can Make Sure It Doesn't Come True." Los Angeles Times, September 16, 2022. https://www.latimes.com/opinion/story/2022-09-15/national-bill-banning-abortions-15-weeks-lindsey-graham-nightmare-nov-8-election.

Edwards, John. "2 Ways Hedge Funds Avoid Paying Taxes." Investopedia, May 20, 2022. https://www.investopedia.com/articles/investing/101415/2-ways-hedge-funds-avoid-paying-taxes.asp#:~:text=Key%20Takeaways,investors%20on%20the%20private%20market.&text=Funds%20are%20also%20able%20to,reinvested%20back%20in%20the%20fund.

Edwards, Lee. "How Ronald Reagan Won the Cold War." The Heritage Foundation, n.d. https://www.heritage.org/conservatism/commentary/how-ronald-reagan-won-the-cold-war.

"Fact Sheet: Drug-Related Crime." US Department of Justice, Bureau of Justice Statistics, n.d. https://bjs.ojp.gov/content/pub/pdf/DRRC.PDF.

"Federal Reserve Board." Structure of the Federal Reserve System—Federal Reserve Board, n.d. https://www.federalreserve.gov/aboutthefed/structure-federal-reserve-board.htm.

"Federal Spending: Where Does the Money Go." National Priorities Project, n.d. https://www.nationalpriorities.org/budget-basics/federal-budget-101/spending/.

"Fentanyl." DEA Drug Fact Sheet, n.d. https://www.dea.gov/factsheets/fentanyl.

Fernando, Jason. "Inflation: What It Is, How It Can Be Controlled, and Extreme Examples." Investopedia, n.d. https://www.investopedia.com/terms/i/inflation.asp.

Flintoff, John-Paul. "Eight Reasons People Don't Get Involved." The Guardian, September 25, 2014. https://www.theguardian.com/lifeandstyle/2014/sep/25/eight-reasons-people-do-not-involved-community.

"Fox Business Channel." Episode. US Debt Per Person and Per Taxpayer, January 3, 2024.

Fox, Alex. "Earth Loses 1.2 Trillion Tons of Ice per Year, a Nearly 60% Increase from 1994." Smithsonian.com, January 29, 2021. https://www.smithsonianmag.com/smart-news/earth-loses-12-trillion-tons-ice-year-nearly-60-increase-1994-180976877/.

Glick, Daniel. "Global Climate Change, Melting Glaciers." Environment, n.d. https://www.nationalgeographic.com/environment/article/big-thaw#:~:text=Even%20without%20such%20a%20major,disaster%2C%22%20according%20to%20Douglas.

Gutierrez, Melody. "California Gets New Rules Covering Medical Malpractice Payments. Here's What Will Change." Los Angeles Times, May 23, 2022. https://www.latimes.com/california/story/2022-05-23/california-new-rules-medical-malpractice-payments-changes#:~:text=Gavin%20Newsom%20signed%20a%20bill,damages%20nearly%20five%20decades%20ago.

Haigh, Marilyn. "Why Does Texas Have so Many Counties? A History Lesson." The Texas Tribune, July 3, 2018. https://www.texastribune.org/2018/07/03/beto-orourke-visited-all-254-counties-texas-why-are-there-so-many/.

"History—Mao Zedong." BBC, n.d. https://www.bbc.co.uk/history/historic_figures/mao_zedong.shtml.

Holthaus, Eric. "Scientists Are Desperately Trying to Figure out How Long We Have until 'Doomsday Glaciers' Melt." Mother Jones, November 23, 2017. https://www.motherjones.com/environment/2017/11/scientists-are-desperately-trying-to-figure-out-how-long-we-have-until-doomsday-glaciers-melt/.

"Home." Private School Review—Established 2003. Accessed March 8, 2024. http://www.privateschoolreview.com/tuition-stats/private-school-cost-by-state.

"Houselessness." ACLU of Southern California, n.d. https://www.aclusocal.org/en/issues/economic-justice/houselessness#:~:text=The%20ACLU%20of%20Southern%20California,needed%20housing%2C%20employment%20and%20benefits.

"How Earth Makes Fresh Water." EarthDate, n.d. https://www.earthdate.org/episodes/how-earth-makes-fresh-water.

How many cities are in the United States? 2024, n.d. https://worldpopulationreview.com/us-city-rankings/how-many-cities-are-in-the-us.

"How Many Schools Are in the U.S (Statistics & Facts)—2024." Admissonsly, February 13, 2024. http://admissionsly.com/how-many-schools-are-there.

"Ice Sheet." Ice Sheet—Continental Glaciers, n.d. https://education.nationalgeographic.org/resource/ice-sheet/.

"In Stark U.N. Report, a Quarter of World Lacks Safe Drinking Water." Associated Press. Accessed March 2023. https://enewspaper.latimes.com/desktop/latimes/default.aspx?token=42e23962a5d74614be16bae3d62d13e7&ytn_ud=90901&stnc_ud=4760863&edu%2C%2C%2C.

Inc., YouMail. "U.S. Phones Received Just under 4.5 Billion Robocalls in August, Says Youmail Robocall Index." PR Newswire: press release distribution, targeting, monitoring and marketing, n.d. https://www.prnewswire.com/news-releases/us-phones-received-just-under-4-5-billion-robocalls-in-august-says-youmail-robocall-index-301619232.html.

Investopedia, Team. "What Causes Inflation?" Investopedia, n.d. https://www.investopedia.com/ask/answers/111314/what-causes-inflation-and-does-anyone-gain-it.asp.

Investopedia, Team. "What Is a Hedge Fund? Examples, Types, and Strategies." Investopedia, n.d. https://www.investopedia.com/terms/h/hedgefund.asp.

Isidore, Chris. Russia's economy is surprisingly tiny. here's why it matters so ..., n.d. https://www.cnn.com/2022/02/26/economy/russia-economic-power-sanctions/index.html.

Jaws. Universal/Zanuck-Brown, 1975.

"Joseph Stalin: Death, Quotes & Facts." History.com, April 25, 2023. https://www.history.com/topics/european-history/joseph-stalin.

JustinTOOLs.com. "Convert Olympic Size Swimming Pool to Cubic Meters (Os Sp to M3)." Convert Olympic Size Swimming Pool to Cubic Meters (os sp to m3)—JustinTOOLs.com, n.d. https://www.justintools.com/unit-conversion/volume.php?k1=olympic-size-swimming-pool&k2=cubic-meters.

King, Ian. "Uncle Sam's Race to Fire China." The Banyon Edge, December 3, 2022.

Lee, Juhohn. "America Has Spent over a Trillion Dollars Fighting the War on Drugs. ." CNBC, June 17, 2021. https://www.cnbc.com/2021/06/17/the-us-has-spent-over-a-trillion-dollars-fighting-war-on-drugs.html.

List of rivers by discharge, n.d. https://en.wikipedia-on-ipfs.org/wiki/List_of_rivers_by_discharge.

Loe, Megan, and Ariane Datil. No, you can't steal up to $950 worth of merchandise in California ..., February 28, 2022. https://www.verifythis.com/article/news/verify/crime-verify/california-prop-47-shoplifting-950-fact-check/536-4d1de58e-bf47-4ede-8c2f-b4d0c1788b86.

Loh, Matthew. "Harvard Economist and Former Obama Advisor Says Russia Is 'basically a Big Gas Station' and Is Otherwise 'Incredibly Unimportant' in the Global Economy." Business Insider, n.d. https://www.businessinsider.com/russian-economy-basically-big-gas-station-harvard-economist-2022-2.

Lori, William E. Secretariat of Pro-Life Activities letter from Archbishop William E. Lori to Lindsey Graham and Chris Smith, September 19, 2022. https://www.usccb.org/resources/Pain%20Capable%2015%20weeks%20September%202022%20final.pdf.

Mann, Brian. "2022 Was a Deadly (but Hopeful) Year in America's Opioid Crisis." NPR, December 31, 2022. https://www.npr.org/2022/12/31/1145797684/2022-was-a-deadly-but-hopeful-year-in-americas-opioid-crisis.

"Mass Incarceration." American Civil Liberties Union, n.d. https://www.aclu.org/issues/smart-justice/mass-incarceration#:~:text=Despite%20making%20up%20close%20to,outpacing%20population%20growth%20and%20crime.

Mitter, Rana. "Forgotten Ally? China's Unsung Role in World War II." CNN, September 1, 2015. https://www.cnn.com/2015/08/31/opinions/china-wwii-forgotten-ally-rana-mitter/index.html.

"More Productive Wells Spur U.S. Crude Oil Production Higher—U.S. Energy Information Administration (EIA)." More productive wells spur U.S. crude oil production higher—U.S. Energy Information Administration (EIA), February 2024. https://www.eia.gov/todayinenergy/detail.php?id=61523#:~:text=Since%20first%20surpassing%20the%20previous,by%200.3%20million%20b%2Fd.

"NASA Figured out How to Weigh Greenland—Now We Know How Much Ice Has Been Lost." World Economic Forum, n.d. https://www.weforum.org/agenda/2022/10/greenland-melting-ice-climate-change-nasa/.

Nelson, Laura J., and Benjamin Oreskes. "Money Talks Is U.S. Senate Race. Meet the Biggest Donors." Los Angeles Times. March 3, 2024.

"New Predictions Show Antarctica's Ice Sheets Could Melt Far Sooner than Expected." World Economic Forum, n.d. https://www.weforum.org/agenda/2020/10/melting-antarctica-glacier-could-sea-level.

"New York State Geography." Department of Labor, n.d. https://dol.ny.gov/new-york-state-geography#:~:text=New%20York%20State%20consists%20of%2062%20counties.

Newburger, Emma. "Biden Suspends Oil and Gas Leasing in Slew of Executive Actions on Climate Change." CNBC, January 27, 2021. https://www.cnbc.com/2021/01/27/biden-suspends-oil-and-gas-drilling-in-series-of.html.

"Panama Canal: History, Definition & Canal Zone—History." History.com, n.d. https://www.history.com/topics/landmarks/panama-canal.

"The People's Republic of China." United States Trade Representative, n.d. https://ustr.gov/countries-regions/china-mongolia-taiwan/peoples-republic-china.

Perez, Maritza, and Betsy Pearl. "Ending the War on Drugs." Center for American Progress, June 27, 2018. https://www.americanprogress.org/article/ending-war-drugs/#:~:text=Ending%20the%20War%20on%20Drugs%3A%20By%20the%20Numbers,-Jun%2027%2C%202018&text=A%20record%2063%2C600%20overdose%20deaths,does%20not%20lower%20drug%20use.

"Police Departments, Funding, Stats & Data." USAFacts, n.d. https://usafacts.org/articles/police-departments-explained/.

Popik, Barry. "'an Elephant Is a Mouse Built to Government Specifications.'" The Big Apple, n.d. https://www.barrypopik.com/index.php/new_york_city/entry/an_elephant_is_a_mouse_built_to_government_specifications.

Rapoza, Kenneth. "What China's 'return to Manufacturing' Policy Means." Coalition For A Prosperous America, March 4, 2024. https://prosperousamerica.org/what-chinas-return-to-manufacturing-policy-means/#:~:text=China%20accounts%20for%20about%2030,its%20Strategic%20Emerging%20Industries%20Initiative.

Roy, Jessica. "Experts and a Victim Address ID Theft." Los Angeles Times, n.d. https://www.latimes.com/business/technology/story/2022-10-26/identity-theft-nightmare.

"Russia Population (Live)." Worldometer, n.d. https://www.worldometers.info/world-population/russia-population/.

Russia's minuscule economy: The mouse that roars, 22AD. https://www.ipi.org/ipi_issues/detail/russias-minuscule-economy-the-mouse-that-roars.

Sawe, Benjamin Elisha. "How Many Counties Are in the United States?" WorldAtlas, August 3, 2018. https://www.worldatlas.com/articles/how-many-counties-are-in-the-united-states.html.

Scharping, Nathaniel. "The Ice Caps Are Melting. Will They Ever Disappear Completely?" Discover Magazine, March 21, 2023. https://www.discovermagazine.com/environment/the-ice-caps-are-melting-will-they-ever-disappear-completely.

ScienceSites. "The Impact of Violent Video Games on the Player's Social Network." ISRA, May 9, 2018. https://www.israsociety.com/blog/the-impact-of-violent-video-games-on-the-players-social-network#:~:text=Overall%2C%20it%20appears%20that%20violent,spreads%20through%20their%20social%20networks.

"Self-Defense and 'Stand Your Ground.'" National Conference of State Legislatures, 2023. https://www.ncsl.org/civil-and-criminal-justice/self-defense-and-stand-your-ground.

Seth, Shobhit. "Why China Buys U.S. Debt with Treasury Bonds." Investopedia, n.d. https://www.investopedia.com/articles/investing/040115/reasons-why-china-buys-us-treasury-bonds.asp.

Silver, Caleb. "The Top 25 Economies in the World." Investopedia, n.d. https://www.investopedia.com/insights/worlds-top-economies/.

Soblik, Tim. "The Fed Is Shrinking Its Balance Sheet. What Does That Mean?" Federal Reserve Bank of Richmond, n.d. https://www.richmondfed.org/publications/research/econ_focus/2022/q3_federal_reserve.

Special report on the ocean and Cryosphere in a changing climate, n.d. https://www.ipcc.ch/srocc/.

"St. Valentine's Day Massacre—Victims, Evidence & Suspects." History.com, January 30, 2024. https://www.history.com/topics/crime/saint-valentines-day-massacre.

Stasha, Smiljanic. "Homelessness Statistics in the US for 2021: Policy Advice." Homelessness statistics in the US for 2021 | Policy Advice | Policy Advice, September 29, 2022. https://policyadvice.net/insurance/insights/homelessness-statistics/.

Stebbins, Samuel. "Which Americans Own the Most Guns: All 50 States Ranked." 24/7 Wall St., June 16, 2023. https://247wallst.com/special-report/2023/06/16/which-americans-own-the-most-guns-all-50-states-ranked/.

Steupert, Mia, and Tessa Longbons. "Fact Sheet: Abortions at 15 Weeks in the United States." Lozier Institute, December 11, 2023. https://lozierinstitute.org/fact-sheet-abortions-at-15-weeks-in-the-united-states/.

Stossel, John. "John Stossel: Here Are Even More Inconvenient Facts about Biden's Magical Thinking on Evs." The Daily Caller, November 19, 2022. https://dailycaller.com/2022/11/17/opinion-here-are-even-more-inconvenient-facts-about-bidens-magical-thinking-on-evs-john-stossel/.

"Structure of the Federal Reserve System." Federal Reserve Board—Structure of the Federal Reserve System, n.d. https://www.federalreserve.gov/aboutthefed/structure-federal-reserve-system.htm.

Sun, Tzu. The art of war. New York, NY: W. W. Norton et Company, Inc, 2020.

Texas cities, n.d. https://comptroller.texas.gov/transparency/local/cities.php.

"Total Government Employees U.S. 2022." Statista, November 3, 2023. https://www.statista.com/statistics/204535/number-of-governmental-employees-in-the-us/.

"U.S. National Debt Spiraling out of Control, Rising $1 Trillion Every 100 Days." The Washington Times, March 4, 2024. https://www.washingtontimes.com/news/2024/mar/4/us-national-debt-spiraling-out-of-control-rising-1/.

"United States Drug Enforcement Administration." Fentanyl | DEA.gov, n.d. https://www.dea.gov/highlight-topics/fentanyl#:~:text=What%20is%20it%3F,is%20also%20diverted%20for%20abuse.

The Untouchables, 1987.

"Vladimir Putin." Wikipedia, n.d. https://en.wikipedia.org/wiki/Vladimir_Putin.

Waggoner, John. "What Are the Tax Brackets for 2023 and 2024?." AARP, February 20, 2024. https://www.aarp.org/money/taxes/info-2023/income-tax-brackets-2024.html#:~:text=There%20are%20seven%20federal%20income,make%2C%20the%20more%20you%20pay.

Walsh, Joe. "U.S. Has at Least 20 Million Assault Rifles. A Ban Wouldn't Reduce That Number." Forbes, March 25, 2021. https://www.forbes.com/sites/joewalsh/2021/03/25/us-has-at-least-20-million-assault-rifles-a-ban-wouldnt-reduce-that-number/?sh=66c9412c4978.

"What the World Would Look like If All the Ice Melted." National Geographic Magazine, n.d. https://www.nationalgeographic.com/magazine/article/rising-seas-ice-melt-new-shoreline-maps.

"Who Pays Income Taxes?" National Taxpayers Union, n.d. https://www.ntu.org/foundation/tax-page/who-pays-income-taxes.

"The World Bank in China—Overview." World Bank, n.d. https://www.worldbank.org/en/country/china/overview.

The world counts, n.d. https://www.theworldcounts.com/challenges/climate-change/global-warming/the-melting-ice-caps/story.

"Xi Jinping." Wikipedia, n.d. https://en.wikipedia.org/wiki/Xi_Jinping.

Yotopoulas, Amy. "Three Reasons Why People Don't Volunteer, and What Can Be Done about It." Stanford Center on Longevity, n.d. https://longevity.stanford.edu/three-reasons-why-people-dont-volunteer-and-what-can-be-done-about-it/

ACKNOWLEDGEMENTS

A massive thank you to my family and friends who suffered through my obnoxious talking about this book and its bad-ass solutions. They were incredibly patient and supportive. It helped more than I can express.

I fell in love with my editor. She became my wife—more than forty years ago! Sandy contributed enormously to the content, ideas, structure, clarity, and especially humor. She is a supremely talented writer and actress who made a fabulous difference in this book.

Steve Harrison and Jack Canfield read a pre-published version of *Bad-Ass Solutions* and electrified me with their encouragement and guidance. As the most successful non-fiction author of all time, Jack's foreword gives credibility to the book that I simply would not have been able to achieve otherwise. As the premier marketing guru of non-fiction books, Steve's assistance and support has also proved invaluable. I can't begin to convey how grateful I am to these two giants.

Patty Aubery provided instant encouragement and a bombardment of marketing ideas and connections. Wow, what a force!

Steve Harrison's critically important author programs and brilliant team at www.AuthorSuccess.com, truly provided the expertise, information, and assistance I needed to publish this book correctly for it have any chance of even being read.

Cristina Smith is an amazing coach with deep knowledge of every aspect of getting the book published successfully. She led me on a critical path and was always cheerfully available and supplied correct and beneficial information. Thank you, thank you!

Valerie Costa did an outstanding job of editing the book for consistency and publishing format. Honestly, her fabulous encouragement and kindness filled me with enthusiasm to do everything necessary to get this book published and promoted. I'm trying to get in touch with my fifth-grade English teacher to let her know that everything she taught us about commas, dashes, and percent symbols has been updated.

Christy Day is an incredibly talented cover designer and book layout expert. She was great fun to work with and her creativity resulted in what I hope you agree is a very exciting cover.

Steve Scholl did an excellent job with the final proofread. Incredibly, he found numerous errors—even after the book had been scoured about fifty times! I guess that's why an artist never thinks their painting is finished.

Maggie McLaughlin was fantastic and extremely kind in advising and finalizing the entire publishing process including presenting the book to the major publishing outlets.

Mark Malatesta provided excellent early coaching along with an education in the horrors of navigating the literary agent and publishing business.

Eternal love and gratitude to Joe and Shirley, who trained me to be totally independent, resourceful, and self-sufficient—then were disappointed when I became those things and needed them less.

THE ASS-END

ABOUT THE AUTHOR

MITCH FRANCIS

As the founder of Francis Development Inc., Mitch developed shopping centers, office buildings, and condominium projects. He continues to own and manage commercial properties throughout the US. He was a real estate major at the University of Colorado and has a California Real Estate Broker license he doesn't use (like everyone in California).

Mitch was the founder, chairman, and CEO of a small publicly-traded company for nearly thirty years. The company was initially involved in creating and operating 3-D motion simulator attractions in the US and Canada, utilizing the most advanced flight simulator and other technologies of the day. Subsequently, the company became the largest ticket broker in Las Vegas, selling more than $1 billion in show tickets, attractions, and dining.

Mitch is an innovative business leader whose inventions have yielded four United States patents, with another three inventions currently patent-pending. All of these inventions have contributed to the successes of his unique businesses. He believes that the two most important ingredients for success as a serial entrepreneur are superior skills in problem-solving and unshakable tenacity.

Mitch has been a founding director of two charitable organizations and remains on those boards. Though important, neither organization deals with the twenty topics addressed in Bad-Ass Solutions.

He grew up in Denver, Colorado, and so of course has a life-long love affair with skiing. He was on the Vail Ski Team specializing in downhill racing. He taught skiing on weekends and holidays while at the University of Colorado at Boulder. Picture him studying on the chairlifts…

Mitch lives in Los Angeles with his amazing wife, Sandy. He found her after she got lost while skiing in a white-out. She says he saved her life, so she was obligated to marry him. It's working out—forty-two years!

For this book, Mitch applied his extreme problem-solving skills to many of the most disastrous problems of our time and was able to develop truly viable and implementable solutions for all of them. These are not mainstream or commonly-known ideas. They just make incredible sense. They are so creative and so provocative; they need to be called Bad-Ass Solutions.

Join Mitch as a bad-ass problem-solver to help make this country, and the world, a better place.

Made in United States
North Haven, CT
28 October 2025